Muslim
Brotherhoods
and
Politics
in
Senegal

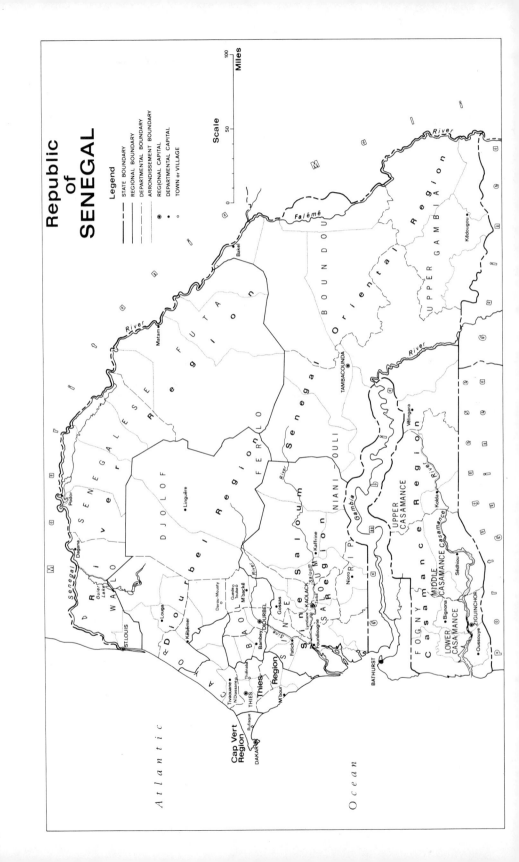

Republic
of
SENEGAL

Legend

STATE BOUNDARY
REGIONAL BOUNDARY
DEPARTMENTAL BOUNDARY
ARRONDISSEMENT BOUNDARY
REGIONAL CAPITAL
DEPARTMENTAL CAPITAL
TOWN or VILLAGE

Scale

0   50   100
Miles

Atlantic Ocean

Cap Vert Region

DAKAR
Rufisque

Thies
THIES
N'Diassane
Tivaouane
Thienaba
M'bour

STLOUIS

WALO

RIVER

Senegal River
Guiers Lakes

Dagana
Podor

SENEGALESE

FUTA

Region

Matam

DJOLOF

Linguère

FERLO

Senegal Oriental Region

BOUNDOU

Falémé

Bakel

MALI

Kébémer
Louga

DIOURBEL Region

Darou-Mousty
Guédiao
Touboa
M'backé
Bambey
DIOURBEL

BAOL

SINE SALOUM

Fatick
Foundiougne
Lyndiane
Gossas
KAOLACK
Kaffrine
Diakhao
Kahone

Region

NIORO
DU
RIP

NIANI
OULI

Gambia River

BATHURST

UPPER GAMBIA Region

TAMBACOUNDA

Kédougou

Gambia River

Kolda River
Sédhiou

UPPER
CASAMANCE

MIDDLE CASAMANCE
Casamance

FOGNY
Casamance Region
Bignona
Oussouye
LOWER CASAMANCE
ZIGUINCHOR

P

My contacts with the Senegalese Muslim brotherhoods were established eight years ago when I first visited Senegal. At that time I was aware only that there existed powerful religious leaders called marabus. The marabu resembled my idea of an oriental king because of his court of advisers, who stood whispering together behind his chair while lay followers and disciples crawled into the royal presence, knelt at the holy feet, and pressed money into the blessed hand before begging for assistance of some kind. I knew, because of the constant rumors floating around Senegal (the so-called Radio Kankan), that certain of the marabus were able to influence political decisions at the highest level; but I did not know why these religious leaders, whose power seemed to contradict the basic goals of the Senegalese government, exerted such a strong influence. This book is a result of my early fascination with the marabus. I began serious research on the political influence of the brotherhoods in 1964 by acquiring an understanding of the historical and theoretical bases of Muslim brotherhoods, and by studying the history of Senegal as far as sources at the Harvard and Boston University libraries would permit. The major part of this study was conducted in Senegal in 1965 and 1966. Ultimately, my sources were primary documents in the Dakar Archives or published by the governments of Senegal or by certain marabus; secondary books and articles on Islam and on Senegal; newspapers and miscellaneous circulars; and, especially, interviews in Senegal with Muslim leaders, disciples, government officials, scholars, and other individuals. The printed circulars and speeches by the marabus, some of the letters and reports by French and Senegalese administrators, and the handbills issued by the Senegalese political parties are not always systematically catalogued in Senegalese libraries. Those sources which I did not obtain from a library and which do not seem to be available in library collections are cited in the footnotes but not the bibliography, as I can only refer the reader to my own collection of papers.

The interviews deserve further comment because of their central importance to this study. Many, if not most, of the people interviewed were involved in some way in transactions between the government and the brotherhoods: thus in most cases it would be bothersome, if not harmful, to the individual concerned to mention his name when citing the interview. In some cases the man (or woman) can be identified in general terms because of his position, but in other cases only the interview, date, and place can be mentioned. All interviews were checked and cross-checked for their veracity, and they are too valuable not to use despite the fact that they cannot be checked by the reader; consequently I am as explicit as possible in my citations, and I offer my interview notebooks to anyone wishing to examine further a particular point or interview.

During the entire period of research a number of people assisted me. The marabus themselves spent many hours answering my questions and trying to make me understand their views of politics. I started out with a secular Western prejudice against these lords who seemed nothing more than exploiters of the Senegalese peasants. I was soon humbled into realizing the superficiality of this view, for many of the marabus are great men whose concern for the welfare of their disciples dominates their daily lives. I wish to thank, then (with apologies for my biases and the limits of my understanding), Al Hajj Abdul Aziz Sy, Serigne Modou Bousso, Al Hajj Saidou Nourou Tall, Al Hajj Modou Moustapha, the late Al Hajj Falilou M'Backé, and especially Al Hajj Ibrahima Niass, whose hospitality combined with his frankness provided my most enlightening experience in Senegal.

The Senegalese scholar whose help and encouragement was most essential to my work is Cheikh Tidjane Sy, whose forthcoming book on the Muridiyya will be a major contribution to the studies on Senegalese Islam. Many other Senegalese—officials, scholars, members of brotherhoods, and so on—spent much time answering questions and providing information. Cherif Babily Aidera, Barra Mame M'Backé, Lamine Diouf, Ibrahima Samb, Christian Mame Dior, Abdoulaye Diop, Ibrahima Faye, Alphonse N'Diaye, Niang Amadou Massemba, Bilkis Niass, and Khady Fall Niass were particularly helpful. So, too, were the personnel in the Dakar Archives and particularly M. Fr. Maurel, the director.

Among the many Americans who assisted me were Martin Klein, Don Essum, George and Mary Brooks, Marc Karp, and especially William Foltz, whose suggestions and criticisms have been essential to my work. I owe a great debt to Ruth Schachter Morgenthau, who originally inspired me to conduct this study and who has advised and encouraged every phase of my work, remaining throughout my sternest critic and most helpful commentator. William Newman and A. A. Castagno gave generously of their time and acted as advisers for this study in its phase as a doctoral dissertation in Political Science and African Studies at Boston University (May, 1967). Dr. Castagno in particular has tolerated constant and lengthy interruptions of his busy schedule and has spent many hours with me going over the

manuscript in all stages. I am also grateful to the women of the
Lecture Note Fund at the University of Pennsylvania who have
patiently and accurately typed several versions of the manuscript,
and to don Claudio Véliz and the Instituto de Estudios Interna-
cionales for providing a quiet work place that greatly facilitated
my revisions. Finally, I acknowledge the assistance of Guy I. F.
Leigh, who spent long hours checking sources and editing the text.

   None of this study could have been undertaken without
generous grants. I am grateful to the Kent Fellowship Program for
a summer grant in 1964, and to the Foreign Area Fellowship
Program for grants in 1964–1965 and 1965–1966. These organizations and the many individuals who helped me are in no way
responsible for errors in fact or judgment that I may have
unwittingly committed. Indeed, I must enter one last caveat here:
it is very difficult for an alien observer, whose own way of life is far
removed from the subject under study, to make valid judgments.
Those who understand the situation in Senegal best are the men
directly involved in day-to-day decision-making processes.
Moreover, the political situation in Senegal is in flux and any
conclusions are therefore somewhat tenuous. Notwithstanding
these factors, I have undertaken this study in the hope that my
perception of politics in Senegal may contribute to studies on
Senegal and on religion and politics in general.

Santiago, Chile   Lucy C. Behrman
1969

Contents

Tables

Illustrations

Muslim
Brotherhoods
and
Politics
in
Senegal

Note on Transliteration

Much confusion exists concerning the use of Arabic and French words in English texts. I have chosen to follow what seems to be the simplest method in current usage. All place names are left as they are commonly known: this means that for Senegalese towns the French spelling is accepted, for example, Kaolack rather than Kawlawkh, which is the correct transliteration of the Arabic word from which the town's name derives. Common nouns from French or Arabic words have been rendered phonetically into English: for example, the word marabout loses the extra consonant and vowel used in French and becomes marabu (in adjectival form marabutic), which is the closest approximation to the sound of the word. Proper names cause more difficulty because so many different spellings exist. I have spelled the names of living men as they are most commonly spelled (Al Hajj Saidou Nourou Tall instead of Saidu Nuru Tall, for example), whereas the names of deceased persons are spelled phonetically in the same manner as common nouns. Falilou M'Backé is an exception throughout as, due to the recentness of his death, his first name is left in the form commonly used during his lifetime.

Introduction

The role of religion in politics has interested political analysts for centuries. Politicians apparently have always manipulated the value symbols and gods of their people to serve the ends of the state and their own personal ambitions. In addition, organized religions of all types have used their authority to exert pressure on the state. Thus, the self-immolation of Buddhist monks and nuns in Vietnam in the early 1960's, which so shocked Western observers, can be seen as one method in a long series of efforts to force, through the pressure of public opinion, a nonbelieving government to concede certain demands. Less dramatically, but with greater success, the Catholic church has managed to exert influence on the various governments of Italy.[1] The role of religion can be approached differently by asking how religious beliefs and values effect the political activities of the ordinary citizen or the official. One can, for example, attempt to isolate the religious element and weigh its importance as a motivating or controlling factor, as has been done in an article on political leaders in Morocco.[2] Or, one can study the philosophies of various major religions and attempt to ascertain and evaluate the political component of each.[3] These approaches, of course, in no way exhaust the studies possible on religion and politics. Rather, what they indicate is that the topic is complex and far from easy to deal with adequately.

I have no intention of discussing the general subject of religion and politics here. I am interested in one small country, Senegal, which has neither the historical greatness of Italy nor the current international significance of Vietnam. My concern is quite precise: I am examining the Muslim brotherhoods in Senegal and attempting to delineate their political role. I will use the different approaches to religion and politics mentioned above but make no attempt to explore all the theoretical and methodological possibilities of any approach. Instead, I shall use whatever aspects of the different approaches seem to cast light on the questions of how and why the brotherhoods exert political influence. Senegal is a microcosm in which it has been possible to examine closely the role of religion: other countries with different religions and religious groups will not have identical situations, but the Senegalese case study suggests questions, methods, and factors to consider elsewhere. Moreover, Senegal is an underdeveloped country which presents a modern front in the form of a

[1] See references to the Catholic Church as a modern pressure group in Joseph LaPalombara, *Interest Groups in Italian Politics* (Princeton, 1964), pp. 306–393.

[2] Douglas Ashford, "The Political Usage of 'Islam' and 'Arab Culture,'" *Public Opinion Quarterly*, 25 (Spring, 1961), 106–114.

[3] Donald Smith, ed., *South Asian Politics and Religion* (Princeton, 1966), pp. 3–48.

Introduction

democratic government and party system but which is basically a peasant-dominated agricultural society overwhelmed by problems of poverty and illiteracy. The influence of the Muslim brotherhoods looms large in this setting and suggests questions about religious and traditional groups that control politics behind the modern facade in underdeveloped areas throughout the world. Western scholars are only beginning to understand what is happening in non-Western politics; a close examination of the influence of a dominant religious group in a single underdeveloped country should provide material to illuminate further the process of political development. Without further justification or explanation, therefore, I shall begin introducing the brotherhoods and politics of Senegal.

Once a year in rural Senegal, the Murid brotherhood[4] holds its annual festival, the Magal. During the days before and after the event the roads leading to the Murid capital, Touba, are choked with huge crowds of travelers, some of whom are in trucks, buses, or cars and many others on foot. Thousands of disciples gather in Touba to celebrate the occasion, which is marked by public speeches by the grand khalif of the Murids on the history of the brotherhood and the moral and political duties of the disciples. The government, too, celebrates the event, and the president of Senegal (accompanied by many ministers and officials) usually appears beside the khalif and makes a congratulatory speech in which the government's gratitude for the assistance of the Murids in carrying out the governmental program is acknowledged. Many writers have attempted to capture the impressiveness of the occasion. Not only are the large numbers of people striking, but so are the fervor and excitement of the crowds and the large sums of money (equaling thousands of dollars) collected by the brotherhood leaders from the disciples at the Magal. Most important, however, the Magal symbolizes two significant factors in Senegalese politics. It indicates the existence of religious leaders who control their followers spiritually and temporally, and it indicates recognition of this fact by the government whose officials come to pay their respects to the marabus. The Murids are the most powerful Senegalese brotherhood, but other orders are also politically important. Many non-Murid marabus, such as the head of the major branch of the Tijaniyya, exert great influence

---

[4] The various brotherhoods will be introduced in Chapters 1 and 3. See also Appendix A.

on national and local political events in Senegal.

The incongruity of the influence of the brotherhoods as contrasted with what appears externally to be the reality of Senegalese politics can be seen by looking briefly at the political history of the country. Senegal's were the longest and most continuous contacts with France of any African colony. At an early date (1848) the residents of the four communes of Dakar, Goree, St. Louis, and Rufisque were allowed to elect a representative to the French Chamber of Deputies. And in 1879 their citizens, who were considered French citizens, were permitted to elect their own mayors and municipal councils. Senegalese in other parts of the country did not have these privileges. Thus the Tukulor ethnic group along the Senegal River, the majority Wolof in the central agricultural area, the Serer in the area north of the Gambia, and the other smaller groups in the Casamance and elsewhere[5] had no political rights; they were considered "subjects" and were not allowed to organize themselves politically. However, they did come in contact with French officials and, more importantly, French customs and values.[6]

The political situation in Senegal was altered by the reforms instituted by the constitution of the Fourth Republic (ratified in 1946). At this time French West Africa became an integral part of the French Republic. The distinction between "citizens" and "subjects" was abolished, and voting privileges and rights of free association, free speech, and free press were extended throughout Senegal. All adult inhabitants of Senegal could now elect representatives to the General Council, renamed the Territorial Council in 1957, and to the Federal Council (to which came representatives from all the territories in French West Africa). In addition, all Senegalese could elect deputies to the two houses of the French Parliament, to the Council of the French Union, and to the Economic Council.

The elected Senegalese officials had little control over the

---

[5] The population of Senegal in 1960 was estimated to total 3,110,000 and to include: 1,103,000 Wolof; 595,000 Serer and Niominka; 422,000 Tukulor; 230,000 Peul, Fula, and Laobe; 216,000 Diola and numerous smaller ethnic groups such as the Bambara, Sarakolé Maure, and Lebou. Louis Verrière, "La Population du Sénégal (Aspects Quantitatifs)," unpub. diss. (University of Dakar, 1965), p. 51.

[6] For information on the colonial period in Senegal and on politics up to independence, see Ruth Schachter Morgenthau, *Political Parties in French-Speaking West Africa* (Oxford, 1964). For the post-independence period, see William Foltz, "Senegal," Coleman and Rosberg, eds., *Political Parties and National Integration in Tropical Africa* (Berkeley, 1964), pp. 16–64.

Introduction

Senegalese government, which remained in the hands of French administrators. Nevertheless, the extension of voting privileges to the countryside changed the character of politics in the country. Formerly, men running for office in the four communes or for the post of deputy in France had concerned themselves mainly with the inhabitants of the communes; now politicians tried to build support in the rural areas. Lamine Gueye, founder of the earliest Senegalese branch of a French party (established in 1936), the Section Française de l'Internationale Ouvrière (SFIO), began making trips throughout Senegal to win peasant support. But his opponent, the highly respected poet Léopold Senghor, was the man who succeeded in organizing the former "subjects" of Senegal into the base of support for his party, the Bloc Démocratique Sénégalais (BDS). By the end of 1951, the BDS had asserted its dominance. It became the party that controlled the Territorial Assembly and eventually took over the government of Senegal. In 1959 the BDS, by then called the Union Progressiste Sénégalaise (UPS), joined with the Union Soudanaise in the formation of the Mali Federation. The federation was granted independence in 1960, but soon thereafter disagreements between the Soudanese and Senegalese politicians led to the breakup of the union. UPS leaders have subsequently controlled politics in the independent republic of Senegal almost unopposed.

The UPS was from the outset extremely modern in outlook and organization. It sponsored progressive platforms that were generally congruent with those of the French Socialist Party (except for the anticlerical plank of the latter group, which did not appeal to UPS leaders). When the UPS leaders took over the government they proposed to reform economic and social conditions in Senegal: to liberate the peasants from servitude and to develop the country economically. The latter has been the major concern of the government, for Senegal was, and is, a poor country whose only wealth comes from one crop, peanuts. There was little in the UPS program to offend the French, who had upheld—at least in theory—the principles of social and economic liberation of the peasants and economic development of the country as a whole. Indeed, the UPS did not come to power in the midst of, or as a result of, a strong anticolonial movement such as that which tore Algeria apart for so many years. As it became internationally more fashionable to do so, UPS leaders criticized the colonial regime and called for self-rule, but no major split between the French and the

4

party occurred despite the mistrust of French officials for the UPS when it was first formed. Senghor and his associates showed themselves to be pragmatic in their recognition of the need of Senegal for continued French assistance. Consequently, even at present there are numerous French officials working on all levels of the Senegalese government.

At first the UPS organization included party units formed by different ethnic, regional, and religious groups; but once the UPS had the majority of votes its leaders felt strong enough to create a more democratic organization based on local units in each village or city *quartier*. The party is now organized pyramidally and is based on cells called committees, above which are subsections, sections, and departmental commissions of coordination. All the commissions in a region (there are twenty-seven departments and seven regions in Senegal) elect the Regional Union. The supposed governing body of the UPS is the Congress, which meets biannually and includes delegates from each departmental commission as well as members of the government and directors of the UPS youth and women's groups. The Congress elects the members of the National Council, which in turn elects a sixty-member Bureau Politique that in fact directs the party.[7]

The UPS organization parallels the structure of the government, and the personnel staffing the highest positions of both organizations overlap. The Senegalese government is modeled on the Fifth Republic. It is a lay state (guaranteeing freedom of worship to all religions), whose constitution proclaims it a democracy in which the people choose the government and are guaranteed liberty and equality.[8] The government is headed by a president, who is elected every four years. He selects the ministers and secretaries who form his cabinet and the former are responsible to him rather than to the Assembly. The Senegalese Assembly itself is unicameral and is elected every four years at the same time as the president.[9] The Assembly technically holds the legislative powers, but in practice approves bills presented by the ministers without question. There is also a judicial system, separate from the legislative and executive branches and headed by a Supreme Court that in theory judges the constitutionality of the laws.

[7] See *Le Militant UPS* (Dakar, 1965), pp. 33–40. and *l'Unité africaine,* July 19, 1960.

[8] *Le Militant UPS,* p. 19.

[9] Each party presents a list of candidates for the entire country, and voters choose between the lists on election day. All adult Senegalese are eligible to vote.

Introduction

Seen in terms of party and government development, then, Senegal appears similar to many other African countries except that in Senegal national parties developed at an earlier date. Moreover, the government of Léopold Senghor has managed to keep control over the country thus far, permitting consistent attempts to implement and extend the reform program—which consistency has not been possible in many neighboring states. But the existence of powerful Muslim orders clashes with this picture of a modern political party and government. In doctrine and organization the Muslim brotherhoods date back to the Middle Ages. The leaders' prayers are believed to send people to Paradise, and consequently the disciples blindly obey orders given them. The marabus' power is cemented further by their assumption of the prerogatives of the former kings and nobles, including the right to payment for the use of land.[10] Some marabus have developed this system into semislavery that extends to every area of life. Many of the more enlightened leaders would like to see living conditions of their disciples improved and therefore they encourage the adoption of improved agricultural techniques. But few if any marabus permit their disciples much independence. Control of the marabus, therefore, indicates a fundamental conflict between the Muslim brotherhoods and the government's modern development program.

At this stage in studies on African politics the existence of powerful traditional (in the sense of non-Western and non-modern) leaders influencing politics behind the modern facade is not, or should not, be surprising. A number of scholars have criticized early writings about African mass parties, in which they were falsely seen as analogous to Western parties and were believed to have organized and reformed traditional society.[11] The existence in Senegal of a government and party system that is Western in form does not necessarily indicate the absence of strong traditional leaders. But the situation in Senegal still remains unique. Other countries with large Muslim populations, Guinea or Algeria, for example, do not have such powerful Muslim brotherhoods. Why should these groups have gained such dominance in Senegal? Moreover, why do they still exert

[10] Valy-Charles Diarassouba, "L'Evolution des structures agricoles du Sénégal (déstructuration et réstructuration de l'économie rurale)," unpub. diss. (University of Paris, 1965), pp. 236–237.
[11] Aristide Zolberg, *Creating Political Order: The Party-States of West Africa* (Chicago, 1966), pp. 9–36.

Introduction

their influence apparently unopposed in any major way, and what are the limits of that influence?

The brief synopsis of Senegalese political history presented above does not answer these questions and, indeed, is perhaps more misleading than helpful because it does not give any idea of the political context in which the brotherhoods operate. Politics in Senegal is more understandable if the political culture ("the particular distribution of patterns of orientation toward political objects among members of a nation"[12]) is outlined. In Senegal this is a culture in which, although the government is Western and democratic in form, the majority of the citizens feel uncertain or negative about the central government and focus their loyalties and expectations on local leaders. Citizens do not feel themselves participant in a democratic governing process; rather, they recognize the authority of paternalistic, authoritarian regional and national rulers who head the clans[13] and brotherhoods. Similar primary structures—clans, families, church groups—are also important in Western countries but they are balanced and influenced by secondary structures that include such organizations as the political parties, trade unions and the government itself. The latter type of organization certainly exists in Senegal: there are unions such as the railworkers' Cheminot, political parties, business organizations like the Chamber of Commerce, Friendly Societies for the protection of urban immigrants from rural areas, and even modern Muslim associations promoting Islamic reform. But these groups have only a minor influence on politics, and they have no significance compared to the primary clan and brotherhood alignments from which political leaders are drawn.

In the Senegalese government, important clan-family-brotherhood alliances are represented in governmental and administrative offices. Official positions, although usually held by Western-educated men, are not earned necessarily because of superior achievement, but because of selection by a certain primary group. The same situation can be found in the United States when government officials hold office because they are appointees of influential men or families. The difference between

---

[12] Gabriel Almond and Sydney Verba, *The Civic Culture: Political Attitudes and Democracy in Five Nations* (Princeton, 1963), p. 13. Admitting the difficulty of defining "political culture" in a precise way, the following discussion is nonetheless included in an attempt to convey a feeling for Senegalese politics as contrasted with politics in more developed nations.

[13] A clan is a group of families or parts of families claiming descent from a common ancestor.

7

the two situations is that there is a widespread belief in the United States that the best trained and prepared men ought to get the jobs. In Senegal, despite the recently formed National School of Administration, public expectation looks to the clan-brotherhood alignments as the proper source of candidates and as the major factor in government decisions. The difference is only one of degree but it is still significant.

The political culture of Senegal also permits and even encourages a certain kind of attitude towards public office on the part of politicians. There is no widespread belief, as in the United States, in the myth that politicians are responsible to their constituents and that the latter have a duty to keep themselves informed and dismiss politicians when they stop acting in the public interest. The word "myth" is used because politicians in the United States are not always controlled by their constituents and often act to further their own and not the public interest. Nevertheless, in the United States there is a tradition of political involvement of citizens and of responsibility of officials that circumscribes the action of the latter and forces them to pay at least lip service to their role as representatives of the people.[14] In Senegal, politicians are responsible to their clans in that they cannot forget to obtain advantages for them. But politicians are not restrained by any tradition of popular control and have not been nourished on the ideal of public service and governmental responsibility. The result is a high incidence of open usage of public office and even public funds to increase private wealth. American politicians in office also obtain money and privileges for themselves and their supporters, but this action is disguised behind their apparent attention to public interest. When a Senegalese politician or a brotherhood leader gains personal wealth, this of course often directly benefits his supporters—to whom, and to whose relatives, he gives money or jobs as they are needed. This fact is true in both countries, but in Senegal, where everyone belongs to one of these groups, such benefits are more important and more striking. In the United States, although the system of clan patronage through government office is widespread, it is considered contrary to the interests of the public as a whole and in conflict with accepted political norms, mores, and values. In Senegal, in contrast, the system is considered natural and acceptable. Questions of public interest are not of concern

[14] See Almond and Verba, *The Civic Culture,* pp. 337–374.

Introduction

to most people who remain oriented to their clans or brotherhood groups.

Senegalese marabus, acting as the leaders of highly organized and powerful brotherhoods, are able to openly demand money and favors from politicians. The fact that the marabus are religious leaders does enter into the situation. The belief in necessary separation between religious and material interests, and in the ideal of otherworldliness in sincerely religious men, exists in Senegal as it does in the United States. Nevertheless, leading marabus traditionally have been wealthy landowners whose positions were reinforced by gifts from their disciples. The most religiously renowned men sometimes give their money away and live in great simplicity. Others, less religiously oriented, show more concern with the earthly benefits extractable from their positions. Both kinds of marabus can be found demanding and receiving money from the government. The more religious marabu makes his demands in the name of his impoverished disciples and the worldly marabu demands what he can get as his holy right.

Marabus have an advantage over other clan leaders in their dealings with the government and with their followers merely from the fact that they are religious leaders. As V. O. Key pointed out, many Church leaders have an edge over leaders of other pressure groups because the former wield the sanctions of excommunication and Hell.[15] Furthermore, in many religious groups the leaders occupy a sacred position that mere mortals find hard to question. In the rational pragmatic culture of the United States, Protestant church leaders, and their Catholic counterparts to a lesser extent, must contend with the opinions of their followers just as the leaders of a secular pressure group like a trade union must at least give the illusion of defending the interest of the association as a whole. In a less pragmatic culture, where religious values rank importantly in daily life, the responsibility of the religious leader to the wishes of his group is emphasized less. Even in the United States it is unlikely that a Catholic group might try to decide policy questions for the church. In Senegal it is even more unlikely that members of a brotherhood would dictate to their leaders. In fact, there is no such thing as a meeting of disciples to decide policy: at a gathering of a brotherhood, members are informed of their leaders' policy decisions. Later a disciple may respectfully submit

[15] V. O. Key, *Politics, Parties and Pressure Groups* (New York, 1958), p. 134.

his suggestions on a particular matter in personal interviews, but under no circumstances would disciples order a leader to act in a certain way.

A marabu can hold powers that few, if any, religious leaders in the West enjoy. Marabus are commonly believed to have certain magical abilities that make them superhuman. It is tempting to deny the importance of magic as a political factor, for although popular belief may credit the marabus with supernatural powers, it seems incongruous that Western-educated politicians would believe such stories. But in fact such a denial is naive. Even in the modern political culture of the United States, the Attorney General of Massachusetts in 1964 hired a New York psychic to help find a dreaded strangler. In Senegal this kind of superstition is even more significant in politics. Most people, including many government officials, believe in the powerful magic of certain men. Stories about magical feats of the marabus add considerably to their stature and sometimes influence government officials in their relations with the brotherhoods. Marabus are able to extort extra privileges and compromises because of their extrahuman powers. Al Hajj Ibrahima Niass, the leader of a major Tijani group, is such a marabu. Educated Senegalese men insist that Niass magically crippled one opponent Senegalése politician and burned alive a clan leader who opposed him. Kwame Nkrumah is known to be a disciple of Niass', although the Ghanaian never became Muslim. Nkrumah's belief in the Senegalese marabu's powers manifested itself in generous gifts of various kinds throughout his years in office.[16] Less powerful than Niass, but important as an example, is Cheikh Tahirou Doukouré, the former Senegalese presidential adviser on religious affairs. The son of a Hamalliyya marabu, Doukouré's rise to political power and subsequently to great wealth is commonly credited to his mystical and magical abilities. Many of the most powerful, well educated, and highly respected members of the Senegalese government believe in his magic, especially in his powers of divination and his ability to cast evil shadows on a man's future.[17]

Despite the power marabus derive from their superhuman abilities and their traditionally high status, however, these Muslim leaders are not omnipotent. In fact, there is no absolute

[16] Interview with members of Niass' brotherhood, Feb. 2, 1966, Kaolack; interview with government official, Mar. 1, 1966, Dakar.

[17] Interviews in 1966 with government officials: Feb. 16, Dakar; Feb. 17, Dakar; Mar. 1, Dakar; Mar. 14, Dakar; Mar. 24, Dakar; Mar. 25, Dakar.

difference between the control exerted by members on their leaders in a brotherhood and that of the members of a modern Western trade union. Even a marabu cannot afford to ignore totally the wishes of his disciples. Similarly, it must be emphasized that the difference between the Senegalese political system and a Western regime is also only one of degree. Senegal, after all, is a country in transition. Recognition of the great power of the brotherhoods should not prevent realization of the multiple, constant changes that are taking place. The government is democratic in form and espouses a modern reform program. Economic development necessities combined with spreading Western education have begun to introduce new criteria for action which challenge the authority of norms of status, custom, and superstition. In certain circumstances in which the demands of modern development oppose the desires of the marabus, politicians carefully maneuver around the request of the latter. Government officials may acquiesce to a marabu in order to gain his help in carrying out a reform the long-term goal of which may contain the destruction of the brotherhood system. The officials' acquiescence is thus in large part functional (to achieve certain ends) as well as traditional and irrational (fear of and respect for the marabu's status and personal magic). Consequently, the influence of the marabus is balanced by other factors, including the desire of many highly placed officials to promote the development of Senegal.

The exact extent of the power of the marabus cannot be easily understood, especially since their authority is not publicly acknowledged by Senegalese officials. It is necessary to examine the relations between the government and the brotherhoods and also between the marabus and their disciples before any precise evaluation can be made. Moreover, an investigation into the reasons for the authority of the brotherhoods must first be conducted as a basis for any evaluation of the current situation. The following chapters begin by analyzing the historical conditions under which the brotherhoods became powerful and the ways in which the present pattern of political relations was established. The contemporary political role of the brotherhoods is examined beginning in Chapter 3: the important brotherhoods are described and their inter-relationships analyzed before their relations with parties, government officials, the government reform program, and modern Muslim reform groups are treated. In sum, this study aims at clarifying the function of the brotherhoods in Senegalese politics.

1 The Foundations of Political Power

The political power of the Senegalese Muslim brotherhoods results from the peculiar sociologic and economic conditions in Senegal at the time the orders were established. But the brotherhoods' organization in itself has favored the development of these orders as significant political units in many countries. The basic characteristics of brotherhoods in general must be examined before the arrival of the orders in Senegal can be evaluated.

The *Tariqa* Organization

Islam as a whole has been called a brotherhood, and the word has been applied to the various Muslim sects. Used here the term brotherhood refers to the mystical Muslim orders (*tariqa*, plural *tariqas*) that spread throughout the Muslim world beginning in the twelfth century.[1] There are hundreds of such orders,[2] most of which accept sunni or orthodox tenets and adhere to one of the four major schools of Muslim law. In West Africa they usually belong to the Malikite school. All the *tariqas* are based on sufism, that is, Muslim mysticism, which had its roots in the very early years of Islam.[3] The early sufis were most concerned with achieving a state of union with Allah. With this goal in mind they developed a series of ascetic practices that each mystic had to carry out in order to reach the desired state of moral purity and spiritualism.[4] Emphasis then was on individual moral and physical discipline as well as mystical theology and ritual. Later, however, mystical theology and ritual assumed paramount importance and ascetic discipline was de-emphasized.[5] This development, according to Louis Massignon, a scholar of Islam, caused sufism to become the intellectual exercise of the few. The rest of the Muslim community lost contact with the mystics and thus potential benefits from sufi orders such as overall patterns of good conduct and personal sacrifice.[6] Massignon sees this separation of sufi orders

[1] Louis Massignon, "Tarika," and "Tassawuf," *Encyclopedia of Islam,* ed. M. Houtsma *et al.* (London, 1929), XLII, 667–672, 681–685.
[2] See partial list of brotherhoods in Massignon, "Tarika," 669–672.
[3] Sufism comes from the word for wool: the early ascetics wore woolen habits. Philip K. Hitti, *History of the Arabs from the Earliest Times to the Present* (London, 1956), p. 433. See also H. A. R. Gibb, *Mohammedanism: An Historical Survey* (New York, 1955), pp. 99–113.
[4] Octave Depont and Xavier Coppolani, *Les Confréries religieuses musulmanes* (Algiers, 1897), p. x.
[5] Louis Massignon, *Essai sur les origines du lexique technique de la mystique musulmane* (Paris, 1914–1922), p. 62.
[6] *Ibid.,* p. 285.

and the community as a symptom of social decadence, which
is the main motif of the present disintegration of the Muslim
world. Nor is Massignon alone in his harsh commentary on
developments in the later sufi movement. Other critics insist
that sufism, which splintered into numerous brotherhoods
warring over small doctrinal points, contributed heavily to the
breakup of the Muslim empire.[7]

But later brotherhoods were also responsible for the spread
of Islam throughout the non-Arab world. In the early years
orthodox Muslims disapproved of the sufi because any relaxation
of Muslim law and tradition, which sufism seemed to condone,
threatened the "true" faith.[8] Gradually opposition began to
slacken as the mystical doctrines became more widely known.
By the end of the tenth century orthodox theologians began to
tolerate sufism, although the enmity between the sufis and
the orthodox community was never completely ended.
Nonetheless, by the twelfth century sufism had achieved
widespread popularity, even influencing sunni Islam to such
an extent that mystical concepts were incorporated into orthodox
doctrines. Furthermore, sufi brotherhoods converted most of
Central Asia, Indonesia, India, and North and West Africa,
among other places, to Islam. Because of sufism Islam became
an international and universal religion.[9] The sufi brotherhoods
in their later stage appealed directly to the average uneducated
man, emphasizing emotions rather than actual behavior and
softening the strict rules of Islam. The orders, which popularized
Muslim traditions and made them understandable to everyone,
also tolerated pre-Islamic beliefs and practices as long as those
beliefs did not contradict the desired goal of union with Allah.[10]
The changes permitted by sufism had the effect of vulgarizing
and distorting Islamic teachings,[11] but they also meant that
sufism could appeal to men at the lowest socioeconomic level.

The brotherhoods also attracted followers because of the
security offered members of the tightly-knit sufi organization.
By the time the orders had spread throughout the world they
were organized into hierarchies with a shaykh at the top

[7] P. J. André, *L'Islam et les races*, vol. II; *Les Rameaux (mouvements régionaux et sectes)* (Paris, 1922), p. 28.

[8] Gibb, *Mohammedanism*, p. 104.

[9] John Alden Williams, ed., *Islam* (New York, 1961), pp. 149–150, 196–198; Gibb, *Mohammedanism*, p. 110, and Massignon, *Essai sur les origines*, p. 5.

[10] Wilfred Cantwell Smith, *Islam in Modern History* (New York, 1959), p. 44, and Gibb, *Mohammedanism*, p. 110.

[11] Williams, *Islam*, p. 169, and Gibb, *Mohammedanism*, p. 110.

assisted by a khalif (head of the order in a given territory, appointed usually by the shaykh), the *muqaddam* (often a territorial leader and delegate of the shaykh), and then various levels of brothers whose positions depended on their study and practice of the orders' doctrines. The base of the pyramid was the mass of lay adherents. The intricacies of the brotherhood hierarchy were known to educated members, but to the uneducated layman the organization did not seem complex. For the average Senegalese member, for example, the mass of followers, lay or not, were (and are) known as *taalibé* despite the fact that this word means student. *Taalibés* were distinguished from the leaders, who were called marabus.[12] The highest leader of a branch of a brotherhood in Senegal was called the khalif or grand marabu. (The word khalif is also used to denote the head of each marabutic family, which can lead to confusion for the outsider.)

Supposedly leadership of the orders went to the most educated and devout individuals, but in actuality leadership positions were usually hereditary and certain families came to dominate the orders. A particularly well educated, devout, and/or charismatic individual might on his own merits rise to a leadership position, just as a particularly undevout, uneducated man might attract few followers; but the general principle of hereditary succession to leadership had become well established in the orders by the time they arrived in West Africa.[13]

The average member of a brotherhood, a brother at the lowest level, was initiated into the order by learning the *dhikr,* that is, the special prayers and exercises prescribed by the founder. Only the select few could go beyond this through the various stages of progression of the soul to achieve *ma'rifa,* or knowledge of God.[14] The mass of lay followers and brothers were not even aware of the stages of mystical progression, although the highest leaders of the orders even in Senegal (which was relatively superficially Islamized at first) were often aware of the levels of mysticism and had achieved

[12] The word *marabu* is a French term from the Arabic word for fortified camp or monastery. A marabu was originally a simple ascetic, but eventually the term became synonymous with a leader of a brotherhood. The word also has been used to denote a holy object such as a tree or a stone or strange (perhaps magical) animals. See Edouard Montet, *Le Culte des saints musulmans dans l'Afrique du Nord et plus spécialement au Maroc* (Geneva, 1909), p. 16; Depont and Coppolani, *Les Confréries religieuses,* p. xii, Louis Rinn, *Marabouts et Khouan : étude sur l'Islam en Algérie* (Algiers, 1884), pp. 70–71.

[13] Depont and Coppolani, *Les Confréries religieuses,* p. 197.

[14] Rinn, *Marabouts et Khouan,* pp. 65–67.

ma'rifa themselves. The majority of disciples, in contrast, were content to rely on their marabu for the benefits of communion with God. They were unacquainted with most of the prescriptions of Islam and merely worked for their marabus, who in turn prayed for them. A few brothers pursued their study of the Qu'ran beyond the elementary stage of blind recitation and these few often became marabus themselves.

The mass of brothers and the lay adherents to any particular order found security in joining an organization which demanded only their obedience and promised salvation in return. This dependence of the followers on their marabus that leads to the apparent ignorance of the mass of followers of Islamic doctrines is what struck most European observers in West and North Africa in the nineteenth century as it does today. This factor is also the key to the political potential of the brotherhoods.

The major reason for dependence of the followers on their leaders stems from the emphasis in later sufism on the ability of the leader of a brotherhood to act as intermediary between Allah and man. Early sufis emphasized individual effort to reach union with the Divine, but later it was stressed that most men could not achieve this union by themselves.[15] It became characteristic of a tariqa for the followers to blindly obey the commands of their leaders in religious matters and in most secular matters as well. That the system, analogous to the relationship between the Hindu student and his guru in India,[16] could be carried to extremes is shown in the popular prescription of the founder of the Qadriyya order, Si Muhammad Abd al-Qadar al-Djilani (died 1166): "You should be in the hands of your shaykh like a corpse in the hands of the mortician. It is God Himself who commands through his voice."[17]

Reinforcing the authority of the leaders was the widespread belief in magical powers of the marabus. Legends about miracles performed by early mystics and about the magical ability of current leaders, who had received divine grace from Allah, grew concurrently with the decline in emphasis on personal efforts at reaching God. Leaders were revered as saints and their tombs became the goals of pilgrimages at which all kinds

[15] André, L'Islam et les races, II, 27.
[16] Depont and Coppolani, Les Confréries religieuses, p. 12.
[17] Quoted in Napoleon Ney, Un Danger européen: les sociétés secrètes musulmanes (Paris, 1890), p. 22; M. Charles Brosselard, Les Khouans: de la constitution des ordres religieux musulmans en Algérie (Algiers, 1859), p. 14; and Rinn, Marabouts et Khouan, p. 90.

of miracles would occur. Edouard Montet observed that nineteenth-century marabus in Morocco had innumerable powers. They could become invisible, walk on water, heal the sick, and resurrect the dead and they were even invulnerable to bullets.[18] The brotherhoods that came into West Africa were oriented around leaders whose ability to perform magical feats is renowned even today. The founder of the Muridiyya in Senegal was believed able to walk on water and to have been transported to Jerusalem and home again in one night through his own powers; Ibrahima Niass is known to talk to the trees, call out devils to attack his enemies, and readily communicate with God.

Not surprisingly, the awe and devotion of the disciples for their leaders was practically demonstrated through material contributions. In North Africa, for example, members paid an offering or *ziara* that was sometimes quite large. They also paid a tenth of their crops to the brotherhood. Land around the motherhouse of the order was worked by the members, who made payments to the brotherhood. The leaders received money for initiation into the order, from people asking favors (a form of *ziara*), and from labor corvées (disciples everywhere were morally obliged to sow and harvest for their leaders). The brotherhoods, and the leaders personally, had large resources: indeed, as noted by Octave Depont and Xavier Coppolani, nineteenth-century authorities on North African Islam, all that a man possessed could be taken by his leader.[19]

Many observers have criticized the brotherhoods for the subjugation of their disciples. Depont and Coppolani somewhat bitterly comment: "The slavery is complete, a slavery both material and moral [which] is spread from one end to the other of the Muslim world. . . ."[20] But, like other scholars of Islam, they are forced to admit that the blind obedience of the disciples to their leaders, and the members' loyalty to the brotherhood as a whole, was the major source of strength of the Muslim orders.[21] The brotherhoods were tightly unified behind their leaders, who spoke and acted with great authority as a result. The marabus were the rural political leaders with whom the French administrators had to contend. So it was that *tariqas* appeared to the French almost as states in themselves inside

[18] Montet, *Le Culte des saints musulmans*, pp. 26–32.
[19] Depont and Coppolani, *Les Confréries religieuses*, pp. 227, 239, 243–244.
[20] *Ibid.*, pp. 203–204.
[21] Brosselard, *Les Khouans*, p. 16.

the French colonial state. At various times and in various places, in North Africa for example,[22] the brotherhoods' political power was translated into a territorial political force which either posed a major threat to French hegemony in an area or provided it with generous support, depending on the circumstances.

The Brotherhoods' Arrival in Senegal

The powerful North African *tariqas* spread to West and Central Africa beginning only shortly after their introduction to the Maghreb. They coincided with and reinforced the general Islamization of the area immediately to the south of the Sahara. Members of the brotherhoods were proselytizing in the West African area prior to the eighteenth century, as records of the individual orders show; however, the brotherhoods did not become extremely important in the area until the nineteenth century.[23]

One of the oldest brotherhoods and one of the first to appear in West Africa was the Qadriyya. Founded by the sharif[24] Sidi Muhammad Abd al-Djilani (1079-1166), the order spread rapidly from near Baghdad all over the Middle East. As Qadriyya branches moved further and further from their place of origin, their emphases began to differ from branch to branch though Qadiri everywhere retained certain common prayers and rituals were known for their stress on philanthropy, charity, piety, and humility. The order was introduced into the Sahel region in the fifteenth century by Muhammad Abd al-Karim al-Maghrib. It was the son of one of al-Maghrib's disciples, Al-Mukhtar ibn Ahmad (1729-1811) of the Arab Kunta tribe, who founded the motherhouse north of Timbuktu which became the center for the order in West Africa.[25]

The second most important *tariqa* to come from North Africa to West Africa was the Tijaniyya order, founded by the sharif Ahmad ibn Muhammad al-Tijani (1735-1815) in Ain Mahdi

[22] Depont and Coppolani, *Les Confréries religieuses*, p. 243; Montet, *Le Culte des saints musulmans*, p. 42.

[23] For a discussion of the different phases of Islam in West Africa see Alphonse Gouilly, *L'Islam dans L'Afrique Occidentale Française* (Paris, 1952), p. 47. See also, for discussion of the eleventh-century phase of the Islamization of the Sudan, Daniel McCall, "Islamization of the Western and Central Sudan in the Eleventh Century," unpub. ms. (Boston University, 1967).

[24] A sharif is supposedly a man descended from Muhammad who has a special gift of grace owing to his descent.

[25] André, *L'Islam et les races*, II, 32–33; Rinn, *Marabouts et Khouan*, pp. 173–200; Depont and Coppolani, *Les Confréries religieuses*, pp. 293–355; Gouilly, *L'Islam*, pp. 97–105; J. Spencer Trimingham, *Islam in West Africa* (Oxford, 1959), p. 94.

(Morocco) in approximately 1781, following a revelation by the Prophet. Al-Tijani claimed, because of his revelation, to have authorization from the Prophet himself and thus to be able to dispense with the spiritual chain used by most shaykhs to link their teachings to those of Muhammad through a series of spiritual masters. He also forbade his followers to swear allegiance to other orders (multiple allegiances had previously been condoned). Al-Tijani's brotherhood eventually became known, in contrast to the Qadriyya and others, for its relatively uncomplicated prayers, litanies, and exercises, the simplicity of which facilitated the understanding of its teachings and practices by uneducated followers.[26]

Following the death of al-Tijani, his spiritual successors quarreled and caused the division of the order between two centers at Fez and Ain Mahdi. It is with the former center that most of the important Tijaniyya branches in West Africa are affiliated. The actual process of conversion of the Western Sudan was begun before the founder's death when a missionary of the Ida Ou Ali ethnic group, named Muhammad al-Hafiz ibn al-Mukhtar ibn Habib al-Baddi, was sent to his home region in Mauritania. He successfully converted his tribe to the Tijaniyya, and his branch of the order influenced considerably the proselytization of the surrounding area including portions of northeastern Senegal.[27] Large scale Tijani missionary ventures associated with commercial activities were conducted throughout West Africa after 1815; but the most important conversion of the period was that of Umar Tall (1794/7-1864). Tall, a Tukulor from the Senegal River area, was named *muqaddam* of the order when he was in Mecca. He returned to the western Sudan and in 1852 launched a holy war with his army of volunteers. He conquered a large part of the area touching on Senegal in the Tukulor-inhabited Futa Toro, which remained solidly Tijani even after his death. The proselytization efforts of Tall's disciples from the Futa were vitally important in the conversion of the Wolof, the largest ethnic group in Senegal.[28]

The Wolof group is the most important in Senegal owing to its size and, more significantly for this study, to the fact that

[26] Trimingham, *Islam in West Africa*, p. 94; André, *L'Islam et les races*, II, 39–42; Rinn, *Marabouts et Khouan*, pp. 416–480; Depont and Coppolani, *Les Confréries religieuses*, pp. 213–288. For discussion and evaluation of the Tijaniyya see Jamil M. Abun-Nasr, *The Tijaniyya: A Sufi Order in the Modern World* (London, 1965).

[27] Trimingham, *Islam in West Africa*, p. 97.

[28] Abun-Nasr, *The Tijaniyya*, pp. 106–128; A. Le Chatelier, *L'Islam dans l'Afrique Occidentale* (Paris, 1899), pp. 167–174.

in general only the brotherhoods with a majority of Wolof disciples have become significant political forces in Senegalese national politics. In contrast, the neighboring Tukulor, who were converted to Islam before the Wolof and aided in the conversion of the Wolof to the Muslim orders, has only locally important marabus who generally do not have the same degree of authority as their Wolof peers. This can be partially explained by the location of the Tukulor on the periphery of Senegal outside the central important economic zone, but by itself this is not an adequate explanation. It is useful to consider the process of Islamization of the Tukulor and compare the process with conversion of the Wolof in order to determine the salient factors in the Wolof situation.

The Tukulor are a sedentary agricultural people located mostly in the Futa Toro from Bakel to Dagana, although a fairly large number of them have migrated elsewhere, for example, south in Senegal to find work.[29] The Tukulor have had, at least since the tenth century, highly organized state systems in the Senegal River area. The ethnic group itself in daily life and in the heritage of ruling positions follows patrilineal designs and is divided according to status groups.[30] This system encompasses at the bottom a captive group, followed by low-caste artisans and musicians (*griots*), then a large group of free peoples dominated by the top group, the *torodbé*, formerly a religious aristocracy that led the ethnic group into holy wars beginning in the eighteenth century.[31]

The exact date of the Tukulor's first contacts with Islam is

[29] Abdoulaye Diop, a Guinean sociologist at the Institut Français d'Afrique Noire (IFAN) estimates that 25 percent of active Tukulor men have migrated to Dakar to find jobs; Diop, *Société toucouleur et migration (enquête sur la migration toucouleur à Dakar)* (Dakar, 1965), p. 4.

[30] I use the term "status group" to mean a group with a well-defined common status. Such groups have certain distinctive rules of behavior although they are not rigidly self-contained. See Martin Klein, *Islam and Imperialism in Senegal; Sine-Saloum, 1847–1914* (Stanford, 1968), p. 8.

[31] For general information on the origins, history, and customs of the Tukulor, see: Felix Brigaud, *Connaissance du Sénégal*, fas. IX: *Histoire traditionnelle du Sénégal*, Etudes sénégalaises no. 9, Centre de Recherches et de Documentation du Sénégal (CRDS) (St. Louis, Senegal, 1962); J. Lombard, *Connaissance du Sénégal*, fas. V: *Géographie humaine*, Etudes sénégalaises no. 9, CRDS (St. Louis, 1963); Henri Labouret, *Paysans d'Afrique Occidentale* (Paris, 1941); L. Geismar, *Recueil des coutumes civiles des races du Sénégal établi par L. Geismar, administrateur en chef des colonies* (St. Louis, 1933); Abdou Salam Kane, "Coutume civile et pénale toucouleur (cercle de Matam)," *Coutumiers juridiques de l'Afrique Occidentale Française*, vol. I: Sénégal (Paris, 1939), pp. 35–115; H. Gaden, "Du Regime des terres de la Vallée du Sénégal au Fouta antérieurement à l'occupation française," *Bulletin du comité d'études historiques et scientifiques de l'Afrique Occidentale Française* (BCEHSAOF), 18 (October–December, 1935), 403–414. For modern statistics, see Republic of France, *La Moyenne Vallée du Sénégal étude socio-économique)*, by J.-L. Boutillier et al. (Paris, 1962).

unknown. Al-Bakri reported that one of the rulers of Tekrur, a partially Tukulor state on the Senegal River, converted to Islam in the eleventh century. This does not mean that the mass of Tukulor converted then, for later Arabic writings refer to the inhabitants of Tekrur as pagans. But the Tukulor at least had been exposed to Islam by the eleventh century. Records indicate that the first known dynasty in the Futa, the legendary Dyaôgo, was Muslim and supposedly made up of people from Mauritania who ruled from 850 to 1000. Thorough Islamization did not take place until the *torodbé* drove out the pagan Peul Denyianké dynasty in 1776. Thereafter the conversion of the Tukulor on all levels was intensified, and a series of chiefs called *almamys* ruled until the end of the nineteenth century when the French took over the Futa.[32] Islam, thus, was a factor of great importance in Tukulor history for many centuries. The ethnic group traditionally has felt itself to be the carrier of Muslim civilization and superior to the pagan peoples around it.[33] From the early eighteenth century the Tukulor, led by the *torodbé*, launched holy wars on neighboring groups. By then they were in direct contact with representatives of Muslim brotherhoods. The Qadriyya order, through the medium of the Ida Ou Ali and later the Kunta ethnic groups, had many disciples among the Tukulor, but with the coming of Al Hajj Umar Tall (Al Hajj meaning one who has made the pilgrimage to Mecca) the majority of Tukulor became Tijani.

Marabus of Tukulor origin founded the important brotherhoods among the Wolof. (For example, both the Sy and M'Backé families, from which have come the major politically important marabus, are of Tukulor origin.) The Wolof are located from Dagana to St. Louis, south into the former kingdoms of Cayor and Baol to the Gambia River, and east into Senegal Oriental. By the fifteenth century the Wolof had migrated from the area northeast of the Senegal River to the regions immediately south of the river. There they established a state (probably between 1200 and 1350) which, particularly in its southern part, included numerous Peul and Serer peoples. The state remained united until approximately 1550, when it was divided into six kingdoms. The heritage of ruling positions was not organized in the same manner for all the kingdoms: they varied from

---

[32] Diop, *Société toucouleur*, pp. 10–11; Vincent Monteil, *L'Islam noir* (Paris, 1964), pp. 62–63; Labouret, *Paysans d'Afrique Occidentale*, pp. 81–84.
[33] Diop, *Société toucouleur*, p. 13.

Djolof, with a strictly patrilineal system, through Walo, Cayor, and Baol with mixed systems, to Sine and Saloum with matrilineal organizations. In their daily lives the Wolof retained fixed matrilineal and patrilineal customs. Like the Tukulor, they were sedentary and agricultural, and they were organized into a status-group system which was very similar to that of the Tukulor. At the apex were the kings and nobles, followed by a much broader group of free men, the *badolo*; the lowest free group was that of the despised artisans and musicians, superior only to the slaves and captives at the bottom of the pyramid.[34]

When Islam first became known to the Wolof is uncertain. Early European travelers to West Africa, beginning with the Venetian Alvise de Ca' da Mosta in the fifteenth century, all note that marabus were present in the court of the Wolof kings although the mass of the population remained pagan.[35] According to Wolof traditions, the first convert to Islam was a descendant of the second king of Walo, named Wade, who went to the Futa Toro in the end of the thirteenth century.[36] Tradition does not say who the next important converts were; however, in the era of the first conversions to Islam the Wolof were infiltrated by marabus (probably of Berber and Tukulor origin) who gained

[34] For general information on the origins, history, and customs of the Wolof, see: David Gamble, *The Wolof of Senegambia,* Ethnographic Survey of Africa, Western Africa, pt. XIV, ed. Daryll Forde (London, 1957); Henri Gaden, "Legendes et coutumes sénégalaises: cahiers de Yoro Dyâo," *Revue d'éthnographie et de sociologie,* 3 (1912), 119–137, 191–202; L. J. B. Bérenger-Feraud, *Les Peuplades de la Sénégambie* (Paris, 1879); M. Campistron, "Coutume ouolof du Cayor (cercle de Thiès)," *Coutumiers juridiques,* I, 117–146; M. J. C. Fayet, "Coutumes des ouolof musulmans (cercle de Baol)," *Coutumiers juridiques,* I, 147–193; Geismar, *Receuil des coutumes civiles;* David Ames, "Belief in 'Witches' among the Rural Wolof of the Gambia," *Africa,* 29 (July, 1959), 263–273; David Ames, "The Selection of Mates, Courtship and Marriage among the Wolof," *Bulletin de l'IFAN,* 18, ser. B (January–April, 1956), 156–168; David Ames, "Wolof Cooperative Work Groups," in Bascom and Herskovits, eds., *Continuity and Change in African Cultures* (Chicago, 1959), p. 237; R. Rousseau, "Le Sénégal d'autrefois: étude sur le Cayor, cahiers de Yoro Dyâo," *BCEHSAOF,* 16 (April–June, 1933), 237–298; Rousseau, "Le Sénégal d'autrefois: études sur le Oualo, cahiers de Yoro Dyâo," *BCEHSAOF,* 14 (January–June, 1929), 133–211; Rousseau, "Le Sénégal d'autrefois: étude sur le Toubé, papiers de Rawane Roy," *BCEHSAOF,* 14 (1931), 334–364; Rousseau, "Le Sénégal d'autrefois: seconde étude sur le Cayor (compléments tiré des manuscripts de Yoro Dyâo)." *Bulletin de l'IFAN,* 3–4 (1941–1942), 79–144; Rousseau, "Le Village ouoloff (Sénégal)," *Annales de géographie,* 42 (Jan. 15, 1933), 88–94.

[35] G. R. Crone, ed., *The Voyages of Cadamosto and other Documents on Western Africa in the Second Half of the Fifteenth Century* (London, 1937), p. 31; Valentim Fernandes, *Description de la Côte Occidentale d'Afrique (Sénégal au Cap de Monte, Archipels),* ed. T. Monod, A. Teixeira Da Mota, R. Mauny (Bissau, 1951), pp. 7, 9; P. Cultru, *Premier Voyage du Sieur de la Courbe fait à la Coste d'Afrique en 1685* (Paris, 1913), p. 30; M. A. Adanson, *A Voyage to Senegal, the Isle of Goree, and the River Gambia* (London, 1759), p. 56; G. Mollien, *Voyage dans l'intérieur de l'Afrique aux sources du Sénégal et de la Gambie fait en 1818 par ordre du gouvernement français* (Paris, 1820), p. 148

[36] Monteil, *L'Islam noir,* p. 94.

positions of respect among the ethnic group. In many cases marabus were considered sacred, their high positions stemmed partly from their ability to read and write.[37] They began to take over the jobs of Wolof magicians, including making amulets to ward off evil and officiating at coronation ceremonies and at celebrations associated with the rites of passage (birth, circumcision, marriage, and death).[38] Consequently, Islamic prayers and formulas were added to traditional beliefs. Throughout the early years of contact, the Wolof were being conditioned by the marabus for an eventual acceptance of Islam.

By the nineteenth century many Wolof had converted to Islam. This was true despite the rejection of Islam by the Wolof ruling classes. The earliest European travelers found Muslim nobles ruling a pagan population, but apparently the superficial Islamization of the rulers disappeared after the fifteenth and sixteenth centuries.[39] A well-known Wolof tradition documents this in its account of a revolt sponsored by the marabus, who sided with the Maures and led the Wolof common people against their kings and nobles. The marabus helped persuade the Wolof to rebel by promising that millet would grow without planting; when this did not take place the Wolofs threw out the Maures and rulers were re-elected from former Wolof royal families.[40] After the kings no longer professed Islam, what remained was a reverence for the marabus, who continued to live among the Wolof. Some marabus seem to have given up their religion under pressure from the nobles, and their only connection with Islam was their retention of the Wolof title *serigne* (for marabu). The marabus remained in the Wolof kingdoms, heading small colonies of followers and living on land for which, unlike other foreign cultivators, they did not pay. They were headmen in their villages and taught Qu'ranic schools. As long as they did not interfere directly in affairs of state they were left in peace by the ruling class.[41]

By the end of the eighteenth century only the warrior and noble group was inalterably opposed to Islam, for other groups among the Wolof had converted. Finally in the late nineteenth century the process of mass conversion, having received

[37] Mollien, *Voyage dans l'intérieur de l'Afrique*, pp. 106–107; Labouret, *Paysans d'Afrique Occidentale*, p. 90.
[38] Sieur de la Courbe mentions the involvement of the marabus in traditional ceremonies in the seventeenth century. Cultru, *Premier Voyage*, p. 117.
[39] Gaden, "Legendes et coutumes," p. 123.
[40] Cultru, *Premier Voyage*, pp. 132–133.
[41] Gaden, "Legendes et Coutumes," p. 123.

considerable impetus from the holy wars of Umar Tall, was complete. Tall's disciples included Maba Diakhu (died 1867), who led a revolt against the Serer government of Rip (in southwestern Senegal) in 1861 and later converted the pretender to the throne of Cayor and the ruler of Djolof, who consequently spread Islam widely in their kingdoms. Other Tijani marabus, like Saermaty, Maba's son (died 1887), Ahmadu Shaykhu (died 1875), son of an earlier marabu of Podor, and Mamadu Lamine, a Sarakolle marabu (died 1887) were of lesser significance but contributed to the Wolof conversion. Their efforts were reinforced and extended—peacefully—by Qadriyya marabus including, most importantly, Shaykh Sidia and his disciples, from Mauritania, who had many followers in the Senegal River area previous to the Tijani wars; and Ahmad Bamba, who founded his own order (derived from the Qadriyya) in 1886.[42]

The Brotherhoods, "Revitalization," and Social Reform

The bare historical facts of Tukulor and Wolof conversion to the brotherhoods do not explain the differences in political importance of the orders in the two groups, but a closer examination of first Wolof and then Tukulor social and economic conditions at the time of conversion offers a partial explanation of the situation. Such an examination also explains why the Wolof, who had resisted mass conversion to Islam for many centuries, should have joined the brotherhoods in the late nineteenth century.[43]

The most significant factor may be that the brotherhoods acted as revitalization movements for the Wolof in the nineteenth century. The process of revitalization has been described by several writers including the anthropologist Anthony Wallace, whose discussion points out the major elements to consider in the Senegalese situation. According to Wallace, a revitalization movement occurs when the social order is in a state of decay or stagnation, when the current beliefs and patterns of behavior of a given social order no longer seem to respond to the actual situation. Social decay is accompanied by general disillusionment and insecurity for the average individual, who finds that what

---

[42] See Le Chatelier, L'Islam dans l'Afrique Occidentale, pp. 167–223.
[43] See Lucy Behrman, "The Islamization of the Wolof by the End of the Nineteenth Century," in McCall, ed., Boston University Papers on Africa (New York, 1968); Behrman, "The Political Significance of the Wolof Adherence to Muslim Brotherhoods in the Nineteenth Century," African Historical Studies, 1, no. 1 (1968), 60–68.

he has been taught to believe, and the people he has been taught to respect, no longer seem to represent adequate defense against the problems of daily life.[44] The process of stagnation and decay may happen because an outside group or outside ideas challenge or undermine old ways of doing things. At other times a given social order merely seems to lose momentum of its own accord. The revitalization movement appears to offer new ideas and new ways of handling changing conditions. Often it espouses new ideology and rejects part or all of the old order. It offers new, or partly new, patterns of behavior and usually a new leader or leaders around whom converts can rally. Revitalization movements often inspire fanatic self-sacrifice and devotion on the part of their adherents—which fanaticism seems appropriate for the difficult process of breaking away from the old social order.[45]

A revitalization movement may or may not take the form or a religious movement. Wallace assumes that all major religions have acted as revitalization movements at one time or another.[46] Thus the rapid spread of Islam in its early years throughout the Arabic peninsula may have occurred because it filled the role of a revitalization movement. Later, like all other such movements, when Islam had been accepted widely as a way of life, it too became subject to stagnation and decay. Eventually it was being challenged by other reformers representing puritan branches of Islam and even other religions and secular organizations. This is the customary cycle of revitalization—agitation against the unsatisfactory old order, rebellion, acceptance, or conversion of the majority (or conceivably failure to attract support and therefore disappearance of the group); finally the revitalization movement becomes the "establishment," the accepted order, and loses its reforming zeal. The cycle can then begin anew.

By the middle and end of the nineteenth century, the Wolof social order had been severely challenged by new forces in its

---

[44] Anthony F. C. Wallace, Religion: An Anthropological View (New York, 1966), pp. 157–166, 209–215. See also Karl Mannheim, Ideology and Utopia: An Introduction to the Sociology of Knowledge, trans. Louis Wirth and Edward Shils (New York, 1966), pp. 192–263. A number of political scientists have observed the same phenomena but state their analyses differently. David Truman and V. O. Key both observe that when the equilibrium of a group is disturbed it will turn to substitute activities or may form a new group in order to regain its balance. Truman, The Governmental Process: Political Interests and Public Opinion (New York, 1964), pp. 30–31, and Key, Politics, Parties and Pressure Groups, pp. 46–49.
[45] See Eric Hoffer, The True Believer: Thoughts on the Nature of Mass Movements (New York, 1966).
[46] Wallace, Religion, p. 30.

environment. The group had enjoyed a highly developed state system and social structure that was connected to its religious beliefs and customs. The arrival and entrenchment of colonialists disturbed the equilibrium of Wolof society and forced its members to look for ways to replace or reinforce the old life.[47] The French introduced new elements into the situation which challenged old values and habits. Under the necessity of conquering the Senegal area, the French broke the power of the former Wolof rulers, the kings and nobles. Those who resisted were beaten in war. Those who did not, or who at least eventually made peace with the colonialists, found themselves auxiliaries of the French—their power was undermined when the French abolished their sources of revenue and made them dependent on the colonial system for their authority.[48] The Wolof kingdoms were broken up into smaller units whose rulers were impotent adjuncts to the French government. With the destruction of the rulers' power the whole related religious and social system of the Wolof was dislocated.

The French were also responsible for the introduction of the commercial peanut crop into the traditional agricultural system, and this crop too contributed to disintegration of the old social order. Traditional Wolof agriculture was closely tied to family living patterns. Land was not individually owned, rather the family as a whole would cultivate fields that it owned and could not sell; the family chief distributed these lands to the others. The major part of working time was spent in the common fields. The cultivation of peanuts for profit added a new factor to the situation: farmers now had a strong monetary incentive to raise peanuts for themselves in the small private plots that ceased to be unimportant addenda to their work in the common fields and instead became the focus of attention. Many farmers apparently continued to pay lip service to the position of heads of the families through annual gifts in money or kind, but the chain of authority and the close family unity had gone. As the French administrator L. Geismar wrote: "Personal possessions, formerly of negligible quantity, now dominate in importance over the collective family goods. From which [fact], by the force

---

[47] A similar process may have taken place among the Fon of Dahomey. See David Apter, *The Politics of Modernization* (Chicago, 1965), pp. 81–122.

[48] Julian Wood Witherell, "The Responses of the Peoples of Cayor to French Penetration, 1850–1900," unpub. diss. (University of Wisconsin, 1964), pp. 160–161.

of things, [comes] a disaggregation of familial solidarity which has had its consequences in all domains."[49]

The disintegrative force of the growth of peanuts began to be felt by the end of the nineteenth century. Peanuts had been grown in Senegal for many centuries, but it was after the end of slavery in 1848 that the French turned to peanuts in the attempt to make Senegal a profitable colony. After 1850 they were produced in significant amounts for export. By the end of the nineteenth century peanut growers in the area producing the largest part of the crop (Cayor) had spread out to find new fields in surrounding regions, thus extending the destructive effect of commercial peanut cultivation.[50]

The impact of the growth of peanuts combined with the effect of the loss of power of the chiefs in undermining the Wolof social order. These were but two of the many ways in which the French presence affected the Wolof—as the very existence of a controlling foreign group with a completely different way of life was bound to affect them. Moreover, outside changes such as shifts in power in the Futa Toro and elsewhere may have added to the general insecurity of the period. In any case, the Wolof social system was in severe crisis and as a result its people were groping for some kind of security, something that would give a focus to their daily lives. Largely because of this insecurity, Islam in the form of brotherhoods took hold among the Wolof in the end of the nineteenth century. The brotherhoods offered an order of life that seemed more adequate than the old one had been for meeting problems of adjustment and adaptation to the new influences brought in by the French and to the general insecurity of the age.[51]

The brotherhoods were well suited to providing security for their new members because of their close-knit organization and the authority of their leaders. The orders did not change most Wolof customs, but they did provide a framework that

[49] Geismar, Receuil des coutumes civiles, p. 35.

[50] Joseph Fouquet, La Traite des Arachides dans le pays de Kaolack et ses conséquences économiques, sociales et juridiques, Etudes sénégalaises no. 8 (St. Louis, 1958), p. 19, and Witherell, "The Responses of the Peoples of Cayor," p. 23.

[51] Jean Suret-Canale and Marcel Cardaire both reinforce this interpretation by their assumption that new religious sects, Islam in particular, attracted followers because of the disintegration of the old ways of life. See Jean Suret-Canale, Afrique noire occidentale et centrale: géographie, civilisations, histoire (Paris, 1964), pp. 128–129; Marcel Cardaire, L'Islam et le terroir africain (Koulouba, 1954), p. 49. See also Paul Marty, Etudes sur l'Islam au Sénégal, vol. I: Les Personnages (Paris, 1917), p. 192.

Muslim Brotherhoods and Politics in Senegal

gave a meaning to the whole which had been absent before.
A new promise of salvation, represented by new leaders
apparently more powerful than the old, made the intrusion
of foreign ideas and ways of doing things easier to accept.
Because organized action was possible for their members,
the brotherhoods also made easier the rejection by the Wolof
of new and old elements that particularly disturbed their lives;
thus the Muslim orders frequently acted as opponents to
colonial domination and in some places they organized to fight
against hated neighboring groups. Military opposition to other
groups has been typical of revitalizing religious sects of all
kinds at various times in Africa, for example, the Christian
Harris Movement in the Ivory Coast and the Muslim Hamallists
(a subgroup of the Tijaniyya).[52] In North Africa, too, at an earlier
date, Muslim brotherhoods had acted as centers of resistance
to French colonizers.[53]

Not all brotherhoods among the Wolof fought the colonialists
in the late nineteenth century, though branches of the Tijaniyya
led by such disciples of Umar Tall as Maba certainly recruited
many Wolof volunteers seeking a way of opposing the advance
of the Europeans. Of equal, if not more, importance among
the Wolof was the Muridiyya brotherhood, which shortly after
1886 became a major symbol of resistance. This order was
founded by Muhammad ibn Muhammad ibn Habib Allah,
who was called Ahmad Bamba, of the M'Backé family. His
brotherhood was feared by the French from the outset, since
Bamba's father had been counselor and teacher to Maba and had
married Lat Dyor's sister (Lat Dyor led the last major resistance
to the French in Cayor). The order attracted numerous followers
of Lat Dyor, Maba, and other resistance leaders. Rumors
circulated about Bamba's plans to overthrow the French and as
a result he was twice exiled. But his periods in exile only seemed
to add to his reputation, and he drew a large following among
those who felt alienated from the French.[54]

[52] The man for whom this brotherhood was named was Sharif Hamalla ould Muhammadu ould Saidina Umar (1888–1942). Following the lead of another marabu, he insisted that true Tijanis should recite the *wasifa* (a prayer of the order) eleven instead of twelve times as was customary in West Africa. He never tried to found a new order, and it was a French misinterpretation to call his followers Hamallists as if they formed a new *tariqa*. Correctly his group is known as "Tijaniyya Onze Grains" (grains being the rosary beads, one for each *wasifa*). The word Hamallist (Hamalliyya) is used here because it is a widely accepted means of identifying the group.

[53] Depont and Coppolani, *Les Confréries religieuses*, p. xxi.

[54] See Lucy Behrman, "Ahmad Bamba, 1850–1927," in Willis, ed., *Studies on the History of Islam in West Africa* (London, expected 1969). For detailed information on the origin, develop-

The Foundations of Political Power

The brotherhoods also allowed oppressed groups within the ethnic groups to assert themselves in a way not permitted before by the old social order. Former captives and women and youths supposedly joined Umar Tall's brotherhood to liberate themselves from control of the old tribal leaders.[55] Elsewhere Hamallism, too, drew former captives as well as people of low social origin and unsatisfied chiefs and marabus who all tried to find a solution to their problems by joining a *tariqa*.[56] In Wolof territory at the end of the nineteenth century the marabus attracted peasants who wished to throw off the oppressive yoke of the nobles and kings.[57] The French administrator Robert Arnaud described the success of the brotherhoods among the Wolof as follows:

In Wolof country, formerly, the intrusion of Islam constituted a real social revolution and was in reality an opposition of the proletarian caste against the aristocracy, a war of classes. The cultivators had the strongest possible feelings of repulsion against the warriors who exploited them. Thanks to Islam they formed a bloc against the aristocracy which had remained fetichist, and for a long time the marabus remained the natural leaders of the crowd against its oppressors. . . .[58]

The success of the brotherhoods among the Wolof, however, was not simply or even mainly due to Wolof peasants having found in the orders a way to oppose their old rulers. *All* dissatisfied elements in the ethnic group turned to the brotherhoods to find a new life. Thus, the Murid movement drew militant warriors and nobles as well as poor freemen and former slaves.[59] The nobles, as the French scholar Paul Marty wrote, saw the Murid movement as an opportunity to regain

---

ment, and major characteristics of the Murids, see Cheikh Tidjane Sy, "Traditionalisme mouride et modernisation rurale au Sénégal: contribution à l'étude des rapports entre socialisme et Islam en pays sous-développés," unpub. diss. (University of Paris, 1965). Also see Vincent Monteil, "Une Confrérie musulmane: les Mourides du Sénégal," *Archives de sociologie des religions,* 7, no. 14 (1962), 77–102; E. Marty, "Les Mourides d'Ahmadou Bamba (rapport à M. Le Gouverneur Général de l'Afrique Occidentale)," *Revue du monde musulman,* 25 (December, 1913), 3–164.

[55] Suret-Canale, *Afrique noire,* pp. 128–129, and Sy, "Traditionalisme mouride," pp. 26–27.

[56] R. L. Moreau, "Les Marabouts de Dori," *Archives de sociologie des religions,* 9, no. 17 (1964), 113–134.

[57] Vincent Monteil, "Lat-Dior, damel du Kayor, (1842–1886) et l'Islamisation des Wolofs," *Archives de sociologie des religions,* 8, no. 16 (1963), 103–104. The myth quoted on p. 23 above can be used as evidence also.

[58] Robert Arnaud, "L'Islam et la politique musulmane française en Afrique Occidentale Française," *Renseignements coloniaux et documents publiés par le Comité de l'Afrique Francaise et le Comité du Maroc* (1912), p. 9.

[59] Marty, *Etudes sur l'Islam au Sénégal,* I, 206.

their lost authority. The former slaves, Marty suggests, had been accustomed to being tightly controlled by the ruling classes and saw in the Muridiyya a new form of security that was no more than a new type of slavery under descendants of their former rulers.[60] Marty probably overlooked the fact that many peasants turned to the Murids to escape from the control of the nobles, but his analysis does indicate the complexity of the motives of those who became Murid; "class" war does not adequately explain the situation. It would be a mistake to ignore the important social implications of the Muridiyya and the other brotherhoods because the new lords, the marabus, broadened the ruling group at least at first. This leavening of the ruling elite is typical of revitalization movements whose leaders are generally chosen by different criteria than those used for the rulers of the old order. Moreover, the brotherhoods, like other revitalization movements, permitted a degree of social mobility which the old order had lacked. Among the Wolof, land ownership and political power in general were now divided between the aristocrats who became marabus and old marabutic families, some of which had earlier been poor and without power. In addition, a peasant disciple, if he worked hard and obeyed his marabu, could hope to be elevated to the position of a lesser marabu—an advance in status not possible in the secular tribal system. Neverthless, the nobility together with the marabutic families provided the bulk of the marabus. The mass of peasants and low-caste artisans remained subjugated as they had been under the tribal system.[61]

Whatever the nature of the social reforms espoused by the Muslim brotherhoods in the middle and late nineteenth century, these groups lost their reformist character shortly after they appeared. The "revitalization" movement gave way to a new established order, and "sclerosis," as Jean Suret-Canale called it, set in. The momentum for change was lost and the marabutic leadership became closely associated with the colonial regime and the old aristocracy. This development had taken place in the Umarian Tijani brotherhood in Senegal before the Murids became important.[62] By the early 1900's it was true

[60] *Ibid.*

[61] Cheikh Tidjane Sy states that Bamba was a reformer who was able to detach himself from the traditional caste system in order to judge men by merit rather than by status. Nevertheless, few low-status men became important marabus even in the early years. See Sy, "Traditionalisme mouride," pp. 56–57. See also below, Appendix B.

[62] Suret-Canale, *Afrique noire*, p. 129.

of the latter brotherhood as well. Colonial officials began
to remark on the alliances that were formed. A 1904 political
report states:

It is thus that we must observe carefully the alliance which is tending
to be formed between the aristocracy . . . and the marabus. The marabus
enrich themselves by alms collections, the aristocracy . . . which drew its
fortune from its arbitrary power . . . becomes more impoverished daily.
The descendants of the old families, therefore, give to the wealthy shaykh
their daughter or relative in exchange for a large *dot*. . . .[63]

A 1915 political report comments:

And it is precisely because these religious chiefs profit from these
situations, that they have an interest in being with us and if necessary
they would be our support. Their interests are intimately connected
to ours. . . .[64]

The Muslim *tariqas* among the Wolof had become part of the
"Establishment" by the early twentieth century. The marabus
replaced the nobles as recognized leaders of the ethnic groups,
and disciples turned to their marabus when they wanted
something done. The marabus had taken over the prerogatives
of the nobles, such as payments for use of the land. The position
of the religious leaders was, of course, more powerful than that
of the secular nobles because of the organization of the
brotherhoods and the loyalty of the members. The leading
marabus in the various brotherhoods over the last sixty years
have taken advantage of their position and asserted their
authority throughout the countryside.

The closing cycle of the revitalization process left the
brotherhoods firmly entrenched among the Wolof. The
revitalization concept may also account for the lack of political
power of the Tukulor marabus. An examination of the
socioeconomic system of the Tukulor Futa Toro indicates that
the brotherhoods did not act as full revitalization movements
in that area. Proof of this assertion can be obtained from
considering the long process of Islamization of the ethnic group,
which process was intensified at different points by forceful
conversion efforts such as those led by the post-1776 *torodbé*.

[63] Dakar Archives (hereafter DA), "Rapport sur la situation politique en l'AOF" (1st trimester), 2G 4.5.
[64] DA, Lieutenant Governor to Governor General (July 22, 1915), no. 695, 2G 15.6.

Membership in the brotherhoods came at the end of the Islamization process when the conversion had been largely accomplished. The brotherhoods were merely a further step in the long drawn-out conversion to and deepening of Islam in Tukulor life. The brotherhoods did have appeal as reforming organizations to the Tukulor. Umar Tall's brotherhood in particular led a popular holy war against neighboring ethnic groups and the French colonialists.[65] In addition, as mentioned above, captives and other underprivileged groups joined the Tijaniyya order because it symbolized possible new status for them that the old order had not allowed. But Islam and the brotherhoods apparently did not come in as replacements for the old socioeconomic system in general. Rather, the brotherhoods became part of the system which already existed.

In the Futa Toro, politics and society in general are directed by important clan leaders. A clan in the Futa will be made up of more than one family (not all of one family necessarily belonging to the same clan). The leaders of the clans head important noble families in whose hands the ownership of the land, divided into large concessions, still remains.[66] Continued dominance by those families, particularly as shown in their continued control of the land, indicates the stability of the old socioeconomic order. The social structure of the Tukulor has not remained unchanged throughout the many centuries since Islam was first introduced, but the changes had not resulted in a loss of power by the nobles by the time the brotherhoods arrived. Thus the fall of the Denyianké in 1776 led to the rule of Muslim leaders called *almamys*, but the change in rulers did not alter the economic and political control of the area by Tukulor clan leaders. The *almamys* themselves were named by the great families and their power stemmed not from their role as Muslim leaders but from their family connections.[67] The marabus in the Futa never had the opportunity of rising to power. Even Al Hajj Umar Tall, who united many clans for a short time in a religious war, did not change the Futa system.[68] The lack of political power of the Tukulor marabus, then,

[65] Abun-Nasr, *The Tijaniyya*, pp. 106–128.
[66] Diop, *Société toucouleur,* p. 11.
[67] *Ibid.*
[68] Other interpretations are commonly given in Senegal. For example, the Tukulor are said to be more educated in Islam and therefore less likely to depend heavily on their marabus than the Wolof. This interpretation seems unsatisfactory given the fact that marabus in North Africa among equally "educated" disciples sometimes had political power similar to that of the Wolof Muslim leaders.

probably stems from the fact that they never replaced the nobles
as leaders of the ethnic group, for the Tukulor social order was
not in the same state of dislocation as the Wolof when the
brotherhoods became important. Of course this explanation
is only a partial one and does not cover such exceptions to the
rule as Al Hajj Saidou Nourou Tall, the most important living
descendant of Umar Tall. Saidou Nourou is a major political
leader in Senegal with a large part of his following in the Futa.
His authority seems to rest on his position as clan leader and
marabu and on his own great political skill. Throughout the
last sixty years he has had extensive relations with the central
government, both the colonial and the Senegalese, and has used
his power over the Tukulor to give him authority in dealing with
the government. Saidou Nourou Tall is not alone in being a clan
leader as well as a marabu and a skilled politician. Many if not
most of the politically important Wolof marabus are all these
things. Brotherhoods contain various clans which are still
important in Senegal; the leading marabus usually are drawn
from members of traditional aristocratic families. No one reason
completely suffices to explain the present distribution of power
among the marabus, though some attempt must be made
to select the most fundamental factors leading to the
brotherhoods' political strength. I think the two major points
made here remain the most important to consider: on the one
hand the history of sufism and the development of the
brotherhoods as tightly disciplined groups indicates a major
cause of the brotherhoods' current political power. On the other
hand, the rise to power of the *tariqas* in Senegal in the late
nineteenth century can only be understood by analyzing
the political, social, and economic conditions at the time
the brotherhoods became important. Among the Wolof and
the Tukulor the significant point seems to be the role filled
for the former by the orders as revitalization movements.
Indeed, in other non-Wolof groups among whom the
brotherhoods attained political power the situation seems to have
been similar to the Wolof situation described here.[69]

---

[69] See mention of Ahmadou Saidou (whose Tijani branch may exemplify a similar
phenomenon); M. Chailley et al., *Notes et études sur l'Islam en Afrique noire* (Paris, 1963),
p. 154.

2 The Impact of the French

The foundations of political power of the Senegalese marabus were established by the end of the nineteenth century, when the French were consolidating their authority over Senegal. It was not just as an indirect impetus in the revitalization period that the French played a significant role, however; rather, through the direct relations between colonial officials and brotherhood leaders in the early twentieth century the present pattern of political authority of the marabus developed and was accepted. In the beginning of this period the French disliked the brotherhoods because of the holy wars associated with them, but the colonial authorities' attitude gradually changed, at first unconsciously and then deliberately through a curious re-evaluation of their position that led to a change in their policy.

Early French Muslim Policy

From their nineteenth-century experience in North and West Africa the French recognized the importance of Islam in policy considerations. They attached an officer to the Political Bureau of the French West African Federation (the AOF, established in 1904) whose sole job was to deal with Muslim problems. Colonial officials were encouraged to record in detail what they knew of each marabu, and every political report sent to the governor general of the federation and then on to the minister of colonies contained a section on Muslim affairs in the AOF and specific problems in Senegal. In turn, a mass of letters and circulars went out from the governor general to the lieutenant governor of Senegal, and to other AOF lieutenant governors and lower officials such as the *commandants de cercle*, outlining ways of handling the marabus. The various instructions sent out were often unclear and contradictory to such an extent that the French scholar R. L. Moreau concluded that there was no Muslim policy.[1] However, it is possible to isolate certain themes which were emphasized and which, if considered together, seem to form a quasi-coherent theoretical framework that French officials applied to the brotherhoods.

Early twentieth-century colonial authorities were aware that their presence in West Africa had helped the spread of Islam.[2] They recognized that they had contributed to the breakdown of the tribal system and thus enhanced the appeal of the *tariqas*. They were aware that the imposition of peace on the Western

[1] Moreau, "Les Marabouts de Dori," p. 123.
[2] Arnaud, "L'Islam et la politique musulmane," p. 4.

Sudan had facilitated the spread of Islam by allowing missionaries to travel unmolested. Moreover, they had openly underlined their belief in the superiority over other Africans of the literate Muslims by choosing them as clerks, guides, and interpreters. Indeed, as Paul Marty wrote: "Through our administration . . . we have done more for the spread of Islam during the last half-century than the marabus were able to achieve during three hundred years."[3] But it was decided in the early twentieth century that the deliberate fostering of Islam had to be stopped, for Islam in the form of brotherhoods constituted one of the last threats to the French West African empire.[4]

The French did not wish to openly oppose the Muslim religion. They insisted on the right of Africans to practice whatever religion they chose.[5] More importantly, the French did not oppose Islam because they felt that persecution would have even more dangerous results than encouragement had had. Persecution would provoke "not open revolt . . . [but] the state of spirit natural to peoples of all races disturbed in their faith, the thirst for persecution . . . and a more intensive proselytization."[6]

French policy, then, was to be neutral, although this did not mean that Muslims would be allowed to spread their religion as they wished. Rather, proselytization was to be restricted in order to prevent Islam from becoming a unified, spreading anticolonial force. The "politique des races" which had been used in other places throughout the French empire (for example in Madagascar) was to be followed. This policy was an effort to keep various ethnic and religious groups separated from each other so that no major anti-French consolidation could take place. Islam, which the French saw as a religion divided into small warring sects differing widely from each other,[7] was to be kept divided. Divisions were to be maintained by ceasing to appoint indigenous chiefs to rule over large territories, since these chiefs often had imposed their religion with their temporal authority. Under the new policy each ethnic group was to be

[3] Paul Marty, *Etudes sur l'Islam au Sénégal,* vol. II: *Les Doctrines et les institutions* (Paris, 1917), p. 374.

[4] J. Brevié, *Islamisme contre "Naturalisme" au Soudan Français: Essai de psychologie politique coloniale* (Paris, 1923).

[5] DA, William Ponty (Sept. 14, 1909), 19G 1.

[6] DA (May 11, 1914), 19G 1. See also Alain Quellien, *La Politique musulmane dans l'Afrique Occidentale Française* (Paris, 1910), p. vii.

[7] DA, Robert Arnaud, "Situation générale de l'Islam en Afrique Occidentale Française," 19G 1.

ruled by someone from within it whenever possible. The ethnic units would relate directly to the French administrators without the intermediary of provincial tribal chiefs. The *cercle* with its French *commandant* was to be the significant administrative unit in the AOF. The *commandant* would make it his business to be in direct contact with the various ethnic groups under his control, thus preventing any interterritorial Muslim buildup and facilitating tax collection and other administrative tasks.[8]

The second part of the Muslim policy emphasized that the French language and French cultural values were to be spread through West Africa. Connected to the French belief in their civilizing mission, this strand of policy maintained that Muslim culture was superior to pagan ways of life but inferior to French culture. In addition, Islamic culture was supposed to be foreign to West Africa and Arabic was considered more difficult than French for Africans to learn.[9] The spread of French culture would have direct political significance, as the adoption of French customs would make Africans more amenable to French rule and would lead to the development of the AOF according to French plans.[10]

One of the early moves to disseminate French culture was the attempt in 1903 to abolish Muslim courts in Senegal. The first Muslim courts had been opened in St. Louis in 1848 (and reformed in 1857), at a time when Islam was still favored by French administrators. The courts had had jurisdiction over Muslims, who elected to abide by their decisions in civil matters such as marriage, inheritance, wills, and donations. The 1903 law decreed that all Africans would come under the same secular French court system. Muslims in the old town of St. Louis , however, protested that they were being discriminated against since Muslims elsewhere in the French empire had their own courts. The officials gave in to pressure, and in 1905 Muslim tribunals reopened in St. Louis and Dakar and in 1907 in Rufisque.[11] But the jurisdiction of Muslim courts remained restricted to a small number of civil matters and only affected the inhabitants of the communes in which the courts were located. In other areas a basically French system prevailed, although concession

[8] DA, Governor General, "Sur la Politique indigène du Sénégal" (Sept. 22, 1909), 19G 1; also Governor General, "Circulaire sur la politique indigène" (Sept. 22, 1909), no. 186, 13G 72, and Governor General to Minister of Colonies, "La Politique indigène en AOF" (1912), 13G 72.

[9] DA, Arnaud, "Situation générale de l'Islam."

[10] *Ibid.*

[11] René Pautrat, *La Justice locale et la justice musulmane en AOF* (Rufisque, 1957), p. 105, and Quellien, *La Politique musulmane*, pp. 218–242.

was made to the Muslims in that *qadis*[12] were chosen as
assessors in cases involving Muslims. Use of Arabic was also
prohibited in the Muslim courts and in administrative
correspondence in 1911: all judgments and letters were thereafter
to be in French, for, as the Governor General explained, Arabic
was the principal factor in the success of Islam. Developing
a knowledge of French would help to limit Islam. Spreading
French would help forge "the most sure weapon with which
to successfully fight against our ineluctable adversaries . . .
marabus or defeated former political chiefs . . . who will not
forgive us for [our] substitution of a regime of liberty and justice
for the shameful exploitation of the masses by a few privileged
ones."[13]

The greatest hope for the replacement of Muslim culture
by French was the proposed introduction of French education
in Senegal and the ending or diminishing in number of the
Qu'ranic schools.[14] At this time in rural areas the only formal
education any child received came from the marabus and their
Qu'ranic schools, of which there was a very large number:
in Senegal in 1912 there were approximately 1,700.[15] But the
general level of education offered was extremely low. Aside
from a few exceptional well-educated marabus, the majority
of teaching marabus had scant knowledge of the Qu'ran or of
Arabic.[16] Most of them, as had long been the custom in Senegal,
were largely preoccupied with other activities—they were
farmers or traders or fishermen and were generally poor and lived
simply, as did their neighbors. One of a marabu's advantages
was that he was expected to pass on his smattering of knowledge
of the Qu'ran and holy matters to children who were sent to
him for this purpose. The children in turn were sent by the marabu
to beg and/or to work in his fields and often spent most of their
time in these occupations rather than in study; it is not surprising
that the majority learned very little. Paul Marty estimated that
ninety-five out of a hundred pupils who had finished a Qu'ranic
school could not read, write, or understand Arabic at all.[17]

[12] A *qadi* is a Muslim educated in Muslim law according to one of the four major schools, who is therefore qualified to judge in a Muslim court.

[13] DA, Governor General to interim Governor General (Jan. 12, 1912), no. 50, 17G 39.

[14] DA, Governor General (September. 14, 1909), no. 982, 19G 1.

[15] Paul Marty and Jules Salenc, *Les Ecoles maraboutiques du Sénégal: La Medersa de Saint-Louis* (Paris, 1914), p. 29.

[16] *Ibid.*, p. 35.

[17] *Ibid.*, p. 35–57. Marty may have been too harsh in his criticism of the Qu'ranic schools; see Ivor Wilkes, "The Transmission of Islamic Values in the Western Sudan," unpub. ms. (Northwestern University, 1968), p. 7.

The Impact of the French

The French wished to reform the Qu'ranic school system radically and to draw pupils into schools where the French language and French ideas were taught. An important decree in 1903 declared that no one could start a Qu'ranic school without authorization from the lieutenant governor of Senegal. Each marabu had to submit to the secretary general a copy of his judicial record, a certificate of good moral conduct, and proof that he was a French citizen or subject. The requirement alone of such documents would exclude a large number of marabus because many had been involved in anti-French campaigns. The 1903 decree went on to require that each applicant take an examination administered by the *qadi* in St. Louis or by administrators suggested by known Arabic scholars. This examination, depending on the requirements established, would eliminate all but a handful of marabus, since very few knew Arabic well. A commission was set up to inspect the Qu'ranic schools and each marabu was required to keep a registry in French of his pupils; as most marabus knew no French, the latter provision would have been very difficult for them to fulfill. The marabus also had to have a certificate proving that their students were attending French schools, and by this provision they would have been left with almost no students because most Senegalese children normally did not attend French schools. Finally, the decree stated that any school with less than twenty pupils would be closed. The majority of Qu'ranic schools had well under twenty students, and therefore this provision was enough to shut three-fourths of those in existence in Senegal.[18]

In the same year decrees were passed establishing primary schools in villages, in regions, and in urban centers. In these schools French, reading, writing, and arithmetic would be taught. An *arrêté* of 1906 offered 300 francs as maximum subsidy to any marabu who would spend at least two hours a day teaching French.[19] Above the primary school level, a superior primary school offering a Certificat d'Etudes Primaires was established for students in the urban areas. There also were to be higher professional schools for master workers and a Normal School to train teachers, interpreters, *qadis*, and chiefs. The latter was divided into two sections, the first for teachers and the second for *qadis*, chiefs, and interpreters. The second, a continuation of Louis Faidherbe's Ecole de Fils de Chefs (established in 1856),

[18] *Journal officiel du Sénégal et dépendences (J.O.)* (Aug. 15, 1903), 481–482.
[19] Marty and Salenc, *Les Ecoles maraboutiques*, p. 81.

was attached to the *madrassa* (Muslim school) of St. Louis created by decrees in 1907 and 1908.[20] The *madrassa* was supposed to train marabus and other Muslims in the elements of Arabic and Muslim law while they were also learning French and their civic duties to the colonial state. It was hoped that the products of the *madrassa* would gradually replace the existent marabus as the Muslim leaders of Senegal, for the former were believed to be ignorant and hostile.[21]

The third major part of early Muslim policy was to end the exploitation of the masses by their marabus. Foremost on the list of exploitations were the alms collections of the marabus, who openly solicited money and gifts from their followers. Traditionally, the Senegalese gave what he could to his marabu as a fee for his children's education or as a contribution after harvest or for a favor from the holy man. Frequently the marabu would also send representatives among his followers or visit them himself in order to collect money. This system appeared to the French, who wished to stop it immediately, as the worst kind of extortion; therefore part of the 1903 law regulating Qu'ranic schools also forbade the marabus to send children out to beg under threat of immediate closure of the school if the provision were not obeyed.[22] In addition, in 1906 the Governor General demanded that all foreign marabus be placed under immediate surveillance and reported to the central authorities.[23] In 1911 Governor General William Ponty stated any marabu with no physical incapacity living off alms alone should be imprisoned for vagabondage.[24] The Lieutenant Governor of Senegal in the same year passed a bill including even more extensive measures. Local officials who had tried to fight the marabutic collections, he stated, had met with little success not only because of ruses adopted by the marabus, but also because of the "obstinate silence" of the victims who insisted in court that their contributions were voluntary. His proposed law would have made it possible to end the marabus' collections even if the donor claimed that he wanted to give his money to the religious leader, for any subscription without authorization of the lieutenant governor was prohibited.[25]

[20] Quellien, *La Politique musulmane*, pp. 252–256.
[21] *Ibid.*, p. 255.
[22] J. O. (Aug. 15, 1903), 481.
[23] DA, Governor General to Lieutenant Governor (Feb. 10, 1906), no. 262, 19G 1.
[24] DA, Governor General, circular (Dec. 26, 1911), no. 117, 19G 1, and Arnaud, "Situation générale de l'Islam."
[25] DA, décret 1911, 19G 3.

The Impact of the French

The marabus were to be cut off from one of their primary sources of wealth: their collection of alms. In fact, the French fully intended to destroy not only the marabus' economic power but their temporal power as well. The French envisaged a gradual reduction of power of all the chiefs including traditional non-Muslim leaders and marabus. William Ponty described this theory in an angry letter to the Lieutenant Governor of Senegal, in whose colony the reduction of the authority of the chiefs was not being satisfactorily pursued:

In a letter of last September fourteenth, I tried especially to define the attitude which we should adopt in regard to these chiefs. According to my instructions we should continue to surround them, as formerly, with exterior marks of honor and of consideration, acquit ourselves of the obligations which we have contracted to them, use their services in making them auxiliaries of our administration, but occupy ourselves constantly with attenuating their authority over the people.[26]

Thus the final and perhaps most important part of the French Muslim policy is stated. Marabus were to be used when needed. They were to be courted with medals and symbolic honors but their power was to be continually reduced.

Had this Muslim policy been carried out, it is probable that there would be few politically important marabus left in Senegal. The prohibitions against alms collections, if implemented, would have removed the basic sources of the marabus' wealth. Restrictions against the Qu'ranic schools would have eliminated the primordial teaching function of the marabus through which they gained respect, money, and free labor and would have impeded the spread of Islam by the *tariqas*. If the marabus, like the chiefs, had been successfully removed from all important ruling positions, they would have lost their control over the people. Finally, if the French language and French culture had replaced Arabic and Islamic culture as was hoped, Islam in Senegal would have been seriously weakened. In sum, the early Muslim policy if successfully carried out would have demolished the power and influence of the marabus, restricted the area of Muslim proselytization, and even undermined the faith of those who remained Muslim by orienting them to French values and morals.

[26] DA, Governor General to Lieutenant Governor (Aug. 27, 1913), 13G 75.

Actual Relations with the Marabus

Throughout the twentieth century, French officials never trusted the marabus and were never sure when or where a marabu-led uprising might occur. The mistrust of officials is shown in the continuous admonitions of the lieutenant governors of Senegal and the governors general of the AOF that the marabus be kept under close surveillance at all times; the admonitions were constantly repeated in administrative reports between 1900 and the end of the Second World War.[27] As time went on the French gained more confidence in their ability to control the areas they governed, but they still dreaded the unrest which a rebellious marabu could stimulate in a particular region. Such minor uprisings did continue to occur throughout the period. Almost every year in some part of Senegal a marabu would turn up claiming to be a mahdi[28] with a mission to chase out the French infidels and bring Islam to its true glory. In most of these instances the ensuing revolt was quickly and mercilessly repressed, since the administrators wished to prevent protracted disturbances that were expensive and often resulted in reprimands from their superiors in France. Indeed, their fears of such rebellions apparently caused the French sometimes to over-react to potential threats to their rule and to punish the offending marabu in an unnecessarily severe fashion. But the dispatch with which the French disposed of rebellious marabus can be contrasted with the normal course of relations between the colonial authorities and the brotherhoods. Only where the French were forced to act, that is, when they were convinced that an uprising was about to occur, did they mobilize against the marabu, who was then rapidly killed or exiled and his following dispersed.

Fode Sulayman Bayaga was one of numerous marabus who pitted themselves against the French and were quickly eliminated. Bayaga, who led a revolt in the upper Gambia region in 1908, was a Sarakolé marabu who had founded a village formed of his Sarakolé disciples in an area inhabited by pagan Peul tribesmen a short time before the revolt took place. The elements

[27] Arnaud, "L'Islam et la politique musulmane," p. 148; also DA: no. 982 (Sept. 14, 1909), 19G 1; "Chapter IV" (May 14, 1914), 19G 1; "Rapport politique du Sénégal," 2G 18.1; no. 1631 (July 10, 1918); "Rapport politique de l'AOF," 2G 24.13; "Rapport politique du Sénégal," 2G 39.34.

[28] A mahdi is an envoy from Allah. The word was broadly used by the French to refer to rebellious marabus in their territory.

of a dangerous situation were present, for his village was in an isolated district difficult for the French to control. Bayaga built himself a fortress-like mosque against the orders of the French, who considered this action provocative. The latter sent an administrator to the village who caused the Peuls to destroy the mosque. At this point the situation developed into a crisis. Bayaga, in Gambia when he learned of the administrative action, mobilized his Sarakolé followers and marched back to his village, where he killed several Peuls and took their leaders prisoner. The French sent out a military column, and on October 12 a confrontation took place in which Bayaga and many followers were killed, the rest of his disciples dispersed, and his village razed.[29] The French method of handling the situation, which may have forced Bayaga to complete intransigence through the destruction of his mosque by pagan Peuls, can be questioned. Leaving aside this value judgment, the incident illustrates a typical reaction by the French in the face of direct challenge to their authority.[30]

In most cases major marabus did not choose to act as Bayaga did, possibly because they recognized the futility of attacking the powerful French rulers. Usually the French and the marabus were able to cooperate peacefully however much they may have mistrusted each other. The Murid order provides an excellent example of how the normal pattern of relations developed because this was the brotherhood most feared by the French but the one which became the mainstay of the French regime.[31]

Almost from the date of the brotherhood's foundation in 1886 the annual political reports from Senegal on the Muslim problem referred to the Muridiyya. Almost every report after its foundation contains some reference to the group, which worried the authorities for a number of reasons. In the early years especially, the French were convinced that Ahmad Bamba intended to create an army to drive out the Europeans. The

[29] DA, letter (Nov. 13, 1908), "Opération de police dans Haute Gambie," 13G 74, and Brunot, letter (May 10, 1908), no. 43, 13G 74; telegram (Sept. 2, 1908), no. 220, 13G 74; telegram (Sept. 9, 1908), no. 200, 13G 74; telegram (Sept. 14, 1908), 13G 74; report to the Minister of Colonies (Nov. 20, 1918), 13G 74.

[30] Bayaga did not attack a European-led post, which was the dread of administrators in outlying regions. An example of that kind of uprising occurred in 1917 when the French administrator at a post in Senegal Oriental was decapitated while the rebellious marabu sat on his horse chanting verses from the Qu'ran. DA, Administrator to Lieutenant Governor, no. 159, 13G 382.

[31] See Behrman, "Ahmad Bamba, 1850–1927."

Murids also worried the French because the latter could not understand the group's dynamism, which overflowed into continuous conflicts with other groups. Moreover, the French were concerned by the colonizing techniques of the Murids, who took over villages and land from unwilling inhabitants and spread their settlements to uncultivated territories.

By 1888 the French were openly concerned about Ahmad Bamba, who attracted considerable numbers of anti-French supporters into his ever-growing group of followers. Under pressure from colonial authorities Bamba wrote a conciliatory letter that denied his interest in the "things of this world."[32] Later, in 1891, he traveled to St. Louis to declare to the Governor his loyalty to the French and to denounce those of his disciples who had most openly agitated against the colonial regime.[33] But the subsequent uneasy peace of the next few years was broken when in 1895 he moved from Baol, where his holy village Touba was established, to Djolof. His arrival in Djolof caused a ferment in the area that colonial officials interpreted as a direct threat to their authority. There was no concrete proof that Bamba planned a rebellion, but the French were convinced by rumors circulating about a Murid uprising; Bamba was arrested and sent to Gabon in September of that year.[34]

The Murid founder was permitted to return to Senegal in 1902, and his return stimulated increased agitation as old and new followers flocked to him. Both the French-appointed Senegalese chiefs and the administrators strongly mistrusted his motives.[35] Because of continued agitation and rumors he was exiled again in 1903, this time to Mauritania, where his spiritual master Shaykh Sidia, head of the Qadriyya, promised to keep watch over him. In 1907 Bamba returned to Senegal and was sent to Thieacine in Louga. Once again his return provoked agitation, and large numbers of followers flocked to his camp. Bamba himself asked the administrators to control the flood of

[32] Marty, "Les Mourides," p. 7.

[33] Ibid., p. 7; also DA, Governor of Senegal to Minister of Colonies (Sept. 16, 1895), no. 1124; dossier on Ahmad Bamba, Director's Office (hereafter Dossier).

[34] DA, Dossier; Director of Political and Administrative Affairs to Governor of Senegal (Aug. 29, 1895); Administrator of St. Louis to Director of Political and Administrative Affairs (July 10, 1895); letter of M. Merlin to Governor of Senegal (Aug. 29, 1895); debate, no. 16, Procès Verbal (extract) (Sept. 5, 1895).

[35] An example of the chiefs' reactions can be taken from a letter written by the Superior Chief of Djolof: DA, Bouna N'Diaye to Secretary General of AOF (June 3, 1903), Yang Yang, Dossier. For the reaction of the administrators see DA, Administrator of Tivaouane to Secretary General (June 10, 1903) and report by Administrator of Tivaouane (Mar. 31, 1905), Dossier.

disciples pouring into his camp,[36] but officials still suspected
him of planning to organize his followers into an anti-French
army.[37] He was threatened with yet another exile if the situation
did not improve, and in 1912 he was moved to Diourbel, which
was more central and therefore supposedly more easily
controllable by the administration.[38]

Beginning around 1912 the administrative reports on Bamba
grew more favorable. Paul Marty wrote in that year that Bamba's
ambitions to form a temporal kingdom had been curtailed
and that he now only wanted to be able to pursue his spiritual
role as head of the Murids and was willing to obey the French
rulers.[39] The authorities, influenced by reports like Marty's,
relaxed their control somewhat and generally permitted the
marabu to receive followers unmolested. But the French never
really trusted him. Bamba helped recruit troops and collect
money for the First World War, and the French appointed
him to an honorary committee on Muslim affairs in 1916 and
made him Chevalier de la Légion d'Honneur in 1919; but much
remained that the Europeans could not understand. Bamba
was kept under close surveillance for the rest of his life and was
never again permitted to reside in Touba.[40] As late as 1923
French administrator P. J. André suggested that Bamba might
be supporting a plot against the French,[41] and amidst the laudatory
reports about the marabu written at the time of his death one
finds the comment of the Governor General in his political
report of 1927 that Bamba's loyalty remained "uncertain."[42]

It is interesting, if difficult, to learn from the welter of documents
on Ahmad Bamba what effect French policy had on him and his
brotherhood and what trends can be observed from the whole
patterns of pressure and response to pressure acted out by
the two sides. On the one hand the French wielded all the
weapons of organized force. The Murid leaders, weaker in a
military sense, responded on the other hand with the strong
support they enjoyed on all issues from their loyal followers.

[36] DA, Administrator of Louga to Lieutenant Governor (Sept. 25, 1907), no. 102, Dossier.
[37] DA, Lieutenant Governor to Governor General (1908), "Rapport politique du Sénégal,"
2G 8.10, and Lieutenant Governor to Governor General (Dec. 2, 1908), ibid.
[38] DA, letter to Administrator of Baol (Dec. 20, 1911), no. C4555, Dossier.
[39] Marty, "Les Mourides," pp. 12–13.
[40] DA, "Rapport sur Ahmadou Bamba et ses Mourides" (Oct. 22, 1915) and Commandant
of Baol to Lieutenant Governor (Apr. 5, 1925), no. 8, Dossier.
[41] DA, P. J. André, "Notes de renseignement" (Feb. 28, 1923), no. 16, 19G 25 (108) Fonds
Modernes (FM).
[42] DA, "Rapport politique de l'ensemble-AOF," 2G 26.8.

Perhaps the best indication of the strength of French influence on the brotherhood as a whole came during the two succession crises that took place after the death of Ahmad Bamba and his son Mamadu Mustafa. The French were interested in who would become khalif. In 1927 they disliked and distrusted Shaykh Anta, Bamba's brother, and favored Mamadu Mustafa, Bamba's eldest son. In 1945, when Mamadu Mustafa died, they favored Falilou over the son of Mamadu Mustafa, Cheikh M'Backé. Significantly, in both cases it was the candidate favored by the administration who won.

In 1923 André wrote: "It would perhaps be good to know . . . who will be his [Bamba's] eventual successors, to know their tendencies, and to take account of whether or not we should favor one candidate more than another."[43] An unusually frank report in 1926 states the choice that administrators felt they faced. First, the French could stay out of the succession and allow influential members of the family to dispute among themselves, which would result in splits and divisions in the brotherhood and doubtless reduce its prestige. The second choice would be to give official support to a candidate who would accept French sponsorship, follow French directions, and keep the brotherhood submitted to French authority. If the second choice were taken then either Balla M'Backé (a brother of Ahmad Bamba) or Mamadu Mustafa would have to be the candidate,[44] and this was apparently the French choice. When Bamba died, a Murid council met that was comprised of his brothers (Serigne Balla Thioro M'Backé, Ibra M'Backé, Shaykh Anta M'Backé), the three eldest sons (Mamadu Mustafa, Falilou M'Backé, and Bassiru M'Backé), and Bamba's cousin M'Backé Bousso and his first disciples (Shaykh Ibra Fall, Yassa Diene, and Balla Fall). The council, after "a discreet intervention by the administration,"[45] chose the eldest son as khalif. Mamadu Mustafa had been designated as successor by Bamba himself,[46] so it is doubtful that the French had to do more than let their support of him be known to the council through the resident in Diourbel. However, they acted most decisively when they exiled Shaykh Anta in 1930, when his maneuvers in support of his own candidacy as khalif threatened to split

[43] DA, P. J. André, "Notes de renseignement" (Feb. 28, 1923).
[44] DA, "Rapport politique du Sénégal," 2G 26.10.
[45] DA, Lucien Nekkach, "Unpublished Report on the Murids," 1G 56, Director's Office.
[46] DA, "Rapport politique du Sénégal" (1927), 2G 27.18.

the brotherhood; he might have succeeded in this or even in dethroning his nephew because of his considerable wealth and power.[47]

The French played even more of a decisive role when Mamadu Mustafa died in 1945. Another Murid council was called, this time composed of the surviving brothers of Ahmad Bamba, the khalifs of the deceased brothers' families, Mamadu Mustafa's brothers and his eldest son, and the khalifs of the Bousso, Ibra Fall, and Yassa Diene families.[48] The 1945 council chose Falilou M'Backé, the next eldest son of Bamba. In this instance it was the brother and not the eldest son of the khalif who succeeded. According to traditional Wolof custom the eldest brother should succeed as head of the family,[49] but this custom had long been modified by Muslim law;[50] the precedent was unclear, and Cheikh M'Backé attempted to take over leadership of the order. The French let the council know through the intermediary of the Lieutenant Governor of their preference for Falilou, although colonial officials were well aware that the precedent was not clear and did not follow the one set at Bamba's death. In fact it was admitted, although not openly, that French support of Falilou constituted a serious departure from the publicly stated ideal of French neutrality in Muslim affairs.[51] But the French were pleased with the council's choice and turned their attention to reinforcing the new khalif by eliminating the threat posed by Chiekh M'Backé, who, together with his uncle Bassiru,[52] was agitating against Falilou. The Director of Political Affairs warned Cheikh M'Backé that he could be exiled as Shaykh Anta had been: "I put him . . . on guard against the intrigues which were planned and which could create regrettable incidents. I warned him very clearly that we would not tolerate any agitation and that, these intrigues coming from certain of his disciples, he has all interest in using his influence to make them cease so that he will not be considered their instigator and so that he will not risk finding himself one day in the situation of his uncle Shaykh Anta . . . ."[53]

[47] Nekkach, "Unpublished Report," and DA, "Rapport politique du Sénégal" (1929), 2G 29.15.

[48] Nekkach, "Unpublished Report."

[49] *Ibid.*

[50] Maghetar Samb, *La Succession en droit musulmane* (St. Louis n.d.); Dépot Légal no. 1806; and interviews with Amadou Moctar Samb, *qadi* in the Muslim Court of St. Louis, and Moctar N'Diaye, his assistant *qadi*, Mar. 10, 1966, St. Louis.

[51] Interview with a former French administrator, December, 1965.

[52] Nekkach, "Unpublished Report."

[53] DA, Director of Political, Administrative, and Social Affairs, "Note pour M. le Gouverneur Général" (September, 1940), 19G 2(1).

Cheikh M'Backé was forced as a result of French pressure to restrict his opposition to his uncle, although his negative attitude never completely changed. The situation became further complicated when Senegalese politicians, seeking support throughout the countryside, sided with the new khalif or with the opponent; their interference will be discussed later. Falilou remained khalif of the Murids and was able to build his position to one of considerable strength.

Clearly, the French administration played an important role in Falilou's rise to power. French intervention in the Murid succession crises is proof of their great influence on the Murids. Together with the evidence that can be drawn from the description above of relations between the Murid founder and the French—the exiles of Bamba, the restrictions against his followers' free visits to him, the mere fact that Bamba, who apparently wanted only to be left alone,[54] had to maintain good relations with the administrators—indicate that the lives of the leaders and the development of the brotherhood would have been very different had the French been less powerful. Yet, it must not be assumed that the French were able to mold the Murids to their will; the relations described above show that they were in fact unable to do so.

The trend to be discerned is, rather, the trend toward increasing cooperation, true for the marabus as much as for the French. In the early years the gap between the two was wide, and the French feared the Murid founder while the marabu quite probably disliked the French. But each side was willing to take what it could from the other. The cooperative trend was intensified because of the emphasis which both the Murids and the French placed on the importance of peanut cultivation. The French began to realize the economic potential of the group for the development of Senegal. A 1911 report was one of the first to comment on its positive potential.[55] Other reports around that time stressed the group's economic danger: one of 1906 noted that Shaykh Anta, on the pretext of having dug a well at Gavouane, was trying to take over the neighboring territory from its owners.[56] In 1913, the administrator at Diourbel warned

[54] See Letter of Ahmad Bamba, June 3, 1903, Dossier; also Behrman, "Ahmad Bamba, 1850–1927," for discussion of Bamba's letters.
[55] DA, "Rapport politique du Sénégal" (May 5, 1911), no. C577, 2G 11.7.
[56] Ibid. (June 27, 1906), 2G 6.4.

The Impact of the French

that Shaykh Anta's property at Gavouane was the center of a
large area of deforestation that threatened wooded areas nearby.[57]
A report in 1916 repeats the warning in noting that Murids
in the Petit Côte were destroying the wooded areas in their
search for land on which to grow peanuts.[58] But gradually
the positive side of the Murids' economic role was given more
emphasis until it became the dominating concern of the French.
The 1926 annual political report notes: "If it is possible to regret
having allowed this Murid power to be established . . . it must
be realized that, from the economic point of view, the action
of Muridism has powerfully contributed to the so accentuated
development of agricultural production in the region of Baol.
And this action, which is beneficial from this point of view,
forms . . . a serious counterweight to the eventual difficulties
which may come."[59] In 1927 the Lieutenant Governor wrote
even more glowingly: "The Murids do not disdain material
progress in any way. They are as good commercial agents as they
are good farmers and speculation does not scare them.
It is not among them that one risks finding that tendency
to lethargy which . . . characterized certain regions of Islam."[60]

The French now began to actually encourage the Murids
by giving the marabus special privileges and concessions
of land. Economic collaboration, particularly in the 1930's,
was openly pursued by the French authorities, who had seen even
the election of Mamadu Mustafa as economically beneficial
to Senegal.[61] Now and then observers warned, as did the 1927
annual report, that despite the economic contributions of the
Murids the French should be careful not to "enthrone" new
Ahmad Bamba's in other regions of the AOF, thus pointing
out their unwitting aid to the power of the Murid founder.[62]
Such warnings, however, usually went unheeded, for the French
seemed most interested in increasing the production of peanuts
by whatever method possible. In the depression years they
stressed heavily the need for more peanuts and found the
Murids a valuable adjunct to their campaign.[63]

[57] DA, Commandant of Baol, "Rapport de Novembre, 1913," Dossier.
[58] DA, "Rapport politique du Sénégal" (1916), no. 1178, 2G 16.5.
[59] Ibid. (1926), 2G 26.10.
[60] Ibid. (1927), 2G 27.18.
[61] Ibid. (Sept. 19, 1929), 2G 28.8.
[62] DA, "Rapport politique de l'Ensemble-AOF" (Sept. 22, 1928), 2G 27.21.
[63] DA, "Rapport politique du Sénégal" (1932), 2G 32.21.

The Exchange of Services

The trends discerned in the Murids' relations with the French are applicable to all the other brotherhoods in Senegal, for the marabu-official cooperation became a general phenomenon. Each brotherhood and each marabu had their own experiences, which differed one from the other, with the colonial authorities. But as the Murids were one of the last Senegalese orders to oppose the French in any significant way, most of the other important brotherhoods were more easily able to establish relations of mutual service with the French.

The French found numerous ways to make use of the marabus, some of which were illustrated in the discussion above. One typical service the marabus performed was helping in the recruitment of soldiers and giving general support to the French cause. Ahmad Bamba recruited four hundred Murid soldiers during the First World War.[64] Al Hajj Malik Sy, the venerable head of the largest Wolof Tijani branch, gave speeches on behalf of the French war effort exemplified by the following excerpt: "Adhere completely to the French government. God . . . has given especially to the French victory, grace and fervor. He has chosen them to protect our persons and our goods. . . . My brothers, do not yourselves be seduced by the words of fools who say to you 'the day of the defeat of French power is coming.' These are pernicious shadows. An affirmed knowledge in God shows the opposite . . . ."[65]

An interesting sidelight to the colonial use of the marabus to inspire loyalty to the government in crisis periods was the exaggerated (in light of the actual situation) French fear of pan-African sentiments. The Senegalese marabus were used as instruments to prevent pan-Islamic anti-European feelings from spreading. They were also regarded as barometers of local opinion: since they apparently knew very little about the rest of the Muslim world they usually registered favorably, but French fears did not die down over the years.[66] The official correspondence in the Dakar Archives concerning the dangers of a pan-Islamic movement in West Africa is voluminous

[64] DA, Lanet, "Rapport confidentiel sur les Mourites" (January, 1914), and Lanet, "Rapport sur Ahmadou Bamba et ses Mourides" (Oct. 22, 1915), Dossier.

[65] DA, Malik Sy (Ramadan 4, 1330 AH), reported Apr. 23, 1913, 19G 2.

[66] Consequently, the French tried to impose strict censorship on Arabic material to prevent the Senegalese from coming into contact with subversive information. See DA, circular (Feb. 16, 1908), no. 31c, 19G 4.

beginning around the time of the First World War. Because of German and Turkish use of Islam against the Allies in the Middle East, the colonial administrators kept close watch on the brotherhoods. In the 1920's the authorities were concerned with the explosive Middle Eastern debate over the Muslim khalifat,[67] although only the Syrians in Senegal seemed to be acquainted with the issue.[68] The Director of Political Affairs could write confidently in 1940 that Muslims in Senegal were generally out of touch with the major international political currents,[69] but a constant fear of the potential danger of such issues remained and pushed the French to depend more heavily than ever on the cooperation of the Senegalese marabus.

The single most striking example of the uses to which a marabu could be put is the case of Saidou Nourou Tall, still one of the most famous marabus in West Africa as a result. An untitled two-volume book of testimonials written by thousands of officials in France and all over West Africa witnesses the varied ways he served the French. He traveled all over West Africa acting as a mediator in disputes among Muslims and among non-Muslims as well. He endorsed health and sanitation campaigns, encouraged the payment of taxes, and, in line with the French preoccupations of the period, greatly emphasized peanut production.[70]

In his turn, of course, Saidou Nourou, like the other major marabus, made use of the French. The administration allowed him various privileges such as free travel on railways or ships and awarded him honors (by 1957 he had received twenty-four medals).[71] Most important he became identified with the power of the colonialists. Consequently, when one wanted a favor from the French, one went to Saidou Nourou, a man whose

[67] Arab nationalists sought to restore the khalif of all Islam in order to unite the Muslims (politically as well as religiously). Efforts to restore the khalif failed after an indecisive Arab conference in 1926.

[68] The administrators in France apparently were more concerned than their subordinates in Senegal; see DA, Minister to Governor General (Dec. 10, 1933), no. 305, 19G 63 (108) FM. But administrators in Senegal were also worried; see DA, André, "Rapport no. 2 à M. le Gouverneur Général" (Mar. 26, 1923), "Rapport sur les tendences actuelles de l'Islam" (Jan. 5, 1923), and "Deux Rapports du Sénégal" (Mar. 29, 1923), 19G 25 (108) FM.

[69] DA, Director of Political and Administrative Affairs to Inspector General of Education (Jan. 10, 1940), No. 77 AP/2, 19G 63 (108) FM.

[70] See DA, El Hadj Seydou Nourou Tall, 2 vols., 19G 29 (108) FM.

[71] His honors included the following: Grand Croix de la Légion d'Honneur, Commandeur du Mérite Saharien, Commandeur de l'Encouragement de la République, Grand Croix de l'Ordre National du Sénégal, and Commandeur des Palmes Académiques. He also received the Order of Tunisia in 1965–1966. DA, El Hadj Seydou Nourou Tall, 19G 29 (108) FM. It is interesting to note that the Vichy regime, which also used Saidou Nourou, did not really trust him. He was accused of having relations with Morocco and Bathurst and of supporting people whose loyalty was in doubt. DA, "Rapport politique du Sénégal" (1940), 2G 40.26.

words would be listened to by the authorities. His stature,
like that of Ahmad Bamba, was enhanced, and he became even
more powerful than before. In areas where the French were
particularly unpopular his collaboration with the colonialists
may have undermined his position,[72] but in general this does
not seem to have been the case.

The French could reward important marabus who were
cooperating with them in various ways, just as they had rewarded
Saidou Nourou. Obviously they could give gifts, and political
donations, expected to help keep the marabus favorable to the
French regime, date back to earliest French colonization.
Even unpopular marabus (to the French, that is) like Shaykh Anta
received money, and others like Shaykh Sidia, who helped
the colonial regime greatly, received frequent gifts.[73] It became
a matter of habit for families of the great marabus to expect
money from the government.

More important than outright grants of money to the marabus
was the increasing French involvement in strictly Muslim affairs—a
matter of discontent for some Muslims but a way in which
individual marabus could use the colonial authorities to obtain
what they wanted. The French became useful agents for Muslim
leaders, providing advice, material assistance for certain projects,
and sometimes force to settle a quarrel, as in the case of the
Murids' succession crisis. Thus, too, the Qadiri leader Bu Kunta
asked the French to support his son Bekkai Kunta as his heir.
Accordingly, when Bu Kunta died in 1914 the French found
themselves saddled with an enormously complicated problem
of succession which they had to straighten out for Bekkai.[74]

The French also became the source of authorization for
mosques, which were prestige symbols for the marabus.
Colonial officials were drawn into quarrels over who should
build a mosque and who should become the imam;[75] in principle
they attempted to remain neutral, but in fact those marabus
who served the French were given preference. The Dakar Archives
contain a large number of documents relating to mosques,
interesting because they show the considerable volume of

[72] Muslim reformers and political radicals in Senegal and elsewhere in the AOF have been
very critical of Saidou Nourou because he identified so much with the French.
[73] DA, decree (Mar. 22, 1913), Fonds secrets (see list of expenditures), 17G 24.
[74] DA, dossier entitled "Succession Bou Kunta," 13G 67.
[75] The imam leads the Friday prayers at a mosque and is considered the leader of his
particular Muslim parish.

transactions over such matters.[76] The letters also show that the French in their dealings over the mosques tried to appear as the benefactors of Islam, often giving money to the mosques though usually in small amounts. Governor General de Coppet gave 100 francs to a mosque in Medina in 1937, for example.[77] Important marabus sometimes received more substantial assistance: Ibrahima Niass demanded and received a special fifty-percent reduction in the tax on the transportation of building materials for his edifice in Kaolack.[78]

Gradually as the years went by, cooperation between the two sides was taken for granted. Symbolically, high government officials began to appear at important Muslim ceremonies. This had not always been the case. An annual political report in 1917 noted that as the marabus gained confidence in the French they tended to stop trying to hide their actions and even invited the administrators to participate in their ceremonies, "although a few years ago the Europeans were systematically excluded."[79] French officials at Muslim ceremonies became an accepted part of Muslim life in Senegal. When, in 1937, the Governor General himself appeared at the Tabaski (festival of the lamb) ceremony, many Muslims of Senegal greeted this as a noble gesture and an honor.[80] The Governor General attended in order to show his administration's sympathy for Islam,[81] and his move was imitated by most subsequent governor generals; this cemented the identification taking place between the marabus and the French. Administrators at every level came to be officially present in Muslim ceremonies, although the Governor General restricted his appearances to national celebrations, refusing, for example, to attend the inauguration of Ibrahima Niass' mosque in order not to let that ceremony lose its purely local character.[82] The big Muslim festivals became the occasion for

[76] For example, see: DA, Lieutenant Governor to Governor General (Apr. 22, 1909), no. 672, 13G 67; Malik Sy to Lieutenant Governor (Sept. 2, 1916), 13G 72; Governor General to Amadou Diagne Latyr (Apr. 11, 1938), 19G 63 (108) FM.

[77] DA, letter no. 619 A/G (Mar. 12, 1937) and Governor General to Administrator (Mar. 22, 1937), no. 275, 19G 63 (108) FM.

[78] DA, letters: Ibra Niass (Mar. 27, 1937); Director of Cabinet (May 3, 1937); Governor General to Inspector (May 12, 1937); Al Hajj Kane (Feb. 18, 1938), 19G 63 (108) FM.

[79] DA, "Rapport politique du Sénégal" (July 6, 1917), no. 1811, 2G 17.6.

[80] DA, Abd el-Kader Diagne to Governor General (Feb. 25, 1937), 19G 63 (108) FM.

[81] DA, Governor General (Feb. 17, 1937), 19G 63 (108) FM.

[82] DA, Governor General to Lieutenant Governor (Feb. 3, 1938), no. 34c; Director of Political, Administrative and Social Affairs (Feb. 22, 1938), no. 365; Governor General to El Hadj Kane (Feb. 23, 1938), no. 365, 19G 63 (108) FM.

major speeches in support of French causes, and in all ceremonies the Muslim leader spoke of the great French contribution to Islam and the solidarity between the colonial regime and the Muslim people.[83]

The Policy Change

Early Muslim policy was ignored by the later colonial officials. In their first goal colonial officials were completely unsuccessful: Islam continued to attract adherents, while the various brotherhoods were able to extend their membership among neighboring Muslim and pagan peoples despite the "politique des races." Membership in the Muridiyya rose from 70,000 in 1912 to 400,000 in 1963.[84] The number of Muslims in Senegal went from approximately 1,026,000 in 1907 to 2,789,320 in 1963, while the total African population rose from 1,120,000 to 3,110,000.[85] Even allowing for different methods of estimation in the different periods—and early estimates may have increased the number of people called Muslim—both the number of Muslims and the size of the population almost trebled.

The second goal, the spread of the French language and culture was not achieved on a broad scale. The marabus discouraged their disciples from attending French schools whenever possible. Ahmad Bamba was forced to pay for a school in M'Backé that taught French to Murid peoples, and he had to send other *taalibés* to the French school in Diourbel.[86] But neither he nor his successors apparently sincerely encouraged Murids to attend French schools; thus the M'Backé school never received much support, even after its removal to Diourbel in 1915.[87] The Franco-Murid school established to teach basic notions of agriculture, as well as French, was received with more enthusiasm,[88] but it was never greatly expanded nor was it duplicated in other villages. The French-sponsored *madrassa* in St. Louis never had more than a handful of students and eventually disappeared. In 1936 the Governor General

[83] For example, DA, "Report of Tabaski Prayer," (Jan. 20, 1940), 19G 63 (108) FM.
[84] DA, Nekkach, "Unpublished Report"; Monteil, "Une Confrérie musulmane," pp. 89–90.
[85] Verrière, "La Population du Sénégal," p. 73, and government of AOF, *Situation générale . . . pour l'année 1907* (Dakar, 1908).
[86] DA, Commandant of Baol, "Rapport sur Ahmadou Bamba et les Mourides" (Oct. 31, 1913), no. 16316 (cabinet stamp), Dossier.
[87] DA, Commandant of Baol, "Rapport sur Ahmadou Bamba et ses Mourides" (Oct. 22, 1915), Dossier.
[88] DA, "Rapport politique du Sénégal" (1932), 2G 32.21.

proposed the creation of another such national *madrassa*, together with a large national mosque,[89] but money for the school was not forthcoming and the war interfered with the plans. The school was never built and the mosque was not started until Senegal had become independent.

The Qu'ranic schools remained virtually untouched by the administration because the strict 1903 and 1906 legislation was never implemented. Paul Marty himself had deplored these decrees, which he thought unrealistic and impractical in that they contradicted the customs and traditions of Senegal.[90] He would have continued to demand a registry of students and to encourage marabus to send their pupils to French schools,[91] but even these limited proposals were not enforced. Not until the Vichy regime was there any attempt to reform the schools along the lines proposed in the early legislation. Vichy was much less tolerant of the marabus than its predecessors had been and sought to limit the Muslim leaders' activities by restricting the Qu'ranic schools, among other measures. The 1940 annual political report echoes many of the criticisms made forty years before, indicating how little the situation had changed. The Qu'ranic schools, it said, did not meet the requirements of health or of intellectual achievement because the marabus were notoriously ignorant. Children were forced to work for the marabu or beg for him and were punished by being beaten.[92] A decree was passed in July 1942 to remedy the situation which sounded much like the 1903 and 1906 laws. It had eight major provisions, requiring: 1) administrative authorization before a school could be opened, 2) registration of all existing schools to be approved before the following January, 3) inspection of all schools by the Chef de Service de l'Enseignement, 4) prohibition of begging by the students, 5) that the marabu have enough money to establish his students without exploitation, 6) that the teaching marabus be Senegalese, 7) prohibition of the location of Qu'ranic schools in an animist territory, and 8) provision that refusal of authorization or its withdrawal be made by the Governor. But by the end of 1943 the Vichy regime had been replaced by a Gaullist government. Many Vichy laws were revoked, among them the provisions

[89] DA, "Rapport politique du Sénégal" (1937), 2G 37.1, and letter, no. 916 AP/a (June 15, 1937), 19G 63 (108) FM.
[90] Marty and Salenc, *Les Ecoles maraboutiques*, p. 75.
[91] *Ibid.*, pp. 74–86.
[92] DA, "Rapport politique du Sénégal" (1940), 2G 40.26.

for Qu'ranic schools on the grounds that the schools transgressed the religious liberty of the Africans.[93]

Thus, the only serious effort to control the Qu'ranic schools was dismissed with the Vichy regime. The French educational system also failed in the plan to draw students away from the marabus. Many parents recognized that their children would profit from learning French and technical skills, so that the French schools did not lack for candidates; however, the French school system grew very slowly over the years because little money was invested in it. Few Senegalese benefited from a Western education and few consequently knew French or were acquainted with French culture.[94]

Another major part of the Muslim policy had been to stop exploitation of the African masses in the marabus' collection of alms. But income from such alms rose to very great amounts in the following years, and the major Murid marabus became extremely wealthy as a result. An official in 1915 complained that Ahmad Bamba spent 200,000 francs in a good year.[95] Forty-one years later his son Falilou received the equivalent of approximately $200,000 from a single festival.[96] The French were helpless to prevent a marabu's collection of alms from followers who lived nearby or who came to ask favors of him. It would seem easier to control the trips of marabus made for the purpose of collecting gifts, but apparently this was not the case. A number of lesser marabus were tried for extortion and fined or imprisoned,[97] but generally the French did not interfere with the major marabus; with the explicit or tacit sanction of the authorities, therefore, marabus regularly collected or sent their representatives to collect offerings. Saad Bu, for example, a well-known Mauritanian Qadiri leader, made frequent profitable trips to Senegal up to 1913, when he was very old and ill and so fat that he could not enter the compartment of the Dakar-St. Louis railway.[98] His peers continued such trips

[93] Interviews with former French administrators, Dakar, December, 1965.

[94] There were estimated to be 12,288 students in Qu'ranic schools in 1906, while only 4,750 students attended French schools. By 1960 the number of students in French schools was higher than that of students attending Qu'ranic schools (109,800 to 65,700); nonetheless, the absolute number of Qu'ranic pupils had risen rather than fallen. See Quellien, *La Politique musulmane*, p. 262, and Verrière, "La Population du Sénégal," p. 84.

[95] DA, Commandant of Baol, "Rapport sur Ahmadou Bamba et les Mourides" (Oct. 22, 1915), Dossier.

[96] Nekkach, "Unpublished Report."

[97] DA, Commandant of Kolda (Dec. 1914), 13G 67.

[98] DA; Lieutenant Governor to Governor General (July 2, 1905), no. 98, 19G 3; Lieutenant Governor to Administrator (Mar. 3, 1906), no. 149, 19G 3; "Rapport politique du Sénégal" (1908), 2G 8.10; *ibid.* (June 18, 1913), 2G 13.8; and Republic of France, *Rapport d'ensemble 1913* (Dakar, 1916).

throughout the years. The Vichy regime, in line with its harder attitude toward the marabus, attempted to control the collection of alms,[99] but its attempts were abandoned when the Free French took over Senegal. The gathering of offerings continued essentially as it had fifty years before. If the system was different at all, the difference was in the interest of the marabus who could travel further on railways in the broad area pacified by the French and could even receive free transportation.[100]

The most important aspect of the French program, to end the marabus' role as temporal rulers by undermining them as political leaders, was never implemented. There were not enough French administrators to fill all the temporal functions carried out by the religious leaders. More important the European officials remained irremediably separated from the people they governed by language, traditions, and thought patterns. They tended to feel superior to the Senegalese, and the latter in turn viewed the French *toubabs* (Wolof for "white foreigners") as alien to their way of life. There was no question of the French officials actually replacing the marabus as the recognized political leaders.

It is important to realize that many aims of the early French policy were approved of by later administrators even after the liberation of Senegal. Many officials deplored the Qu'ranic schools and especially the unlimited control by the marabus that so often appeared to the Western-educated observer as cynical exploitation. But the early Muslim policy was replaced by another Muslim policy based on a different set of priorities. In the early 1900's the brotherhoods appeared to threaten the hegemony of the French, but gradually, as the French hold over Senegal was consolidated, fear of the brotherhoods faded. Thus in 1911 the political report could say tentatively: "An Islamic movement directed against our authority [seems to be] difficult if not impossible to organize and in any case the people scarcely think of such a thing."[101]

The administration never completely trusted the marabus, but the French grew confident of their ability to control the brotherhoods. Destruction of the authority of the marabus no longer seemed as important as before. The brotherhoods themselves, in the final stage of the revitalization process, no

[99] DA, "Rapport politique du Sénégal" (1940), 2G 40.2.
[100] Not all marabus could receive free transportation; only those whom the administration wished to support received such privileges.
[101] DA, "Rapport politique du Sénégal" (Aug. 22, 1911), no. 1011, 2G 11.7.

longer presented as fanatical and revolutionary an aspect
as they had earlier, and their growing conservatism reinforced
the more positive impressions of the French. It grew to be more
important to use the marabus in whatever ways possible in
ruling Senegal; and this became the major plank of the Muslim
policy that was consistently pursued throughout the
twentieth-century colonial period.

The colonial authorities were most concerned with running
Senegal peacefully and at the least possible cost to themselves.
The French government had no money to invest in West Africa,
so the administrators made do with what they had; their best
resource in Senegal seemed to be the marabus, the use of whom
as auxiliaries of the French became necessary for the smooth
running of the colony. By the Second World War the tone
of official comment in regard to Islam had completely changed.
The Governor General wrote in 1937:

> This is no longer the time for doctrinaire discussions on the
> Islamization of West Africa . . . it is now an accomplished fact. . . .
> [Moreover] the morale of the Prophet creates . . . a discipline . . . which
> constitutes against their [the Africans'] disorganization [when] confronted
> with European doctrines which are difficult to assimilate, a protection
> which it would be imprudent to ignore.
> These facts make one ask oneself if it would not be better not only to
> maintain a benevolent neutrality in regard to Islam, but also to give it . . .
> active support.[102]

In the pattern of relations established between the French
and the marabus it almost seems as though the marabus had
the advantage. In one sense, of course, as the French became
more involved in Muslim affairs the marabus found themselves
more restricted; they could not do exactly what they wanted
but were bounded by the limits of French law. If they challenged
these limits as Bayaga had done they could be destroyed.
But if they did not revolt against the French, the marabus had
a considerable amount of independence and were free to relate
to their followers as they had always done. Moreover, their
position was reinforced by privileges granted them by the

[102] DA, Governor General de Coppet to Minister of Colonies (June 15, 1937), no. 916 AP/a,
19G 63 (108) FM. The personal biases of the governors general (and other administrators), of
course, affected the policy proclamations. Thus de Coppet probably favored Islam more than
did his immediate predecessors or successors. Nevertheless, he is not inconsistent with the
general trend toward a more favorable French view of Islam.

The Impact of the French

colonial officials and they were recognized by all as the appropriate intermediaries between the people and the government. Indeed, the marabus strengthened their political position in Senegal by becoming allies of the French.

3 The Power structure and Inter-relationships of the *Tariqas*

The pattern of political relations established by the French and continued by Senegalese politicians cannot be understood without some description of the inner mechanism of the brotherhoods. The success of French and Senegalese officials, after all, has been based on their intimate knowledge of the affairs of the *tariqas*, which affairs underlie and explain many of the complicated political machinations that make up daily Senegalese politics.

Significant Senegalese Brotherhoods

There are four important brotherhoods in Senegal: the Tijaniyya, the Muridiyya, the Qadriyya, and the Layenne. The Muridiyya is the most unusual of these orders, which in part explains its current political dominance. Ahmad Bamba, the founder, had been a Qadiri before his revelation led him to establish the new brotherhood; he distributed Qadiri prayers and litanies although he had adopted his own *wird*[1] by 1907.[2] The innovational force of the order, however, seems to come from the attitude of the Murid marabus toward work and discipline, rather than from prayers and litanies. Traditionally, a Senegalese marabu used his students to provide labor in his fields, especially during the rainy season and the harvest months immediately thereafter (June through November or December). Adult disciples generally also helped in the fields, particularly in sowing and harvesting periods. Some marabus were very concerned with the instruction of their disciples and paid little attention to their fields. Others, such as Bu Kunta, apparently exploited this system to the utmost and ignored their duty to educate their disciples.[3] But Murid leaders went beyond other marabus and made such work a virtue and not just a duty. Ahmad Bamba is frequently quoted as saying "work is part of religion" or "work as if you would never die and pray as if you were to die tomorrow."[4] Such a doctrine is not contrary to the laws of Islam (rather, as Vincent Monteil indicates, it is similar to a *hadith* from the Prophet);[5] however, it produced a fundamental change in peasant work in the fields. This change is related to another (probably apochryphal) quotation from Bamba, "work for me and I shall pray for you." There is no evidence that Ahmad Bamba ever encouraged his disciples

[1] The *wird* includes the special prayers and litanies of the order.
[2] Monteil, "Une Confrérie musulmane," p. 88; Sy, "Traditionalisme mouride," pp. 59–63.
[3] See Marty, *Etudes sur l'Islam au Sénégal*, I, 337–364.
[4] Monteil, "Une Confrérie musulmane," p. 95, and Sy, "Traditionalisme mouride," pp. 54–55.
[5] Monteil, "Une Confrérie musulmane," p. 95.

to give up Muslim prayers and rituals, but many Murids so interpreted his doctrine and cited the third quotation as authority. Not only among the Baye-Fall, a Murid subgroup known to outsiders for its fanaticism, intensive labor, and scorn for Muslim education,[6] but also among the main group of Murids, the majority do not even observe the required five prayers a day. In this they are not too different from the Tijani disciples, who often do not observe the proper prayers and rituals. But among the Murids, including the most renowned Murid scholars, there seems to be a much greater emphasis than among the Tijani or other orders on the demonstration of devotion to Islam through work for and obedience to the marabus.[7] The result of the unique Murid emphasis has been a discipline and unity that have made the order the most aggressive and dynamic in Senegal. Followers were, and are, attracted to the Muridiyya because of the vitality of the group and also because the duty of the disciple, who only has to work in the fields, is simplified.

The field work of the disciples is generally the growing of peanuts. The early Murid marabus' stress on peanuts was logical since, by the end of the nineteenth century, the importance of peanuts was increasing. This was the only crop that could enable a farmer to obtain some of the new goods and food gradually spreading throughout Senegal.[8] The Murid leaders were unusual in that they ambitiously organized their disciples into hardworking production units and became some of the largest producers of peanuts in Senegal.[9]

The Murid brotherhood was much admired and emulated. It was so successful that outside observers have tended to lose perspective when comparing it to other brotherhoods, endowing the Muridiyya with unique characteristics that actually are not unique. The devotion and obedience of the disciples to their marabu is mentioned as a Murid innovation[10] although blind obedience of disciples is common to sufi brotherhoods and extreme subjection of disciples, similar to the Murid relationship,

[6] For information on the Baye Fall see Sy, "Traditionalisme mouride," pp. 93–96.
[7] Interviews with Modou Mustafa M'Backé, Dec. 9, 1965, Touba, and Modou Bousso and brothers, Nov. 21, 1965, Guede.
[8] Monteil, "Une Confrérie musulmane," p. 95.
[9] For further information see Sy, "Traditionalisme mouride," pp. 64–92, and A. Bourlon, "Mourides et Mouridisme 1953," in Chailley et al., Notes et études sur l'Islam, pp. 66–72.
[10] Bourlon, "Mourides et Mouridisme," p. 55; Pierre Rondot, L'Islam et les Musulmans d'aujourd'hui, vol. II: De Dakar à Djakarta: L'Islam en devenir (Paris, 1960), p. 55; Marty, "Les Mourides," pp. 106–112.

has been observed elsewhere. What is different in the Murid order is only the organized fashion in which this obedience is expressed through directed work and regularly solicited gifts.

Nor have the Murids been able to completely dominate Senegalese Islam. On the contrary, other brotherhoods have remained important. The Tijani groups taken together (including the Hamalliyya) actually have the largest number of disciples, estimated at 1,037,088 in 1958.[11] The Murids follow the Tijani with approximately 423,273 members, the Qadiri supposedly number 302,957 and the Layenne 15,430.[12] Even at the time when the Murids appeared the most aggressive the reputation and influence of one Tijani marabu rivaled that of Ahmad Bamba. The marabu was Al Hajj Malik Sy (1869-1922), head of the major Tijani branch centered at Tivaouane. Malik Sy had a double spiritual tie to the Umarian Tijani and to the Ida ou Ali through his dual initiation by a disciple of Umar Tall and an Ida ou Ali representative. He made a pilgrimage to Mecca, a most unusual venture in his day, in 1889 and settled in Tivaouane in 1902. Malik Sy was extremely well educated in Islamic literature and juridical studies and was the author of numerous scholarly treatises on law, theology, and sufism. His center became known for the advanced Islamic education it offered and for its abundant library. Malik Sy's erudition did not make him markedly different from Ahmad Bamba, who was also highly educated and the author of numerous religious works. Moreover, Murid disciples could take advanced courses in the Islamic sciences at Touba or at the nearby town of Guede with the M'Backé Bousso family. But Malik Sy stressed more than Bamba did the traditional Muslim virtues, including the rituals and prayers of Islam and the value of Muslim education.[13]

The best-known leaders of the Qadiri *tariqa* were similar to those of Malik Sy's Tijani branch in their greater emphasis (as opposed to the Murids) on teaching. When Bamba first established his order some of the Qadiri marabus, such as Shaykh Sidia in Mauritania, were highly renowned for their learning and piety and had large followings in Senegal, especially in the Senegal River area. But the Qadiriyya was replaced by the Muridiyya in many areas, therefore it is at present only locally important, like the

---

[11] F. Quesnot, "Les Cadres maraboutiques de l'Islam sénégalais," in Chailley *et al., Notes et études sur l'Islam,* p. 194.

[12] *Ibid.*

[13] Marty, *Etudes sur l'Islam au Sénégal,* I, 175–210.

Layenne group; and, like the latter, it does not have as much influence nationally as do the Murids and the Tijani.[14]

The Murid emphasis on work and discipline remains a vital distinction between it and other brotherhoods.[15] Though splits exist between various Murid leaders, the influence of the group has not been fragmented as much as that of other Senegalese orders. The Tijani brotherhood in particular has within it conflicting subgroups, centered around the homes of different families. Most important is the Abdul Aziz branch (he is the son and heir of Malik Sy), though other subgroups are also significant. Each subgroup is often further split by factions in the same family. Members of the faction remain inside the subgroup but often tacitly oppose its leader or at least voice different emphases in their secular and religious teachings. The Qadiri and Layenne, perhaps because of their smaller size, do not have as many important subgroups as the Tijani; but they and even the Muridiyya do have subgroups and factions.

Almost all Senegalese are Muslim and belong to a *tariqa,* even those living in the Casamance, but the greatest density of Muslims is to be found in the peanut zone and the Senegal River region. Here one also finds the greatest density of marabus of all orders except the Layenne. A recent population study, compiled from the 1960 census, included 5,060 Senegalese who listed themselves as marabus and in a few cases priests (all non-salaried and were self- or family-supported).[16] The number seems large despite the large numbers of marabus estimated by Paul Marty in 1912.[17] Whatever the actual number of marabus may be, the significant factor is that most of them are poor farmers with little influence. Only a few hundred marabus were influential in 1912 and only a few hundred are significant now. Of the latter, only a handful have

[14] None of the brotherhoods in Senegal are discussed here in detail, although information on the major ones illustrates the basic points made. Such fascinating groups as the Layenne or the Tijaniyya branches in the Casamance can not be examined here. For information on the Layenne, see G. Balandier and P. Mercier, *Les Pêcheurs Lébou: particularisme et évolution,* Etudes sénégalaises no. 3 (St. Louis, 1952).

[15] Because of this emphasis the Murids have developed special structural features, the most important of which is the *dara,* a group of young *taalibés* not yet initiated and called *taqdar.* These *taalibés* leave their families to go off to create new areas of peanut cultivation on previously unworked land, under the direction of a marabu who provides them with food and seeds. Eventually they are initiated into the order and thereafter they live in the new villages with their families, as do other disciples, giving part of their crops and the product of the village field set aside for the marabu to their leader. See Sy, "Traditionalisme mouride," pp. 81–92.

[16] Verrière, "La Population du Sénégal," p. 100.

[17] He estimated approximately 1,700 teaching marabus; Marty and Salenc, *Les Ecoles maraboutiques,* p. 29.

national political power, and they are usually the khalifs or their immediate relatives who head the major brotherhoods.

The Power Structure of the Brotherhoods

The way in which important marabus exert influence on their disciples can be explained through examination of the structure of relations in the orders. The differentiation between *taalibés,* marabus, and khalifs in Chapter 1 can be amplified by distinguishing between lay followers who contribute to their marabus but live and work in their villages and full-time disciples who leave home, at least temporarily, and live in the motherhouse of their order. The full-time disciples dedicate themselves totally to religious studies and to fulfilling the wishes of their marabus, and as delegates of the marabu they often possess certain authority over lay members. The lay followers and full-time disciples rarely all come together except in the fields of the marabus to harvest or plant, or when the annual festival of the order is held. At these times all the followers of the order hear their khalif speak to them, perhaps to thank them for their work and donations and to advise them of their duties. For the rest of the year, however, the lay disciples as a group see only their local marabus, who pass on instructions of the higher leaders and see to the disciples' immediate spiritual and temporal needs. The local marabus themselves pay allegiance to the marabu above them, up to the khalif who directs the order.

The major marabus of any Senegalese brotherhood have always met in councils to decide important matters: at the death of Ahmad Bamba and Mamadu Mustafa, for example, the most important marabus met to decide the succession.[18] A council met in the early fifties when the Tijani khalif Abubacar was involved in a serious disagreement with his two brothers Mansur and Abdul Aziz, and a council was called at the death of Bu Kunta to decide his succession.[19] The councils are not formalized or regular but occur when the khalif or a group of important marabus are aware of a problem disturbing members of the brotherhood. Sometimes the meetings involve regular discussion or confrontations between opposing points of view. But at others the khalif merely lets his opinion be known to his assistant leaders on some issue or other.

[18] Nekkach, "Unpublished Report."
[19] DA, dossier entitled "Succession Bou Kounta," 13G 67.

The retainers who constantly surround a khalif can influence his point of view on any subject and are vitally important parts of the decision-making process in a brotherhood. Moreover, they often act as intermediaries between the khalif and the disciples or the state representatives, and as intermediaries they have great power. The former khalif of the Murids, Falilou M'Backé, for example, had a complicated group of assistants including Serigne Amadou Fall, who was in charge of the finances of the khalif's household; Al Hajj Bousso (Falilou's nephew), who was in charge of the fields (he also acted as chauffeur), Bamba Gueye, who until recently represented the khalif in Dakar on the ministerial level; Modou Mustafa, the khalif's eldest son, who acted as a general representative; and, most important, Al Hajj Dramé, the general secretary who represented the khalif in dealings with President Senghor. In addition, the khalif had representatives (who sometimes were and sometimes were not marabus) in each of the major towns in Senegal and a large group of less important retainers including trusted assistants who accompanied him when he traveled and handled the followers that came to see him.[20]

Many of the other marabus in Senegal have sets of assistants and representatives, although they are usually not as numerous as Falilou's were. Some marabus are not interested in politics and may not have representatives charged with dealing with the government. Others, though very wealthy and powerful and involved in politics, prefer to handle their own affairs personally and only have one or two assistants. Marabu Ibrahima Niass, however, has many retainers assigned tasks similar to those of Falilou's retinue. A man who is related to him is in charge of Niass' household finances and a general secretary oversees his affairs. He has another assistant to manage his fields and a representative in each village or town where there are disciples. He also has representatives among his disciples in Ghana, Nigeria, Mauritania, Gambia, and Mali.[21]

The councils of marabus and the clusters of retainers around each major leader are two major sources of policy formulation within the brotherhoods. These are informal groups, but they are in fact much more influential than the various formal organizations which have become appended to the *tariqas*.

---

[20] See Sy, "Traditionalisme mouride," pp. 97–113.

[21] Interview with Niass' disciples, Jan. 15, 1966, and with Mor Abdiou N'Diaye (Niass' general secretary), Jan. 21, 1966.

The *Tariqas*

For example, a more formal and modern type of council was formed among the Murids in 1947 called the Council of Murid Administration, established to handle investment of Murid funds.[22] At origin the council had eleven members, all of whom were descendants of Ahmad Bamba, and it was presided over by Falilou with Bassiru as vice-president and Cheikh M'Backé as secretary. It concerned itself with a number of undertakings including supervision of the construction of the grand mosque at Touba. The council was never publicly dissolved, but it did not become very significant in the ruling pattern of the leaders.

The Council of Murid Administration symbolizes an interesting trend in the Senegalese brotherhoods of adapting modern formal organization and modern techniques to brotherhood needs. The major reason for the adaptation is that the leaders of all the *tariqas* have been constantly involved with the French since the end of the last century and have been influenced by Western ideas and customs. (An obvious result of this contact with the French has been Murid emphasis on the production of peanuts and on money-making in general.) Thus, the council took on the formal structure of a Western association with a president and vice-president in charge; but it was controlled by power relationships established in *tariqas* in the Middle Ages and reinforced by precolonial tribal custom. The khalif and his assistants directed the organization without any question of their right to do so.

Similarly, modern formal organizations were created within the brotherhoods when marabus organized their own cooperatives in the late forties and fifties. These *were* modern organizations on paper but in actuality they were not cooperatives at all, since the members did not share the profits. Like the cooperatives, the *dahira* (singular *dahiratu*), which are organized in towns to raise money for the brotherhoods, have elected officers (a president or presidents, a commissioner or director, and often a secretary and treasurer for each); but in reality they are dominated by appointees of the major marabus. Neither the *dahiratu* nor the cooperative is a fundamental part of the decision-making process in the brotherhoods except inasmuch as its leaders are involved in the informal councils of marabus or have the personal trust and confidence of the khalif. Members of these "formal" groups have no voice in the management

---

[22] Nekkach, "Unpublished Report."

of their organizations or of the brotherhood as a whole. Like the general membership of the brotherhood, the members of the "formal" organizations merely accept decisions of the major leaders as expressed by intermediary marabus or delegates of the khalif.[23]

In summary, the power structure of a Senegalese brotherhood is relatively simple. Decisions are made at the top by councils of marabus or, more regularly, by the khalif on the advice of retainers and trusted councillors and are transmitted to the lesser marabus and through them to the mass of disciples. All the Senegalese *tariqas* are organized in this fashion, but it is important to note that there is a significant difference between the Murids and other groups in their degree of marabu control over disciples. The Murids are more highly disciplined than other groups and their marabus enjoy tightly unified support for any policy they wish to adopt. This fact has great political significance: politicians are aware that they must win the support of the Murid leaders if they want cooperation from Murid disciples. In other *tariqas* the members do not feel it necessary to obey their marabu's every word except in religious matters and, similarly, the marabus in charge are less likely to insist that their disciples act in some specific way regarding the government. Many Tijani marabus are exceptions to this pattern; but, nonetheless, government officials know that although opposition by a leading non-Murid marabu can cause discontent with the government among his followers, it is less likely to result in total opposition as could be the case if Murid leaders pitted themselves against the government.

One must not, however, overexaggerate the importance of this factor. All the major *tariqas* in Senegal have potentially great influence on national politics. Indeed, the political strength of a brotherhood depends also on the character and inclinations of the leaders. Thus it is commonly recognized in Senegal that the last khalif of the Tijanis, Abubacar, was more interested and involved in politics and also had a more forceful nature than his younger brother and successor, Abdul Aziz. The Tijanis, during the reign of Abubacar, appeared more dynamic and were more influential in national politics than they are at present. Among the Murids, Falilou was viewed as much more forceful than his predecessor Mamadu Mustafa; and it is assumed

[23] See Appendices C and D on the *dahira* and the marabus' cooperatives.

that Abdu Lahat, who succeeded Falilou as khalif in 1968, will
not have as much political influence as Falilou had. Ibrahima Niass
personally pushed his branch of the Tijani into an important
political role, which his father and brothers never were able to do.
Saidou Nourou Tall is another marabu who has used his position
to build up his brotherhood and his own importance as a
political leader. In contrast, Sidi Lamine Kunta, heir to the
Bu Kunta khalifat and extremely wealthy with numerous
faithful *taalibés,* is reputedly unwilling to mix in politics and has
kept out of political affairs as much as possible. The discipline
of a *tariqa* must be reinforced by forceful, politically involved
leaders if that group is to be powerful in Senegalese national
politics.

Intrabrotherhood and Interbrotherhood Disputes

The political influence of *tariqas* in Senegal would be easier to
analyze if the simple knowledge of who the khalif is and who
his favored retainers or most trusted marabus are could suffice
to explain the inner politics of any one brotherhood. In fact,
however, all the brotherhoods are split by bitter feuds among
different marabus each of whom is trying to increase his own
personal influence and prestige. So it is that the power alignment
within any one brotherhood can only be understood if the splits
among the major leaders are known, for each leader uses his
own following for his own purposes. The mass of followers owe
their loyalty ultimately to the khalif of their *tariqa*, but the more
immediate loyalty of each goes to his local marabu or to the man
who initiated him into the brotherhood. In a conflict the disciples
may well follow their initiator and not their ultimate leader.
Therefore the marabus can and do use their disciples to fight
each other although they may present a united front to outsiders.

One of the major causes for divisions within a brotherhood
has been the question of succession. The struggle of Shaykh Anta
and Cheikh M'Backé to inherit the khalifat of the Murids is an
excellent example but certainly not the only one.[24] In the major
branch of the Tijanis, Al Hajj Malik Sy left five sons to contest
his succession when he died in 1922. His favorite and the one
with whom he had associated most was his second son, Mansur
Sy; but it was Abubacar, the eldest, who inherited the khalifat.
Despite relative peace in the early years, by the end of the

---

[24] See Chapter 2.

Second World War the khalif Abubacar strongly distrusted
his brothers Mansur, the second, and Abdul Aziz, the third
youngest, both of whom, he felt, were conspiring to take over
the brotherhood. The quarrel came into the open in 1951,
when the khalif's brothers refused to appear with him at the
annual religious ceremony in Tivaouane.[25] The breach was not
closed until 1952, when a grand council of all the Tijani leaders
including Saidou Nourou Tall and Ibrahima Diop, an important
Tijani leader in Dakar, was held.[26] The reconciliation was publicly
recognized in January, 1952, when the Avenue El Hadj Malick Sy
in Thies was dedicated and both Abubacar and Mansur presided;[27]
but it was short-lived, and relations rapidly grew tense again
between the brothers. In the spring of 1956, a year before
the khalif died, the dissension between Abubacar and Mansur
flared up in a violent attack by the khalif's disciples on his
brother's compound.[28] Although the incident was broken up
by the police, friendly relations were not established.

Mansur Sy, who should have succeeded his brother in 1957,
died four days after Abubacar's death, leaving Abdul Aziz to
become the new khalif of the major Tijani branch. He was not
unopposed for the third of Abubacar's sons, named Cheikh
Tidjane Sy, claimed the position. Cheikh Tidjane, like Cheikh
M'Backé, argued that he, not his uncle, had the right to succession
and backed up his arguments with the support of his father's
taalibés. Cheikh Tidjane had no grounds for his claim because
he was not the first son; nevertheless, he caused the khalif
extreme difficulties and, had it not been for the firm support
of the major Tijani marabus like Saidou Nourou, Abdul Aziz
might not have been able to remain in office.

The Tijani Niass family faced similar difficulties when Al Hajj
Abdoulaye Niass, father of the present khalif, died in 1922.
His eldest son Muhammad, succeeded him, but Ibrahima, a
younger son, was the most forceful leader. Ibrahima established
an independent branch of the Tijani, which separated from
his brother's between 1928 and 1930. Later he collected disciples
from many different countries in West Africa, building his order
into a powerful group. The hostility between Ibrahima and

---

[25] Referred to in Abun-Nasr, The Tijaniyya, p. 149. Information also from interview with
Abubacar Sy, son of Mansur Sy, Oct. 21, 1965, Dakar.
[26] Interview with Abubacar Sy, ibid.
[27] AOF, Feb. 4, 1965.
[28] Interviews with Tijani leaders, Mar. 2, 1966, Dakar; see also reference to fight in Réveil
islamique, no. 17, June, 1956.

his brothers flared openly when Umar succeeded Muhammad in 1957. Violent fights occurred between the sons of the present and former khalifs and Ibrahima's *taalibés* on this occasion, but they were quickly suppressed. Peace was established, and today Umar even attends Ibrahima's festivals,[29] though it is still believed that he and his adherents are jealous of his powerful younger brother.[30]

Various less important leaders line up in support of one or another candidate in a succession struggle and sometimes such quarrels threaten to split the brotherhood into warring factions. Thus the sons of Mansur Sy supported Abdul Aziz against Cheikh Tidjane as did, at least tacitly, the elder sons of Abubacar. Among the Murids, Falilou supported his uncle Shaykh Anta against Mamadu Mustafa and, later, Cheikh M'Backé found adherents among his father's *taalibés* and also among the Baye Fall, who split over the matter.[31] Nor is it only succession crises that cause enmities within a brotherhood. Minor leaders war among themselves constantly in attempts to increase their own prestige, as Bamba's brother Shaykh Thioro did in expressing open hostility to his brothers Shaykh Anta and Ibra M'Backé.[32] The sons of Ibrahima Niass also are reportedly not in agreement with each other.

The divisions in each *tariqa* are reinforced by the jealousy and enmity between the various brotherhoods or branches thereof. To some extent this is a doctrinaire opposition. Many Tijanis, for example, feel that the Murid order distorts Islam. But as important, if not more so, as disagreements over doctrine are the personal ambitions of various important marabus. Furthermore, in some cases *taalibés* of one group are united against another in hopes of increasing the power and prestige of their own brotherhood—Murid and Tijani disciples have warred since the founding of the Muridiyya. The founder of the major Tijani branch in Senegal openly disapproved of the Murids, and the present khalif criticizes them sharply if not openly.[33] Ibrahima Niass is equally critical of the Murids. Moreover, he is critical of his fellow Tijani, denouncing the title of khalif held by Abdul Aziz as not part of Islam. He refuses to recognize

[29] For example, he attended Ibrahima's Gamou in 1966.
[30] Interviews with Niass' disciples Jan. 11 and 15, 1966, Dakar.
[31] Nekkach, "Unpublished Report."
[32] DA, letter from Shaykh Thioro (June 4, 1914), Dossier.
[33] Interview with the khalif Abdul Aziz Sy, Dec. 5, 1965, Tivaouane.

the authority of that Tijani branch and openly castigates the political machinations of Saidou Nourou Tall.[34] Sidi Lamine Kunta and Ahmadou Saidou have also been known to express hostility to the major Tijani branch by criticizing Saidou Nourou for his great involvement in politics.[35]

Not suprisingly, Senegalese marabus have eagerly taken part in quarrels of brotherhoods other than their own to further their personal interests. Consequently, the disagreement between Abdul Aziz and the former Murid khalif Falilou leads one to suspect the motives for the friendliness that existed between Falilou and Cheikh Tidjane. This friendliness has been explained as having arisen from the khalif's admiration for Cheikh Tidjane's dynamism and education,[36] but the political advantages of the alignment can be clearly seen: Falilou supported Cheikh Tidjane in order to weaken Abdul Aziz.[37] Falilou's actions were not without precedent, for Abdul Aziz himself reportedly made friends with Mamadu Mustafa in a maneuver which may have aimed at helping Abdul Aziz in the inner struggles of his own *tariqa*.[38] At an even earlier date Ahmad Bamba and other marabus were said to have intervened in the succession crisis when Bu Kunta died in order to attract more disciples for themselves.[39]

The Involvement of Politicians in Brotherhood Disputes

The interference of French officials and then Senegalese politicians in the inner power struggles of the brotherhoods has been a constant factor since the French established their control over Senegal. The French favored marabus who seemed most amenable to their rule. They supported the candidacies of Mamadu Mustafa and then Falilou M'Backé, for example, and helped the favored son of their former assistant Bu Kunta to keep his place as head of the family. Senegalese politicians continued this pattern of interference but for slightly different reasons. They supported a marabu because he could offer

[34] Interview with Ibrahima Niass, Jan. 29, 1966, Kaolack.
[35] Interview with an Islamic scholar, Mar. 2, 1966, Dakar.
[36] Interview with an assistant to Falilou, Nov. 20, 1965, Touba.
[37] Interview with government official and Murid disciple, Nov. 9, 1965, Dakar. See reference to friendship in Sy, "Traditionalisme mouride," pp. 183–184.
[38] DA, letter from Commandant of Diourbel (June 13, 1939) in untitled book on Saidou Nourou Tall, vol. II.
[39] DA, "Rapport politique du Sénégal" (2nd trimester 1914), no. 2707, 2G 14.6.

them money and votes and sometimes because he promoted a cause which they were backing: in the late twenties and early thirties Blaise Diagne, who was in the French parliament, favored Mamadu Mustafa, who was also allied with the administration. Diagne's opponent, Galandu Diouf, who was considered radical and dangerous by many French officials, favored Shaykh Anta, who had a similar reputation and therefore symbolized opposition to the French. Lamine Gueye, who also apparently sided with Shaykh Anta at the time of his exile, was in the opposition at this time and may have wished to attract opposition supporters to himself through defending a marabu feared by the administration. Later, when Galandu Diouf was in parliament, he and Abubacar Sy openly cooperated with each other, and Lamine Gueye, in opposition, reportedly received some assistance from the Murid *tariqa*.[40]

Lamine Gueye in the pre-World War II period had been friends with Abdul Aziz, Ibrahima Niass, Mansur Sy, and also Abubacar Sy. None of the elder Sys openly involved themselves in the split between Lamine Gueye and his younger colleague Senghor after the war; but it soon was evident that the khalif, perhaps because of Gueye's association with his hated brothers, perhaps because of the prodding of his son Cheikh Tidjane, was favorably inclined toward the BDS. Abubacar's next two brothers remained loyal to Lamine Gueye. The alignment was not open at first and Cheikh Tidjane even published one of his *causeries* on Islam in the SFIO newspaper, the *AOF*, in 1950;[41] But it was more easily recognizable as time went on, especially after 1951, when an incident occurred that tightened the lines between the two sides. Apparently the Socialists planned to hold a rally in Tivaouane. As their trucks headed toward the rally site, a few Tijanis stoned the vehicles and SFIO men (called "Red Berets") sprang from the trucks and attacked the khalif's compound in retaliation. The incident caused much ill feeling among the khalif's followers against the SFIO and may well have damaged the chances of that party in the 1951 elections in Tivaouane. Cheikh Tidjane, meanwhile, became openly associated with the BDS. He published a series of articles in

[40] See DA: letters from Blaise Diagne (July 23, 1929), (2) 13G 2, and Buernier (Aug. 4, 1929), (2) 13G 2; "Rapport sur l'incident de Diourbel (affaire Cheikh Anta M'Backé)," Feb. 14, 1930, (2) 13 G 2; police report (Feb. 20, 1930), (2) 13G 2. References to these alliances can be found in Abun-Nasr, The Tijaniyya, pp. 147–148.

[41] Cheikh Tidjane Sy, "De l'Education morale des Musulmans africains," *AOF* (Oct. 14, 1950).

Condition humaine, the party newspaper, which supposedly
were religiously oriented but also quite openly supported
the BDS.

At the same time as the BDS and the SFIO were involving
themselves in the Sy family quarrels, they also took sides
in the Murid succession struggle in the late forties and early
fifties. Mamadu Mustafa had just died and Cheikh M'Backé
was exerting his considerable influence to prevent his uncle
from establishing himself as khalif. Both Lamine Gueye and
Léopold Senghor undertook early pilgrimages to woo the
Muslim leaders, but it was Senghor who obtained the loyalty
of Falilou M'Backé, the newly appointed khalif, by promising
to cooperate with him should the BDS come to power. Falilou
did not openly support Senghor in his break with the SFIO,
but the marabu had reached an understanding with the BDS
head that was reinforced by the Socialists' association with
Cheikh M'Backé. Lamine Gueye had been friends with Mamadu
Mustafa and his son Cheikh M'Backé, and Cheikh had
accompanied him on a pilgrimage to Mecca in 1947 with Abdul
Aziz.[42] The Socialist leader's first loyalty was to Cheikh M'Backé,
who seemed a good ally because he was powerful. Gueye did
not want to make an enemy of Falilou, but the latter was in
sympathy with Senghor and consequently Socialist support
of Cheikh M'Backé became more open and determined.

On their side, BDS leaders did not wish to alienate Cheikh
M'Backé any more than necessary. They resorted to depreciating
evidence of an alliance between the young marabu and the
SFIO leaders. For example, Cheikh Tidjane wrote in *Condition
humaine* in 1951 that Cheikh M'Backé could not be involved
with the SFIO "saboteurs" because he had other things to do.[43]
An earlier article by Amadou Diop stated that Lamine Gueye,
unable to gain support from the country at large, was trying
to use the marabus to get votes. This policy was condemned
in the article even though both parties were attempting to get
help from the marabus, and the author concluded that Cheikh
M'Backé and his uncle Bassiru could not possibly be connected
with such crude political maneuvers.[44]

---

[42] Quesnot, "Les Cadres maraboutiques," p. 136. See also "Un Grand Pionnier de
l'agriculture sénégalaise Al Hadj Cheikh Amadou M'Backé," *AOF* (May 16, 1952).

[43] Cheikh Tidjane Sy, "Aimer Son Pays," *Condition humaine* (May 24, 1951).

[44] Amadou Diop, "Voyage socialist en lieux Mourides . . ." *Condition humaine* (Mar. 24,
1951).

The *Tariqas*

The BDS won by a large majority in the Diourbel-Touba region in elections for the French Assembly in 1951. Cheikh M'Backé openly opposed the BDS, but Falilou, while not in open support of it, tacitly favored it and his supporters voted for it. In March, 1952, in a violent effort both to help the SFIO and to further his own position, Cheikh M'Backé launched an attack by his *taalibés* on Falilou's compound. Several members of the khalif's entourage were seriously injured but the compound was not taken. The BDS, of course, publicized the fight, which they blamed on the SFIO. Cheikh M'Backé because BDS leaders again did not wish to alienate him, was not openly condemned.[45] But his attack discredited him in the Murid milieu, and Falilou took the opportunity to broadcast the event by convoking the principal Murid leaders and criticizing his nephew. His action was interpreted as an avowal of support for the BDS, which subsequently won the Territorial Assembly elections in the Diourbel region.[46] Bassiru, whose support of his nephew had fluctuated, ceased to side with Cheikh M'Backé, who found himself expelled from the Council of Murid Administration.[47]

For a while SFIO leaders continued to give open support to Cheikh M'Backé,[48] but they could do nothing to restore his lost prestige. Severely weakened in his quarrel with Falilou, Cheikh was forced to restrain his efforts to take over the khalifat. Nevertheless, the young marabu remained hostile to his uncle throughout the succeeding years.[49] In 1956 a move toward reconciliation was effected by one of the khalif's elder sons. Cheikh M'Backé was led to pay a visit to his uncle symbolizing the apparent truce between them. A few months later he appeared with Falilou at the annual Magal, and outwardly, at least, the unity of the family was restored.[50]

By this time, the support Cheikh M'Backé had received from the SFIO had disappeared. In fact, the SFIO had faced numerous electoral defeats at the hands of BDS leaders, and eventually in 1958 it was forced to merge with the BDS (called the BPS since

[45] *Condition humaine*, Mar. 27, 1952.
[46] *Condition humaine*, Apr. 9, 1952.
[47] Nekkach, "Unpublished Report."
[48] See "Un Grand Pionnier de l'agriculture sénégalaise."
[49] See reference to split in Oumar Dieng, "Le Magal de Touba," *Réveil islamique* (November, 1954), and "L'Institut Islamique de Touba et la politique musulmane française," *Réveil islamique* (June, 1956).
[50] *Ibid.*

1956). The merger called itself the Union Progressiste Sénégalaise (UPS)[51] and was dominated by Léopold Senghor, his assistant Mamadou Dia, and other BDS leaders. Cheikh M'Backé now had to find support among politicians not tied to the dominant party, allied with the Murid khalif. He contributed money and support to Cheikh Anta Diop, who formed an opposition party, the Bloc des Masses Sénégalaises (BMS), in 1961 that became part of the Force National Démocratique Sénégalaise (FNDS) in 1963.[52] Cheikh M'Backé's part in the opposition party was not openly acknowledged by the UPS leaders, who, as usual, avoided clashing directly with the powerful marabu although secular BMS leaders were treated without ceremony.[53]

By the time of the Murid Magal in July, 1962, many BMS leaders were officially considered outlaws. Furthermore, the government had made broad hints that they suspected the party of involvement in a recent plot against the regime.[54] Cheikh M'Backé, nonetheless, chose this moment to underline his support of the BMS and therefore his disagreement with his uncle, who was allied with the UPS. When the Magal ceremony was about to begin and all the government representatives, including Prime Minister Mamadou Dia, were seated and the khalif had entered. Cheikh M'Backé drove up in a car with Cheikh Anta Diop. Mamadou Dia ordered that Cheikh Anta not be permitted to enter. But Cheikh M'Backé would not allow the police to prevent Anta's entry and he signaled to his adherents among the Baye Fall, who, according to one version of the incident, picked up the car in which the marabu and Cheikh Anta rode and carried them in, pushing aside the government police. The affair evoked consternation among the Murids. Some interpreted Cheikh M'Backé's late entrance as a deliberate slight toward the khalif and an open declaration of hostility to the Murid leader and his associated UPS friends.[55] Others insisted that Cheikh M'Backé was always late and that this was no special slight but agreed, nonetheless, that the event indicated continuing ill feeling between the khalif and his nephew.[56] The official UPS paper, *L'Unité africaine,* made no

[51] *AOF,* Apr. 2, 1958.

[52] The BMS was dissolved in October 1963; *L'Unité africaine,* Oct. 16, 1963.

[53] For example, Cheikh Anta Diop and two companions were thrown into jail for attacking a UPS official even though it is somewhat doubtful that they did so. See "Après les Incidents de Louga et Pikine . . ." *L'Unité africaine* (Aug. 22, 1962).

[54] "Six Comploteurs anti-nationaux arrêtés," *L'Unité africaine* (Mar. 16, 1962).

[55] Interview with Murid scholar, Oct. 7, 1965, Dakar.

[56] Interview with government official and Murid follower, Dec. 3, 1965, Dakar.

mention of the incident at first[57] but later condemned what
had occurred. Not surprisingly, the paper did not mention
Cheikh M'Backé, but blamed what had happened on the BMS,
which "distorts the political climate of Senegal."[58] Cheikh M'Backé
was not arrested and continued to express opposition to his uncle
in different ways, though not as blatantly as at the 1962 Magal.[59]
But his opposition, at least publicly, was much more restrained,
and the UPS leaders made attempts to win him to their side. In
the early sixties he even had conferences[60] with President
Senghor, who is reported to have given him financial assistance.
Despite the conferences, there is little reason to doubt that
Cheikh M'Backé maintained this opposition to his uncle.
Quite probably a new, more powerful alignment of politicians
that challenged the UPS and thus the khalif would have received
his open support.

Cheikh M'Backé was not the only Murid marabu who attempted
to use an opposition party to enhance his position vis-à-vis
the khalif and his UPS allies. Less well known is the stand
reportedly taken in 1962 by the eldest son of Falilou, Modou
Mustafa, in support of the opposition party, the Parti du
Regroupement Africain (PRA), supposedly in an effort to increase
his own prestige. He was not strong enough to oppose his
father, who is reported to have placed him under house arrest.
Very little is publicly known about the affair, but whatever
happened, it is evident that shortly thereafter Modou Mustafa
was a trusted agent of his father in dealings with the government.[61]

Alignments between the important marabus and politicians
have strongly affected intergroup struggles. The politicians must
move with great care, since, even more than in cases of quarrels
within a group, they cannot afford to be completely identified
with one set of marabus or one brotherhood. Nevertheless,
various incidents have demonstrated that politicians have at
times sided with one group against another.

Probably the most important political alliance has been that
between the Murid khalif and the President of Senegal. The latter,
of course, needs the help and cooperation of Tijanis of all groups,

---

[57] *L'Unité africaine,* July 25, 1962.
[58] "Après les Incidents de Louga et **Pikine**."
[59] Thus he made a peaceful appearance at the 1963 Magal. See Republic of Senegal,
*Compte rendu de la cérémonie inaugurale de la Grande Mosquée de Touba et de la
première prière de Vendredi le 7 Juin 1963,* by Cheikh Ba Baidy (Thies, June 1963), p. 5.
[60] For example, in March, 1966, as reported in *Dakar Matin,* Mar. 16, 1966.
[61] Interviews with government officials, Murid disciples, and Murid personnel: Oct. 7, 1965,
Dakar; Oct. 4, 1965, Dakar; Nov. 3, 1965, Dakar.

but he has still been forced to side with the Murids on various occasions—for example, in the bitter struggle over the new mosque in Dakar. The mosque, first proposed in 1936, was to be Tijani but a religious symbol for all the Muslims of Senegal as well. It was a popular project and received wide publicity at the time of independence. All the major marabus supported it and the Murids contributed as much money as any other *tariqas'* leaders.[62] But the agreement among the many marabus over the desirability of building the mosque was broken over the questions of how large it should be and who should control it. It was widely rumored that Mamadou Dia planned to make this the largest mosque in Senegal, complete with a Muslim Institute and the Hostelry. Reportedly the Murid khalif was somewhat reluctant to see this Tijani mosque outshine the new Murid mosque in Touba,[63] but the more important question was, who was to be imam of the mosque and receive the prestige and power which that position would give?

The imam of Dakar, Al Hajj Amadou Lamine Diene, had held his position since 1941.[64] He was an associate of Abubacar Sy and tended to favor Cheikh Tidjane in his struggle with Abdul Aziz. He was also the logical choice for imam in Dakar. Diene had been head imam before the mosque was built and, according to the usual laws of Islam, should have been allowed to retain that office. An imam normally cannot be removed from office unless he becomes senile or goes against the doctrine of Islam according to Malikite law, which offenses Diene had not committed. But the leaders of the Abdul Aziz branch of the Tijanis wanted to replace Diene, who, they said, was not well educated in Arabic or Muslim science and therefore was a poor representative of the Tijani *tariqa*. More important, they wished him removed so that their own men could be installed.

Saidou Nourou Tall intended to have Abdul Aziz himself become the official imam, assisted by Mourtada Tall, Saidou's nephew. Abdul Aziz was apparently quite ready to follow Saidou's suggestions in the matter. Technically Saidou, who had been initiated by Al Hajj Malik Sy, should have been the loyal follower of Abdul Aziz, but the latter is not politically oriented and so Saidou directs him in political matters.

---

62 See *L'Unité africaine*, Jan. 30, 1960.
63 Interview with Murid official, Dec. 9, 1965, Touba.
64 Quesnot, "Les Cadres maraboutiques," p. 145.

The *Tariqas*

Saidou's interest in the mosque resulted in the election of Abdul Aziz to the office of imam by unanimous vote at a meeting of the Association of Imams of Cap Vert. But the Association was controlled by Saidou and not all its members had been present when the vote was taken, besides which it is not the only association of imams in the region. Opponents of the candidacy of Abdul Aziz quickly pointed out these facts as reasons for the invalidity of the vote.

Falilou, in the meantime, was not pleased by Saidou's proposal. He apparently did not want Abdul Aziz and Saidou Nourou to control the mosque directly, as this would give their branch of the Tijanis added prestige and power. The Murid khalif's opposition was supported by Cheikh Tidjane, who did not want to see his uncle's power increased. Ibrahima Niass also opposed Abdul Aziz as a candidate for imam. The mosque was inaugurated, although it was still unfinished on March 27, 1964, in the presence of King Hassan II of Morocco and with Abdul Aziz presiding at the prayers.[65] But Murid pressure was placed on the government, specifically on Minister of Foreign Affairs Doudou Thiam, a Murid who had reportedly threatened to resign if Diene were not made imam. Eventually Senghor conceded the matter to the Murids and Lamine Diene was acknowledged as imam.[66] The mosque crisis demonstrated the strength of the Murid tie with the government, to the chagrin of the main branch of the Tijanis. Abdul Aziz showed no public dissatisfaction at the government's decision; but this was not true of Saidou Nourou, a supporter of the UPS from its foundation, who showed his displeasure through a distinct coldness in his dealings with government officials.[67]

Examples of government and party officials siding with the Tijanis against the Murids are more difficult to find because the UPS has always been allied with the Murids. However, in late spring 1965 Léopold Senghor appeared at the annual Tijani festival in celebration of the birth of Muhammad, the Gamou. It was the President's first appearance in many years at this festival, and he cut short his usual summer trip to Paris to attend. He spoke warmly to the Tijani khalif and ended

[65] *Afrique nouvelle*, Apr. 3–9, 1964; *L'Unité africaine*, Apr. 2, 1964; *Dakar matin*, May 12, 1964.
[66] Interviews with government officials, Murid disciples and leaders, and Tijani disciples and leaders: Oct. 5, 1965, Dakar; Oct. 7, 1965, Dakar; Oct. 21, 1965, Dakar; Nov. 3, 1965, Dakar; Jan. 7, 1966, Dakar. See also *Dakar matin*, May 13 and 15, 1964.
[67] Interviews with government official and Muslim scholar, Jan. 7, 1966, Dakar.

by criticizing the divisions in Senegalese religion and pledging the support of his government for religious unity.[68] His presence at Gamou at this time, when he and the Murid khalif were in disagreement over the khalif's personal secretary,[69] was widely interpreted as a threat of governmental support for the Tijanis against the Murids. Falilou's only representative at the festival, notably, was an envoy to Cheikh Tidjane's private Gamou.[70]

Muslim Unity

The involvement of politicians in brotherhood affairs began during the colonial period, and in time officials and politicians became adept at playing one brotherhood off against another. Radical Muslim students today condemn the French for having sought to "diviser pour regner,"[71] but present-day politicians also see the usefulness of this policy. In one way, of course, the situation today is quite different from that which prevailed earlier: the French were not Muslim and were alien to Islam and the African peoples, whereas Senegalese politicians are largely Muslim and are in sympathy with Islam. Nevertheless, Senegalese rulers are aware of the powerful opposition to modern reform that conservative marabus could create if they were unified, and thus the government has an interest in dividing in order to rule just as its colonial predecessors had.

In reality, the chances of Senegalese marabus to unite and remain unified for any period of time are slight, since the enmities within any group and between different brotherhoods are deep-rooted. Only a serious threat to Islam as a religion or to the institution of the brotherhood would provide enough common ground for an alliance between the Senegalese *tariqas* unless the present pattern of relations were fundamentally altered. At one point in recent history such an attack was feared by marabus in Senegal, and for a short time it seemed that a viable alliance might be created; an alliance was in fact formed, after the Enabling Act of 1956 had brought responsible government to Senegal and placed the UPS in control. Despite pacts between various marabus and politicians, Muslim leaders

[68] *Sénégal d'aujourd'hui,* Aug. 1965, pp. 28–30.
[69] See Chapter 5.
[70] Interviews with government officials and Murid personnel, Nov. 3, 1965, Dakar.
[71] "L'Islam aoefien et le colonialisme," *Réveil islamique* (July 1954).

still feared that an African government might seek to alter
the pattern of relations set up by the French and might attempt
to reform the brotherhoods and injure the position of the
marabus. In order to be sure that they could continue to
control the situation, several marabus decided to form a council
of marabus. Saidou Nourou Tall engineered the new council,
which was formed in December, 1957 (though it did not
coalesce until November, 1958) and called the Council of
Islamic Reorganization.[72] On paper the organization, now known
as the Superior Council of Religious Chiefs, was extremely
impressive. Its intention was to "protect, guard and maintain
the dogma of Islam in the true sense." It proposed three additional
important goals: 1) to control and verify the Constitution
of Senegal, which had to be submitted to the council for
approval in order that Islam might be given absolute liberty,
2) to act as mediator in all differences that might arise between
Muslims or religious leaders or between the latter and the
administration, and 3) to defend the interests of Muslims
associated with the public and judicial authorities.[73]

The council was directed by a commission which could
convoke the General Assembly on matters of significance.
Most of the important marabus in Senegal were named as
officials. The Tijani president was Saidou Nourou Tall and the
Murid president Falilou M'Backé. The vice-president was Bassiru
and the two secretaries general were Ibrahima Niass and
Cheikh M'Backé. Abdul Aziz was treasurer general and one of
his two assistants was Mamadou Awa Balla, a cousin of the
Murid khalif. There were twenty-one members of the Director
Council, including Cheikh Tidjane Sy and Sidi Lamine Kunta.[74]
The council was a formidable organization, with its aim of
controlling the government's actions in any area that touched
upon Islam or upon the brotherhoods and their leaders. Had
it remained united it could have dictated to the government,
for the marabus listed as its members controlled the major
part of Senegal's Muslim population. It also would have

[72] Quesnot, "Les Cadres maraboutiques," p. 137.
[73] Typescript copy of the resolutions of the Council of Islamic Reorganization.
[74] Ibid. Also named as council officials were Chams Eddine Diagne, a wealthy Dakar
marabu; Ibrahima Diop, also from Dakar; Mustafa Sy, relative of the Tijani khalif; and Cheikh
Mandione Laye, head of the Layenne order. Named honorary presidents were Sharif Tidjane
Muhammad al-Habib, head of the Tijani *tariqa* in Morocco; Cheikh Sidia al-Hajj Abdoulaye,
Mauritanian head of the Qadiri branch from which the Muridiyya derive; and Cheikh
Talibuya, son of the former important Mauritanian marabu Saad Bu.

represented a triumph for the marabus, who had never succeeded in overcoming their differences. Despite a few meetings in Tivaouane and N'Diassane, the Kunta center, however, it was stillborn. A major reason for the failure apparently was Falilou M'Backé's lack of cooperation: he had agreed to join and, indeed, was a president, but he was doubtful about the organization and had less confidence in it than in the close relationship between himself and Léopold Senghor. Without his support the council was almost inevitably doomed, for the Murids were politically the most powerful Senegalese *tariqa*.

A second cause for the council's failure lay in the political astuteness of the Senegalese politicians, particularly Léopold Senghor. It was logical that government leaders should seek to undermine the council, since they viewed it as potentially dangerous, but they could not oppose it openly. What occurred is illustrated by the following event. One of the first demands of the council leaders was for forty Muslim seats in the eighty-man legislature, that is, for forty appointees of the council leaders in the Assembly. Rather than dealing with the council heads as a group, Léopold Senghor reportedly saw each member alone. He stressed the fact that forty Muslim members in the legislature were not nearly enough for a Muslim country; he confused and divided the marabus on this matter, although the Muslim members he proposed could not be controlled by the council. Further, Senghor promised different kinds of aid to the individual council members, quietly tying them to his government separately and dividing them from each other. His policy was nothing more than the old, but successful, colonial policy.[75]

The Superior Council of Religious Chiefs was not officially dissolved, although it rapidly fell into disuse. It was the first and last serious attempt by the Senegalese marabus to unite for political action. It had no follow-up, perhaps because the marabus lost some of their fear of the Senegalese government and became convinced that, even in independent Senegal, life would continue as it had for the last fifty or sixty years. There was one other attempt to unite the marabus, but it was made by Mamadou Dia in 1962 and was an obvious and

[75] Interviews with government officials, Murid disciples and leaders, Tijani disciples and leaders, and Muslim scholars: Oct. 30, Nov. 3, 1965, Dakar.

The *Tariqas*

unsuccessful effort on his part to use marabus for political
support in his struggle with President Senghor.[76] So it is that
the brotherhoods in Senegal remain torn by external conflicts
with other brotherhoods and internal quarrels among marabus.
The Murids have maintained the most united front of any
tariqa because of their doctrinaire emphasis on loyalty and
discipline, but even that group contains bitter differences of
interest between major leaders. The perpetual dissension between
the marabus is the primary weakness of the Senegalese *tariqas*.
It is also an essential factor in the past and present politics
of Senegal.

[76] See Chapter 4.

4 The Political Parties and the Marabus

The involvement of politicians in the affairs of the brotherhoods can be looked at from a slightly different perspective than the one employed so far. Rather than continuing to give examples showing that various party leaders' and politicians' interests have been furthered through their interrelations, one can ask specifically how these interrelations affect the parties themselves. What kinds of programs or platforms result from close ties with the brotherhoods? Exactly how important have the brotherhoods been in the policies and activities of the UPS?

Early BDS and SFIO Efforts to Win Marabu Support

Marabus in the early twentieth century such as Ahmad Bamba, Shaykh Anta, and Bu Kunta were approached by Senegalese politicians who were running for office in the four communes and wanted money for their campaigns and the support of urban disciples of the orders.[1] However, it was not until the vote was extended to the countryside that the marabus became determinant factors, as the Senegalese scholar Cheikh Tidjane Sy (a specialist on Senegalese Islam) points out.[2] In this period immediately after the Second World War, when politicians wanted Muslim leaders to provide rural votes for the new national parties, the importance of the brotherhoods was emphasized in party platforms and propaganda. The politicians stressed their own deep religious sentiments, their support for Islam in particular, and their desire to help the marabus. The first trips of the party leaders to attract followers in the countryside were highlighted by receptions given by the marabus. Articles that spoke glowingly of the contacts with the "masses" ("how can we not vibrate with love at [our] contact with these working people whose confidence and optimism is so touching?")[3] underlined the marabus' approval of the politicians. For example, Mamadou Dia describes one of Léopold Senghor's first trips to the Murid region as a great success, particularly because of the "perfect communion" between the BDS leaders and

---

[1] Ahmad Bamba was asked for support in election campaigns on a number of occasions. His interest in such matters apparently was not great, but other contemporary marabus such as Shaykh Anta and Bu Kunta became quite involved in some elections. See DA, Commandant of Baol, "Rapport confidentiel sur les Mourites" (January, 1914), and Commandant of Baol, "Rapport sur les Mourides . . . Mars, Mai, Juin 1914" (July 1, 1914), Dossier.
[2] Sy, "Traditionalisme mouride," p. 143. See Appendix A.
[3] "L'Acceuil de Sine-Saloum," *Condition humaine* (Apr. 7, 1948).

the Murid marabus.[4] A similar article in the SFIO paper in 1949 stresses the acclaim that Lamine Gueye received from Abubacar Sy in Tivaouane.[5]

Condition humaine and *AOF* were full of notices about events of interest to Muslims. Muslim festivals such as the Murid Magal and the Tijani Gamou were enthusiastically reported, and the inauguration of a mosque or the reception of honors by Muslim leaders were warmly congratulated. Causes sure to appeal to Muslim leaders were supported by the parties: for example, it was reported that Léopold Senghor was sponsoring the increase of Arabic teaching in Senegal, the creation of a Franco-Arabic *madrassa*, Arabic study in secondary schools, and the establishment of an Arabic Institute at Dakar University, as well as scholarships for Senegalese students to study Arabic in France and North Africa.[6] His proposition echoed an earlier SFIO proposal with similar goals.[7] On another occasion Senghor spoke for the creation of Muslim tribunals in the major towns of Senegal, saying that the present system was no longer valid for the country.[8] The Socialists in turn publicized the defense of Islam by the SFIO deputy Djim Momar Gueye against the accusations of François Mauriac, who apparently had likened the Muslim religion to Communism.[9]

The fact that Léopold Senghor was Catholic, of course, was stressed greatly by the SFIO. The party had an advantage from this point of view, since Lamine Gueye was a Muslim who had made the pilgrimage to Mecca in 1947 with some of the most important marabus in Senegal: Senghor, therefore, was put on the defensive. His party emphasized that there was no division between Muslims and Catholics in Senegal, only between religious and nonreligious men. The lines between the two parties on this issue were quickly drawn, with the SFIO trying to make the elections into holy wars against non-Muslims and, on the other side, the BDS indignantly

[4] Mamadou Dia, "Trois Jours à travers le Baol," *Condition humaine* (May 26, 1948).

[5] Sar Amadou Boubacar, "Tivaouane en fête acclame Lamine Gueye," *AOF* (May 16–22, 1949). On this occasion the BDS denied that Gueye had had a warm reception in Tivaouane—a typical method of reprisal for both parties. See Guiby, "A Propos de 'Gueuleton' de Tivaouane," *Condition humaine* (May 31, 1949).

[6] L. S. Senghor, "L'Organisation de l'enseignement arabe en AOF," *Condition humaine* (Aug. 23, 1949).

[7] "L'Enseignement arabe en AOF," *AOF* (Sept. 9, 1948).

[8] "Lettre du deputé Léopold Senghor à Monsieur le Ministre de F.O.M. tendant à la création de tribunaux musulmans," *Condition humaine* (July 25, 1950).

[9] Djim Momar Gueye, "M. François Mauriac, je ne suis pas d'accord . . ." *AOF* (Aug. 11–Sept. 1, 1950).

1. The late khalif Falilou M'Backé

2. Students memorize verses from the Qu'ran written in ink on their boards

3. Ibrahima Niass blesses a disciple during the annual harvest of his fields

4. The Touba mosque during the annual Murid Magal

5. Lamine Gueye, Saidou Nourou Tall, and Falilou M'Backé

6. Political speech of Cheikh Tidjane Sy

7. Falilou M'Backé with President Senghor in the place of honor beside him at the annual Murid Magal

8. Murid disciples going to work in their marabu's peanut fields

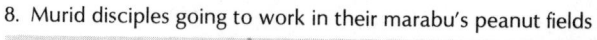

9. Peanut storehouse in the field of a Murid marabu; the marabu is in white at right

denouncing this policy while attempting to cast aspersions on the Socialist leaders' religious sincerity. Both groups, meanwhile, continued to publish reports of their many contacts with Muslim leaders.

The Socialists' method of denigrating Senghor was clearly demonstrated in an article in 1949. The BDS leader was accused of dividing the country into Catholics and Muslims with the aim of taking advantage of the Muslims in order to give the Catholic minority more power. The article also claimed that Senghor was pretending to sympathize with the Muslims so that he could take advantage of them.[10] A later article similarly accused the BDS leader of favoring Catholics and cited as evidence the parliamentary alliance of the BDS with the MRP in France.[11] The BDS leaders responded by condemning Lamine Gueye for profaning Islam and for trying to take advantage of the marabus in order to build support; in addition, the BDS continued to stress that there was no division between Catholics and Muslims in Senegal.[12] Gueye, according to several articles, was trying to bring religious quarrels to a country which had chosen both Catholics and Muslims to represent it in the past and thus traditionally had eschewed such quarrels.[13]

By the end of 1951 it was evident that the SFIO had lost ground throughout Senegal, but the emphasis on religious themes remained strong on both sides. SFIO leaders were openly preaching holy war against the BDS and the latter responded by alternately condemning such tactics and sniping at Lamine Gueye, who, Condition humaine noted, preferred to marry a Catholic rather than a Muslim, by civil rite rather than in a mosque.[14] After the BDS had won the 1952 Territorial elections the religious issue was dropped for the most part. Both party papers continued to sponsor causes dear to the Muslims but accusations and counteraccusations were abandoned.

[10] Ousmane Socé Diop, "Le Dijad de Serigne Léopold ou la politique du chef du BDS," AOF (Jan. 13, 1949).

[11] AOF, July 14, 1951; the MRP is of course the Mouvement Républicain Populaire.

[12] Amadou Diop, "Voyage socialist en lieux Mourides, tentative de Profanation de l'Islam," Condition humaine (Mar. 24, 1951), and Ibrahima Sow, Défie jete au peuple," Condition humaine (June 5, 1951).

[13] See Cheikh Tidjane Sy, "Méfiez-vous de la dépravation," Condition humaine (Apr. 24, 1951).

[14] See Alioune M'Bengue, "Politique de pression sur les consciences," Condition humaine (Mar. 27, 1952), and "Drôle de défenseur de l'Islam que Lamine Guèye," Condition humaine (Mar. 27, 1952).

The disappearance of the religious fights from the papers coincided with the establishment of fixed alliances between marabus and politicians. A marabu allied himself with the political leader who appeared most able to support his brotherhood and his personal ambitions. Neither party's propaganda about religion had had much effect, although some marabus distrusted Senghor at first because he was Catholic.[15] But it was, in fact, the Catholic Senghor who managed to win the support of the most powerful marabus. He allied himself primarily with Falilou M'Backé but also with Abubacar Sy, Cheikh Tidjane Sy, Saidou Nourou Tall, and a network of lesser marabus throughout the country. Gueye, too, had his allies, including Cheikh M'Backé, Abdul Aziz Sy, and Ibrahima Niass, but these marabus, though influential, were unable to offset those who backed Senghor. Gueye, moreover, was not as assiduous as Senghor in cementing his ties with the marabus through concrete gifts and promises of help for the future. Nor did he try to extend his relations to marabus on lower levels of the brotherhood hierarchies. Senghor's marabutic support, much stronger than Gueye's, weighed heavily in the defeat of the SFIO.

Senghor also seems to have been more aware than Gueye of the necessity of choosing leaders for his party who were representative of the different religious, tribal, and social groups.[16] For example, the struggle between the BDS and the SFIO to win the support of the influential Tukulor union in Dakar, UGOVF, and its leader Saidou Nourou Tall, is typical of the means Senghor used to attract religious and ethnic leaders throughout Senegal. This maneuver was difficult for Senghor because Dakar, like St. Louis, remained largely faithful to its old leader, Lamine Gueye. But Senghor wooed UGOVF by stressing his desire for a Tukulor assistant in the BDS and later by appointing Mamadou Dia, a Tukulor whose family came from the River Region.[17] The Socialists, in contrast, attempted to reason with the Tukulor by insisting that the SFIO represented all ethnic and religious groups. A 1949 article in the *AOF* states that the

[15] Interview with Ibrahima Niass, Jan. 29, 1966, Kaolack.

[16] The mosaic of ethnic, religious, and social representation is recorded in the lists of party cells in *Condition humaine*. See, e.g., *Condition humaine*, Apr. 5, 1949; Aug. 15, 1950; Nov. 7, 1950.

[17] At first Senghor chose a Lebou (Abbas Gueye), but he stressed to the Tukulor his desire to find an assistant from that group. Interview with Tukulor leader, Jan. 19, 1966, Dakar.

The Political Parties and the Marabus

Party could not give way to "regional bribery" and could not favor any one ethnic group over another because it stood for all groups.[18] UGOVF leaders seemed unimpressed by this kind of reasoning and their support went to the BDS. Lamine Gueye attracted only the Centrale de Fouta, a small splinter group of Tukulor,[19] and he hurt any chances of getting further Tukulor support by alienating Saidou Nourou Tall reportedly by opposing a trip proposed by the latter to Guinea.[20] In 1953 UGOVF split into warring factions and thus lost its political control of the Tukulor, but Senghor had already received valuable support from the group in the years before its division.[21]

Minor Parties and the Brotherhoods

Once the BDS had the majority of votes it was able to democratize its structure and eliminate the explicit representation of status, ethnic, and religious groups in the party.[22] Thus Serer and Wolof sections of the BDS, and *griot* (musician) and blacksmith sections, were replaced by cells organized on the basis of localities. But Senghor and his assistants never actually ceased their efforts to have the party hierarchy represent the important social and ethnic divisions in Senegal; representation was merely made tacit as opposed to explicit. In particular, Senghor never ignored the marabus, whose support remained essential to the UPS. His recognition of their importance was, in fact, a major reason why the BDS and than the UPS was able to defeat the many small parties based around intellectuals and on urban groups that sprang up to the left of his organization in the fifties and sixties. These parties were able to play on dissatisfaction in different regions, for example in the River Region and in the Casamance, but they never had broad-based support outside of the cities. They were usually highly critical of the UPS for not reforming the country but were themselves apparently unsuited to the task because they were unable to attract many followers.

---

[18] Diop Boubacar Obeye, "Le Parti d'abord," *AOF* (Mar. 7–13, 1949).

[19] Diop, *Société toucouleur*, p. 226.

[20] Interview with Tukulor leader, Jan. 19, 1966, Dakar. Many Guineans opposed this trip as well.

[21] Saidou Nourou Tall split UGOVF by opposing the president elected in 1953 and demanding that his own candidate be given the office. Diop, *Société toucouleur*, pp. 226–227, and interviews with Tukulor leaders, Jan. 19, 1966, and Feb. 16, 1966, Dakar.

[22] Referred to in Diop, *Société toucouleur*, p. 227.

One need only look at the experience of the Parti de Regroupement Africain-Sénégal (the PRA-Senegal) and the Parti Africain d'Indépendence (PAI) to see how these parties related to the Muslim leaders. The PRA-Senegal, the more important of the two, was formed in 1958 by a group of left-wing intellectuals when Léopold Senghor refused to campaign for independence from France. It existed for eight years, a long period of survival in Senegalese politics, but it was repeatedly defeated in the national elections. In June, 1966 the PRA leaders finally acknowledged defeat and merged with the UPS. Shortly before this, one of the most outstanding leaders of the party pointed out in an interview that the PRA had failed because it was alien to the masses: PRA leaders had never accepted the idea of wooing the marabus and this was their mistake, for the marabus were the only ones close to the people in the central zone of Senegal.[23]

A brief look at some of the handbills published by the PRA and the party paper, *Indépendence africaine*, tends to support the PRA leader's analysis. The handbills, in general, criticized the government for corruption among its officials and for handling the elections unjustly, stressed that the PRA wanted freedom for the "People," and denied the various UPS charges of collusion with the enemies of Senegal. There was little or no emphasis in the sheets on Muslim matters, and certainly on none that dealt with the interests of the marabus.[24] *Indépendence africaine* paid more attention to religious matters, but not in a manner calculated to give assurance to religious leaders. An early issue published a resolution passed at the Conference of African Peoples in Accra in December, 1958, which the PRA evidently supported. Part of the resolution condemned tribalism and religious separatism and even noted that certain traditional African institutions (perhaps the brotherhoods) were not compatible with democracy because they supported colonialism and were organs of "corruption, exploitation and repression

[23] Interview with leader of the PRA-Senegal, Oct. 13, 1965, Dakar. See notice of merger with UPS in *Afrique nouvelle*, June 16–22, 1966.

[24] Articles in party newspapers and circulars, of course, were not widely distributed in rural areas; moreover, the marabus usually do not read them, although some of their assistants do. But the PRS papers, like the BDS and SFIO papers, can still indicate propaganda themes stressed by the party leaders. See the following for examples of PRA-Senegal manifestos: July 31, 1960, Imprimerie (Imp.) Diop, Depot Légal (D.L.) 915; Oct. 23, 1963, Imp. Chams Eddine, D.L. 6; Oct. 30, 1963, Dakar; Nov. 1963, Dakar; Nov. 15, 1963, Imp. Dakar, Md. No. DL 6; Nov. 15, 1963, Imp. Dakar, Md. No. 1494–11063, D.L. 3; Dec. 1963, Imp. Chams Eddine, D.L. 8; Jan. 1964, Imp. Chams Eddine, D.L. 9; Feb. 1964, Imp. Chams Eddine, D.L. 10; Nov. 1964, Imp. Chams Eddine, D.L. 14.

which strangle the dignity . . . and the will of the African to emancipate himself."[25]

At one point the PRA leaders used an old SFIO tactic and attempted to show that Léopold Senghor as a Catholic was trying to make the Government Catholic while using Mamadou Dia, a Muslim, as a shield. The article published on this subject said that neither the "profiteers" of the UPS regime, who pretended to be *taalibés* of great marabus, nor Mamadou Dia could prevent the reaction which must arise among Muslims against the policy of "clericalism" that was obviously dictated by the needs of French imperialism.[26] This theme, however, was not stressed by the PRA. More common were articles accusing the UPS of being an alignment of clan leaders which left the "masses" out of consideration.[27] In such articles the marabus were openly classified as bourgeoisie acting in collaboration with the UPS.[28]

Thus the PRA made no special effort to win the cooperation of Muslim leaders, but its members did not dissociate themselves from the marabus who supported them when events pushed one or another of the religious leaders to try to find an opposition party with which to ally. For example, in 1959 PRA leaders explored a possible alliance with the Parti de Solidarité Sénégalaise, a marabu-backed party that will be described below. PRA leaders also accepted the support of the Murid khalif's son, who sided with them in 1962. In the 1963 elections the PRA leaders combined their list of candidates in a unified opposition list entitled Démocratie et Unitié Sénégalaise (DUS) that included remnants of the BMS supported by Cheikh M'Backé and disciples of Cheikh Tidjane Sy, who had come out against the government. But the DUS and its components did not have organized support in the rural areas and were soundly defeated in the 1963 elections.[29]

The PAI is more radical than the PRA. It is Marxist-Leninist in doctrine and is accepted as a Communist party by the Communist parties in France and the Soviet Union. It has consistently made attempts to win Muslim supporters in general and the reformist Muslim associations in particular. But the

[25]*Indépendence africaine*, Jan. 10, 1950.
[26]*Ibid.*, Nov. 21, 1959.
[27]*Ibid.*, Mar. 5, 1960; Aug. 20, 1960.
[28]*Ibid.*, Sept. 17, 1960.
[29]Republic of Senegal, Ministry of Interior, *Livre blanc sur les elections présidentielles et législatives du 1er Décembre 1963* (Dakar, 1964).

PAI leaders, like the PRA men, have not given much attention
to attracting marabus whom the leaders view as a negative
group in Senegal and as part of the "exploiting classes."[30]
The PAI, founded in 1957, has its base of support at the
University of Dakar. It has managed to attract many Muslim
students by supporting causes such as the increased teaching
of Arabic in Senegal.[31] Articles in the party paper, La Lutte,
have tried to show that those marabus who helped the PAI
would gain from their cooperation. Moreover, all Muslims
have been guaranteed freedom of worship, increased numbers
of mosques, modern religious schools, and an institute of research
on religion should the PAI take control of Senegal. But the
PAI paper has also stated that all payments to chiefs, religious
and otherwise, would be terminated under PAI authority and the
working class and peasants liberated. Such a program as a whole,
then, could hardly be expected to appeal to the marabus.[32]

UPS leaders have been quick to point out that the PAI,
as an atheist Marxist party, is a danger to Islam and to the
marabus, and the PAI has made various gestures to contradict
this accusation. A long article in its newspaper Momsarev
in 1959 entitled "The PAI and the Religious Collectivities"
insisted that those who said the PAI was against religious
collectivities were lying. Imperialism is the enemy of the PAI,
religion a private affair; religious chiefs are the victims of
colonialism, and it is in their interest to fight against colonial
exploitation. The paper also stated, however, that the PAI
was against all marabus who use their prestige to enslave the
Senegalese people and to block progress in the country. Only
those marabus whom the PAI considered "progressively inclined
patriots" in the tradition of Al Hajj Umar and Ahmad Bamba
had nothing to fear from the PAI.[33] Not surprisingly, PAI arguments
have not inspired confidence in the marabus and no major
marabus have supported the Marxist group. From 1959 on
PAI leaders have attempted sporadically to get the opposition
parties to unite[34] but with little success. The party was declared
illegal after the elections in July, 1960, and thereafter remained
under cover. Supporters of the party voted for the DUS list
in 1963 which de facto meant cooperation with certain marabus,

[30] "La Structure de la société," La Lutte, no. 8, 1957.
[31] Cheikh Niane, "L'Enseignement arabe," La Lutte, no. 6, 1957.
[32] "Projet de programme du Parti Africain de l'Indépendence," La Lutte no. 15 (March, 1959).
[33] M'Baye Diop, "Le PAI et les collectivités religieuses," Momsarev, no. 4, 1959.
[34] See Momsarev, June 1960.

The Political Parties and the Marabus

but in general the PAI has remained an isolated unit of radicals which rouses enthusiasm among certain elements in the student body of Senegal but has never gained a following outside of the major cities.

The Threat of the Conservative Marabus

Although radical groups like the PRA and the PAI on the left of the UPS have never seriously challenged the hegemony of the latter, the UPS has been forced to adopt certain features of the radical parties' programs. UPS leaders have had to be very careful, however, not to frighten the conservative groups within and outside the UPS by making too many concessions to the forces of the left. Indeed, the UPS has been constantly under threat from conservative marabus and other traditional leaders who see its reform programs as a challenge to their positions and to the old way of life. At any time powerful marabus can decide that the government party, in spite of its gifts of money and other material aid, is pursuing a policy contrary to their interests and then can move into opposition. Thus, major marabus have opposed the UPS publicly on various occasions and this opposition is extremely difficult for the government party to handle. After all, a powerful marabu, even if unsupported by other marabus, can cause great difficulties. He is a religious leader and as such cannot be treated, as are PRA or PAI leaders, with the constant threat of forceful repression. Only after extreme provocation can a marabu be thrown in jail, and in such a case the result will almost inevitably be open opposition of his followers to the party, as the example of Cheikh Tidjane Sy indicates.

Sy has been more of a problem than even Cheikh M'Backé, which is ironical since Sy was one of the first marabus to openly take sides in the political fight against the SFIO in support of Léopold Senghor's party. But Cheikh Tidjane has exhibited a most pragmatic attitude in politics, remaining loyal to the UPS only when it has served his own personal interests to do so. Up until 1957 his alliance with the UPS was openly acknowledged, but thereafter he deviated on several important occasions. Léopold Senghor did not support Cheikh Tidjane in the succession struggle which occurred at the time of the death of Abubacar Sy in 1957 and this may have contributed to Cheikh Tidjane's alienation from the UPS. In any case, he

93

apparently felt strong enough to challenge the UPS in the national elections—hoping, probably, to strengthen his own position within his brotherhood by taking an independent political position.

Cheikh Tidjane was joined in his opposition by Ibrahima Niass and an important Muslim trader, Ibrahima Saidou N'Daw, also from Kaolack. Niass and N'Daw must have hoped to improve their own positions by opposing Senghor; but their opposition was also based on more general considerations, including fear of effects of the alliance with the radical Union Soudanaise recently established by the UPS.[35] Ibrahima N'Daw had been one of the early supporters of the BDS but gradually had grown to distrust President Senghor. The support of the latter for Valdiodio N'Diaye, N'Daw's rival in the Sine Saloum, had hardened the lines between the old trader and the UPS.[36] Consequently, N'Daw became a founder of the Parti de Solidarité-Sénégalaise (PSS) along with Cheikh Tidjane and Ibrahima Niass. Niass, who had broken with N'Daw when he first became connected to the UPS, joined his former comrade in the PSS because he mistrusted Léopold Senghor and wished to back a conservative Muslim party.[37]

Cheikh Tidjane was most active in the ensuing events. He attempted in vain to make peace with Abdul Aziz in order to attract his support for the PSS,[38] and later, in elections for the assembly in early 1959, he ran against Léopold Senghor in Thies. Cheikh Tidjane received few votes (the contest between Valdiodio N'Diaye and Ibrahima Saidou N'Daw in Kaolack, however, was more closely fought), and the UPS won the elections with eighty-five percent of the vote. Despite the defeat of the PSS, Cheikh Tidjane continued to actively oppose the UPS and eventually provoked an incident in Tivaouane when he refused to obey a government order forbidding him to hold a public meeting of his followers (supposedly for religious songs). He resisted the police who attempted to prevent his meeting, and his disciples, reportedly armed in some cases with hand grenades, rioted and attacked the home of a sister of Abdul Aziz.[39] The police calmed the situation and Cheikh Tidjane was

[35] The leaders of the Union Soudanaise, with which the UPS allied to form the Mali Federation in 1959, emphasized more strongly than did Senegalese politicians the need for radical economic and social reforms.
[36] Interview with government official, Dec. 8, 1965, Touba.
[37] Interview with Ibrahima Niass, Jan. 29, 1966, Kaolack.
[38] Interview with Abubacar Sy, Oct. 21, Dakar.
[39] Ibid.

arrested. UPS leaders, recognizing the arrest as a drastic move, immediately made a public declaration justifying its action.[40] At the same time the UPS youth group, the Mouvement de Jeunesse de l'UPS (MJUPS), came out firmly on the side of the government's arrest, noting that the "people" had been uneasy for a long time because of the "religious fanaticism" shown by this "so-called" religious chief who served the cause of the reactionaries.[41]

Cheikh Tidjane was not in jail for long. His uncle Abdul Aziz immediately went to see Mamadou Dia to find out if he could be released in the interests of the Sy family as a whole;[42] by the beginning of 1960 the rebellious marabu had been released. Meanwhile, the PSS was in the process of breaking up. L'Unité africaine published accounts of the defections of PSS leaders in 1959 including several minor Murid leaders who had become associated with the party.[43] At the end of 1959 the PSS joined another small opposition party, and in early January, 1960, Cheikh Tidjane and Ibrahima Niass made a public declaration of support for the UPS.[44] In July Cheikh Tidjane, now at liberty, led the PSS into the UPS.[45] The Tijani was absolved from his actions of 1959 and in August, 1960, when the Mali Federation broke up, he publicly supported the Senegalese government.[46] He was later given a mark of extreme favor in his appointment as Senegalese ambassador to the United Arab Republic.

The UPS reaction to Cheikh Tidjane Sy was most significant: on the one hand the party was harsher with the Tijani marabu than it had been with Cheikh M'Backé, but this is easily explained by the following facts. 1) Cheikh Tidjane directly and openly disobeyed a government order and started a riot, which Cheikh M'Backé had not done, and 2) Cheikh M'Backé was a more powerful marabu than Cheikh Tidjane. On the other hand, the leniency of the government toward the Tijani was very evident: he defected from the UPS and fought the government, but as soon as he had declared himself in favor of the UPS

[40] "L'Arrestation de Cheikh Tidjane Sy qui s'est rendu coupable d'un acte de rébellion caractérisée," L'Unité africaine (June 30, 1959).
[41] "A Propos les Incidents de Tivaouane: déclaration du mouvement des Jeunes de l'UPS," ibid.
[42] Interview with Abubacar Sy, Oct. 21, 1965, Dakar.
[43] See L'Unité africaine, Aug. 1 and 8, Nov. 7 and 21, 1959.
[44] Ibrahima Niass, "Cheikh Tidjane et Ibrahima Niass donnent leur appui à l'action gouvernemental," L'Unité africaine (Jan. 16, 1960).
[45] "Cheikh Ahmed Tidjane Sy apporte l'adhésion du PSS," L'Unité africaine (July 16, 1960).
[46] L'Unité africaine, Aug. 27, 1960.

he was forgiven and rewarded with an important ambassadorial post.[47]

The problems of the UPS with Cheikh Tidjane were not ended when he became ambassador. He appeared to be incapable of running a modern embassy or responding to the tasks required of him as ambassador, and by the end of 1962 he had allegedly spent eighty-one million CFA, almost the entire budget of the embassy, "for private purposes." The affair was not publicized at first but Cheikh Tidjane was called back to Senegal. His recall began another period of opposition to the government by him and his followers. Dissatisfied with his treatment at the hands of the government, at the end of 1962 he joined those who had supported former Prime Minister Mamadou Dia against President Senghor. In 1963 Cheikh Tidjane began traveling around Senegal making speeches and publishing articles against Léopold Senghor in which he virtually encouraged holy war against the government. He went so far as to write letters to President Senghor and other major officials that accused the President personally of a number of immoral and criminal acts.[48] The UPS reacted to Cheikh Tidjane's actions at first by issuing warnings against the group forming around the marabu (called a party by some).[49] But he did not heed the warnings and was arrested for a second time in September and jailed. The government, as in the previous arrest, justified its actions in radio speeches and newspaper articles condemning the marabu in no uncertain terms and saying, for example: "It is painful to say, but it is necessary to say it: the attitude of Cheikh Ahmad Tidjane Sy is determined by his thirst for money. . . ."[50] The government articles also included the Murid khalif's written support of Sy's arrest.[51]

Again Cheikh Tidjane remained in jail for only a short period of time. Abdul Aziz and other members of his family appealed for his release and eventually Falilou also asked for clemency.[52] The young marabu was freed in the beginning of 1964 and allowed to resume his normal activities. In a short time his actions had

[47] The government had reasons for appointing Cheikh Tidjane other than merely to reward him. His extensive knowledge of Arabic and his position as a religious leader were thought to be advantageous for an ambassador in Egypt.

[48] Interview with member of Muslim reform group who possessed copies of the letters, Mar. 2, 1966, Dakar.

[49] "A Visage découvert ou la vaine agitation," *L'Unité africaine* (Aug. 28, 1963).

[50] "Simple Erreur de régime," *L'Unité africaine* (Sept. 25, 1963).

[51] *L'Unité africaine*, Sept. 25, 1963.

[52] Interview with government official and Muslim scholar, Jan. 9, 1966, Dakar.

The Political Parties and the Marabus

been officially forgotten, and President Senghor paid a state call on him on the occasion of his annual Tijani Gamou in July, 1965. In the fall of that year it was widely rumored that Cheikh Tidjane had received a generous loan from the government.[53] Whether or not he did receive the money, he certainly conferred with the president on several occasions, which indicates his complete reinstatement in official favor.[54]

Few if any of the major marabus could be expected to throw themselves into politics in the way Cheikh Tidjane has done, but other marabus, even if they stayed out of elections, could cause their *taalibés* to refuse to cooperate with the government party. Consequently the UPS has had to make intensive efforts to keep the powerful marabus satisfied with its policies and its general attitude toward the brotherhoods.

UPS Need for the Marabus

The UPS has been constantly faced with two major sources of opposition: on the left various radical parties, and on the right conservative leaders, primarily the marabus. Its leaders have tried to remain in the middle, hoping to provide a compromise solution to the problems of Senegal which the two sides will accept. But it has favored the right group because its members, the marabus, control the majority of Senegalese votes and have important economic resources at their command. Indeed, it is interesting to note that in any crisis period in recent Senegalese politics the politicians instantly turn to the marabus to assure themselves of the Muslim leaders' support. This was most evident when the Mali Federation was dissolved. In fact, the first public mention of the coming dissolution of the federation was made at the Murid Magal.[55] Significantly, the major government speech by Mamadou Dia at this festival was entitled "It is Necessary to Think First of Senegal." Léopold Senghor also spoke at the festival and in the course of his speech noted that the Senegalese must tighten their ranks and strengthen their unity, thus reinforcing the impression given by Mamadou Dia that leaders of the government party of Senegal felt the need to defend their country against the leaders of the Union Soudanaise.[56]

---

[53] Interviews with Tijani leaders and government officials, Nov. 10, 1965, Dakar.
[54] See *Dakar matin*, Nov. 12, Dec. 17, Dec. 27, 1965.
[55] William Foltz, *From French West Africa to the Mali Federation* (New Haven, 1965), p. 177.
[56] *L'Unité africaine*, Aug. 20, 1960.

Muslim Brotherhoods and Politics in Senegal

On August 21, 1960, the Mali Federation broke up and Modibo Keita, the Soudanese president, was placed under arrest. Senegal was plunged into a crisis situation, for Keita had made friends among Senegalese radicals who felt that he could reform Senegal. Furthermore, the Soudanese leader had even made contacts with the major Senegalese marabus; most of the important marabus did not side with Keita in the crisis, however, but rallied to the UPS. Falilou sent truckloads of disciples to Dakar in case the government should need their assistance, and all the important marabus sent declarations to the government assuring the officials that they supported the policy of the UPS leaders. Even Al Hajj Ibrahima Niass, who had been quite friendly with Modibo Keita, came out in favor of the UPS. The party leaders, of course, published the notes and telegrams from the marabus to show that they had retained control of the countryside. The Senegalese papers including *Dakar matin*, *Paris Dakar*, and *L'Unité africaine* were full of statements from the important marabus. In the August 27 issue of *L'Unité africaine* there was a large section entitled "All the Religious Chiefs Condemn the Aggression of Modibo Keita." Notably, Falilou M'Backé was quoted as supporting the government with this statement: "In my personal name and in the name of the entire Murid Brotherhood, I take on myself the duty of thanking you . . . for having saved Senegal. . . ." In the same issue the eldest son of Ibrahima Niass voiced his father's support and Cheikh Tidjane Sy assured the government that his *taalibés* were mobilized to protect their national territory. Even Cheikh M'Backé sent a message stating his confidence in the UPS and the government.[57]

Once the breakup of the Mali Federation had become an accepted incident and Senegal was independent, the marabus slipped into the background. The newspapers continued to comment on their activities and festivals, but their political role was not openly stressed again until the next major crisis in Senegal, toward the end of 1962. At this time the power struggle between Léopold Senghor and Mamadou Dia came into the open and the latter was defeated and removed from office. The unrest in Senegal because of the struggle between Senghor and Dia was much more serious than during the period following the breakup of the federation. Leaders throughout

[57] *Ibid.,* Aug. 27, 1960.

The Political Parties and the Marabus

the countryside were seriously divided between Senghor and Dia, the two most powerful men within the UPS. Quite logically both men attempted to use the marabus to reinforce their positions; thus the Muslim leaders played a role of paramount importance in the events which took place.

The actual reasons for the split between Dia and Senghor cannot be thoroughly understood until someone who was intimately involved in the affair publishes a detailed account. At present, President Senghor and the other UPS leaders who triumphed over the group of Dia followers insist that the former prime minister was trying to take over Senegal. Many of those who favored Mamadou Dia claim, quite to the contrary, that it was President Senghor who decided that he wished to rule Senegal without Dia. According to this view, Senghor undercut Dia's support in the government and Dia, to prevent a vote of no confidence, was forced to dissolve the Assembly, which was packed with Senghor's men, in order to make a plea to the members of the party. Thus Dia did not intend to overthrow the government at all, merely to defend himself. In any case, by 1962 Mamadou Dia, who originally had been no more than an assistant to Léopold Senghor, was beginning to hold power in his own right. As president of Senegal during the Mali Federation and then prime minister of the republic of Senegal he had directed the day-to-day working of the government for several years. He had become closely identified with the widely renowned Senegalese Plan worked out by Father L. P. Lebret and a highly trained team of assistants. In fact, Mamadou Dia had come to symbolize those elements in the UPS who wished most strongly to reform the country. Léopold Senghor, in contrast, although his policy differed little from that of Dia, was popularly associated with the conservative elements in the party.

The general malaise between the two former partners became most evident by the spring and summer of 1962. Mamadou Dia undertook a widely publicized trip abroad and on his return to Senegal toured the country. He was apparently trying to build up his own support among the rural leaders of Senegal. It was Senghor who, after the Second World War, had gone to meet "the people" and their traditional leaders; Mamadou Dia had merely been his companion on these trips but had never received the widespread support from leaders and disciples that President Senghor enjoyed. Mamadou Dia was quite evidently attempting to rectify this situation in 1962. One of the Prime Minister's potential attributes among the rural people was the fact that he was Muslim and could appeal on those grounds to his fellow Muslims.[58] A Tijani, his closest ties were with that brotherhood; specifically, he had become close to Abdul Aziz over the years and the relationship between these two men had been similar to that between Senghor and the Murid khalif. When Abdul Aziz wanted something done he contacted Mamadou Dia (for example, he appealed to Dia when Cheikh Tidjane was first arrested).[59] The Tijani khalif therefore sided with Mamadou Dia, but his support was not sufficient to insure the Prime Minister's victory, particularly since Aziz had always attempted to stay out of politics and did so even during the 1962 crisis.

Mamadou Dia had to appeal to the marabus of Senegal as a group in order to get assistance against Senghor, and he had to convince them that he was not too radically inclined. His major appeal came in 1962, when he called publicly for the symbolization of Muslim unity in Senegal by a council of all Muslim leaders to be held after the rainy season ended. He made the appeal at the annual Tijani Gamou in Tivaouane; Abdul Aziz immediately responded by promising his "total support" for the projected congress of marabus and by saying that he would be "the first soldier" of Mamadou Dia in his effort to bring unity to the Muslims.[60] Dia then proceeded to make appeals by letter and in personal visits to the other major marabus of Senegal. The most important man to win over was the Murid khalif, but Falilou M'Backé remained faithful to Léopold Senghor, which was a serious blow to the efforts of the Prime Minister. Falilou apparently distrusted Dia, although it is difficult to know exactly why. It is rumored that Dia had refused a loan to the Murid khalif, and that he had made a speech at Podor promising to jail those who took money from the state which Falilou interpreted as a threat to himself and his followers. It is said, too, that the khalif was displeased with Mamadou Dia because of the Dakar mosque, which the

---

[58] Even Dia's opponents mention that he had a widespread and deserved reputation for piety. Interview with Tijani scholar and opponent of Dia, Dec. 1, 1965, Dakar.

[59] See above, in Chapter 4.

[60] L'Unité africaine, Aug. 22, 1962.

[61] Interview with Murid student, Oct. 14, 1965, Dakar, and with Murid government official, Dec. 9, 1965, Touba.

The Political Parties and the Marabus

Prime Minister was sponsoring.[61] Whether or not these reports are accurate, the khalif refused to support either the council of marabus proposed by Dia or the Prime Minister himself.

The split between President Senghor and Mamadou Dia was publicly acknowledged in a speech made by the latter at Diourbel. So violent was the Prime Minister on this occasion that most men who were involved in politics at the time can remember his exact words. Interestingly enough, there is decided disagreement over to whom the speech referred. The wording seems obviously meant for President Senghor, and many people so interpret it;[62] others assume that the speech was aimed at the Murid khalif and was a direct challenge to his position.[63] Mamadou Dia said:

> I wish this evening to speak like the poet, but you know I am not a poet. I will say it then as I think it: Imbecile! you who had no confidence in the dynamism of your country. Imbecile! you who have no confidence in the future, in the moral values of your country, although everything makes us lift our heads [and] believe in better tomorrows. Imbecile! you who have no confidence in the efficacy of our methods to build African socialism. . . .
>
> For my part I have more confidence than ever . . . in the value of our choice. . . .
>
> We shall not respond to a certain campaign. We will not let ourselves be turned aside from the goals we have fixed . . . for we others, we have no time to lose. . . .[64]

It matters little in the context of this discussion at whom the speech was aimed. Rather, what is significant is that the speech could be interpreted as against Léopold Senghor *or* against the Murid khalif, for this dual interpretation indicates that the split between UPS leaders was evident and that the Murid leader had remained faithful to the President.

Crucial events followed the Diourbel speech rapidly. The UPS held a meeting of its National Council at the end of October in which it made a weak effort to deny that a split existed in the party. Mamadou Dia insisted at the meeting that there could be no disagreement between himself and Senghor, "my brother, my companion of battle for 17 years." The President, too, denied "rumors" about dissension in the

---

[62] Interviews with close relative of Falilou, Dec. 1 and 20, 1965, Dakar.
[63] Interviews with government officials, Oct. 14, Oct. 9, Dec. 20, 1965, Dakar.
[64] "Sur les Chantiers de la révolution agricole," *L'Unité africaine* (Oct. 17, 1962).

party.[65] A month later, however, the situation dissolved completely. A motion of censure was raised against Mamadou Dia in the Assembly. It apparently had only thirty-nine signatures at first (to remove the Prime Minister from office it would have had to have forty-one, a clear majority of the Assembly). Mamadou Dia dissolved the Assembly. He was blamed thereafter for trying to overthrow the government, especially since he had used the gendarmes, who were loyal to him at first, to clear the Assembly and to arrest four of its members. Whatever his intentions, Dia failed. The majority of the Assembly, including many of the ministers (who resigned so they could vote on the motion of censure), followed Assembly President Lamine Gueye and voted against Dia in a special Assembly session. The army rallied to President Senghor, and Dia was given no chance to appeal to the National Council of the UPS but was outvoted in the sessions of the Bureau Politique called by President Senghor. The Prime Minister was arrested on December 17 and the affair was over.[66] Senegal was left in a very unsettled state after the arrest, but Falilou M'Backé immediately broadcast his support for Senghor in a radio speech. The few telegrams in support of Mamadou Dia sent by various minor marabus before the Prime Minister was defeated were suppressed, and gradually the major marabus, including Ibrahima Niass and Saidou Nourou Tall, joined Falilou in publicly stating their support for the government headed by Senghor.[67] The Dia affair had demonstrated once again the tight alliance between Senghor and the marabus, especially Falilou M'Backé. Mamadou Dia had failed to attract wide enough support among the marabus to balance the Murid khalif, and this lack was instrumental in his final defeat.

It is not, of course, only during major crises like the Mali Federation breakup or the struggle between Dia and Senghor that men seek the aid of the marabus to strengthen the UPS at a particular moment or to bolster their own position in the party. Frequently UPS leaders maneuver to better their positions and try to use the marabus to help them. At the end of 1965, a disagreement split Léopold Senghor and Ousmane N'Gom, a member of the Assembly from Thies, secretary of organization

[65] Le Conseil national du 21 Octobre a raffermi la cohésion du parti et dissipé toute équivoque," *L'Unité africaine* (Oct. 31, 1962).
[66] See *L'Unité africaine*, Dec. 26, 1962; also interview with government official close to both Senghor and Dia, Jan. 7, 1966, Dakar.
[67] *L'Unité africaine*, Dec. 26, 1962.

The Political Parties and the Marabus

of the UPS, and member of the party Bureau Politique. It was widely reported that Ousmane was attempting to find support for his position in the party and at large; as part of his program he visited the Murid khalif, and some reports say that he offered the khalif money but was refused because the khalif had been promised an even larger sum by the president. Even if the latter reports are false, Falilou M'Backé apparently did refuse to support N'Gom in his struggle with Senghor, although the marabu continued to receive the politician and gave indications of approval of him.[68]

The Independence of the UPS

Despite the importance of the marabus to party leaders in disfavor, like Ousmane N'Gom, or in crisis or election periods, the UPS is not controlled by the marabus. In the first place, it is based on a much larger coalition of forces than just the followers of one marabu or of several marabus. The party leaders attempt to attract rural people in all regions of Senegal, not just in the marabu-dominated central peanut zone, and they attempt to draw the Western-educated in the towns and villages as well. Second, because the marabus are persistently at odds with each other the party leaders are able to balance one group of marabus against the other or against other rural leaders in different regions. Third, the party structure remains separate from the brotherhoods. Of course, even within the modern organization of the party, marabus or their appointees hold office in certain regions. For example, the sons of Ibrahima Niass and his secretary are officials in the UPS in Kaolack. And, at important party conferences, like the UPS Congress held in Kaolack in 1966, delegates of the marabus, such as the general secretaries of the khalif of the Murids and of Ibrahima Niass, are to be found actively politicking for their masters. Nevertheless, the party structure is not directed by the marabus and has a certain independence largely because the majority of its leaders at all levels are Western-educated men and are not delegated by the marabus.

Finally, and most important, UPS leaders are not merely

[68] Interviews with Murid leaders and government officials, Jan. 25, Feb. 16, 1966, Dakar. One mark of favor shown Ousmane was his placement in a position of honor at the 1966 Magal, as William Foltz has pointed out (author's private correspondence, 1967).

103

trying to control Senegal; they intend to develop the country and improve the state of its economy. Their goals are strongly influenced by Western ideas and they think in terms consistent with modern development in any country, although they affirm that theirs is a uniquely African solution to the problems of underdeveloped areas. UPS leaders insist that they wish to use the essential ingredients of African society in combination with elements of Marxian socialism. One of the major bases of African society to Senghor is the community system of organization, the spirit of which is to be translated into mutual societies and cooperatives. Senghor also intends to combine moral and religious values which he sees as inherent in African society into his program of reform. As far as he is concerned there can be no separation between socialism and religion in Africa, for they are interdependent. Senghor and other UPS leaders also emphasize that personal responsibility must be developed throughout Senegal. The privileges of the elite throughout the country must be removed, according to the party leaders, as the position of the masses must be improved.[69] Mamadou Dia expressed this view in 1960: "It is necessary that we force ourselves to reduce social parasitisms: family parasitism, caste parasitism, so that each active citizen recovers his normal earning capacity. . . . If we don't begin to open this new road, we risk compromising our future."[70]

The philosophy of the UPS leaders leaves no room for privileged feudal lords like the marabus. It calls for animation of the rural masses and for their education in modern methods of farming and in the possibilities of collective action. This, indeed, was the view at the base of the Senegalese Plan published in 1960.[71] Léopold Senghor, though perhaps more moderate than Mamadou Dia and more willing to move slowly in reforming Senegal, believed in the value of the plan and its goals. After the defeat of the former prime minister, the President denied publicly rumors that he intended to ignore the plan and its aims by saying that those who spread such rumors were "criminals." He introduced a second plan in January, 1965,

[69] See Léopold Senghor, *Nation et voie africaine du socialisme* (Paris, 1961), esp. pp. 69, 82. Also see Senghor, "Rapport sur la méthode du parti," *Condition humaine* (July 18, 1953).

[70] Mamadou Dia, "Le Président Dia trace un programme pour la politique d'indépendance," *L'Unité africaine* (June 11, 1960).

[71] See *Rapport général sur les perspectives de développement du Sénégal,* 2 vols. (Dakar, January 1963).

that has maintained the theoretical goals and means of action of the first plan.[72]

Any evaluation of the relations between the marabus and the UPS must not assume that the party is the servant of the marabus. UPS leaders need the support of the major marabus, who, as a result, have a great deal of influence in the party; but the politicians are still working toward the modern development of Senegal, a goal that may very well destroy a large part of the Muslim leaders' power. Furthermore, UPS leaders are continually trying to win the support of the people in Senegal apart from their leaders. Through continued journeys in the rural areas, the spreading of Western education, and the use of modern communications media, they assume that knowledge of party goals will be spread to an ever wider group of people. In the long run they would like to be able to offset the traditional leaders with a block of popular votes not dependent on the marabus. This development would severely diminish the influence of the Muslim leaders on the UPS and in party politics in Senegal in general.

[72] Léopold Senghor, "Rapport du Secrétaire Général," *L'Unité africaine* (Jan. 7, 1965). Also see *L'Unité africaine,* Jan. 23, 1963.

5 The Government and the Brotherhoods

The desire of UPS leaders to diminish the authority of the
marabus is not an easy one to put into practice. The brotherhoods
continue to play an essential role in local, regional, and
national politics. The government of independent Senegal,
like its French predecessor, uses and is used by the marabus
in its daily activities, but the situation in independent Senegal
is not identical to that which prevailed during the colonial regime.
The French used the marabus because that was the easiest
and least expensive way to rule Senegal; Senegalese politicians,
in contrast, are in a more critical dilemma. On the one hand,
the marabus are so powerful that the politicians cannot afford
to challenge them. The French had their army and all the powers
of a Western state to back up the policies they introduced—and,
if all else failed, they could withdraw to France. The Senegalese
have no powerful force behind them and consequently are more
reliant on their good relations with rural leaders. On the other
hand, the politicians are under considerable pressure to improve
the economic position of the people as a whole. The French,
particularly just before and after the Second World War,
attempted to improve the economy of Senegal, but colonial
authorities were hampered by lack of money; and, after all,
the interests of Senegal were secondary to the interests of France.
Thus the Senegalese have a stronger motivation to reform
the country than the French had. The situation of the independent
government of Senegal is therefore ambivalent: the Senegalese
are weaker in regard to the marabus than the French were
but they have a greater interest in undermining the power
of Muslims leaders.

Marabus in Local and Regional Politics

The heaviest concentration of powerful marabus is in the
peanut regions of Diourbel and Sine Saloum, followed by Thies.[1]
Only a few of these marabus are really powerful and only
these few can expect that the president or ministers will listen
to their requests. Many other marabus, in contrast, may receive
marks of favor from the *préfet* but do not exert much influence
on how the administrators handle their tasks. The power of
the marabus varies according to the strength of the brotherhood
and the forcefulness of its individual marabus.

The brotherhoods have the strongest influence on the local
and regional government in the Diourbel region because it is
the center of the Murid brotherhood. Their power can be seen

[1] Verrière. "La Population du Sénégal," p. 73.

107

in the fact that the peasants go to their marabu when they wish something done. Even in Diourbel, however, where the Murid brotherhood is probably more influential than the regional administration, people turn to the government officials in certain cases, for example, to obtain simple government permits. Indeed, as one governor suggested in an interview, people turn to their marabus for out-of-the-ordinary requests which may demand state help that they cannot expect to get if they merely appear at a state office—unless, of course, the *préfet* happens to be a relative or friend.[2]

Unfortunately, it is impossible to measure the volume and importance of cases that go directly from the peasants to the government compared to those processed by the marabus. One is forced to rely on the evidence presented by numerous interviews, corroborated by visual evidence. A visit to the governor's office in Diourbel, for example, compared with one to the khalif's residence in Touba, would indicate that the khalif receives more requests of greater significance than does the governor. On a brief visit to Touba one can frequently see long lines of disciples during visiting hours of the khalif and his major subordinates, coming to ask their master for a favor.

A few examples drawn from my visits to Touba show the types of problems with which the khalif and his assistants must deal. One woman asked to have her niece transferred to a better school in Dakar; a French technician asked for intervention in the National Assembly in order to obtain more well-building credit in the region; a man appeared begging the khalif to secure cooperation of the proper authorities to find his lost horse; a student asked help for a man about to lose his job in the Ministry of Rural Economy.[3] Cheikh Tidjane Sy gives three more typical examples in his study on the Murids, including A., from Gossas, who had been in the police force and removed for an error on his part and who now wished to be reinstated; L., from N'Dindy Abdou, who brought his sick child to the khalif to ask for his prayers; and M., president of a cooperative in Darou Mousty, whose accounts were found missing 200,000 CFA and who consequently wished the khalif's help.[4]

---

[2] Interview, Feb. 6, 1966, Kaolack.

[3] Interviews with brotherhood and government officials, Oct. 8, Nov. 21, 1965, Touba. Interviews with government officials, Oct. 9, 1965, Jan. 10, 1966, Dakar; Mar. 15, 1966, Dagana.

[4] Sy, "Traditionalisme mouride," pp. 100–101.

The Government and the Brotherhoods

The examples given above are mostly small matters, but they are the kinds of issues that commonly arise in regional politics and they indicate that the khalif and his assistants intervene in a wide variety of circumstances. It matters, of course, whether or not the khalif is able to satisfy these demands; it seems in most cases that he can do so with little difficulty. Regional and local officials appear to have great respect for the khalif and tend to respond to his appeals unless his requests are directly contrary to the law. In the latter case the administrators may attempt to reason with the marabu, but they may be forced to concede to his request.[5] Significantly, even government officials are to be found among the men waiting in the khalif's courtyard. The *chefs d'arrondissement*, the *préfets*, and the governor himself (in a crisis situation, that is) all come to ask the khalif's assistance in carrying out their jobs. The *chef d'arrondissement* of an area near Touba explained in an interview in 1965 that he and the *préfet* sought the khalif's help when, during the last Magal, Peul nomads attacked Wolofs who were settling on their land.[6] Other *chefs d'arrondissement* have offered many similar examples, and on one visit to Touba in the late fall of 1965 I saw a *préfet*, a *chef d'arrondissement*, and the Water Commissioner from Louga all waiting to see the khalif for help in their particular duties.

In the region of Diourbel, then, the khalif of the Murids is the most powerful ruling body. Administrators visit him, not vice versa. The khalif's assistants and subordinate marabus are also powerful, and their requests, too, are respected by the *préfets* and the *chefs d'arrondissement*. At times it almost seems as if the local and regional administration has become an appendage of the powerful organization, the Murid brotherhood. This is a false impression but easy to sustain if one is present at several Murid festivals at which the state police, under the direction of Murid leaders, have to organize the masses of disciples merging on the khalif's compound while the *préfet*, who is often present, is ignored.

The Murid brotherhood is not all-powerful even in Diourbel, however, and there are occasions when even the khalif's requests are turned down or at least side stepped. Examples of such cases are hard to find, although it is said that a loan was refused to the

[5] Interview with government official, Feb. 6, 1966, Kaolack.
[6] Interview with chef d'arrondissement, Oct. 8, 1965, Touba.

109

Muslim Brotherhoods and Politics in Senegal

Murid head in 1962.[7] It is possible, however, to cite cases in which the requests of less important Murid leaders have been rejected: the khalif's powerful sister Sokhna Muslimatou was unable to obtain money from the regional government for the construction of a factory to produce cous-cous, the staff of which would have been Murid women working under Sokhna's direction. Reportedly the Regional Development committee refused the request because its members felt the result would be exploitation of the women in the factory.[8]

As one moves out of Diourbel, the brotherhoods are less the central focus of local and regional government and the regional and local administration take on greater relative importance. A former governor of Thies has noted that the Tijani marabus are less disposed than Murid leaders to intervene in the affairs of the government and are less powerful when they do intervene;[9] but the difference between the Murids in Diourbel and the Tijani elsewhere is not absolute. Important Tijani marabus also request favors for their followers and are often obeyed. In a Tijani region people are more likely to go directly to the government with their demands because the Tijani brotherhood is less organized, less disciplined, and therefore less powerful than the Murid. One is less likely to find *chefs d'arrondissement*, *préfets*, or other regional officials waiting for a Tijani marabu to assist them in their duties, although this does occur. Furthermore, as one moves away from the central peanut regions of Senegal the power of the marabus declines further, for ethnic group and clan leaders who are not necessarily marabus tend to act as leaders of the people outside the government structure. Major marabus may be shown marks of respect—Ibrahima Niass could automatically take the *préfet's* car and chauffeur in early 1966 when his own Mercedes 600 broke down.[10] Requests of the important Muslim leaders are often granted: for example, in early 1966 Cheikh Tidjane Sy asked for and received state aid in building a well

[7] The request was turned down by the Regional Development Committee, which nevertheless felt obliged to forward it to Dakar to the central government authorities. This refusal is supposedly one reason why Falilou did not support Mamadou Dia in the 1962 Crisis. Interview with Murid leaders and government officials, December, 1965, Touba.

[8] Not all government officials viewed the factory as antiprogressive. Another attempt, which may eventually be successful, has been made to obtain funds for the khalif's sister through the central government. Interview with government official, Oct. 8, 1965, Touba.

[9] Interview with the governor of the River Region, Mar. 10, 1966, St. Louis.

[10] Interview with Ibrahima Niass, Feb. 1, 1966, Taiba.

on his land in Sine Saloum.[11] In all the mainly non-Murid regions, however, the brotherhoods' influence but do not dominate politics.

All the major marabus have a relative advantage over their counterparts in the administration, as well as greater authority in some situations, because the marabus are permanently located in their regions, while the administrators change frequently. The theory behind this frequent change, and behind the general prohibition against working in one's home region, is that an administrator cannot then make the region to which he is assigned his private fief. Nevertheless, this policy can hamper an administrator's knowledge of the region and therefore his control of it.[12]

Part of the pressure which the powerful marabus exert throughout Senegal is in the selection of candidates for office in the local, regional, and national government. Many requests that come to the marabus, such as those mentioned above to the Murid khalif, deal with promotion to a new post or preservation of a man's old job. The Murid leaders and other powerful marabus have a distinct interest in who is appointed to their regions in the major administrative positions: for example, Falilou showed considerable interest in the governorship of his region. Right after independence the Governor of Diourbel was Ibrahima Tall, one of the four Senegalese elevated to the post of governor in the colonial period and widely respected. But Tall was not the "khalif's man," and according to numerous reports he did not work well with Falilou, tried to force his hand, and sometimes ignored his requests. The situation was not tense, but after Mamadou Dia was defeated Falilou was rewarded (for his support for President Senghor) with a new governor, Médoune Fall. Fall was widely regarded as a protégé of the khalif and relations between the administration and the Murid brotherhood rapidly improved. Later, with Falilou's approval and perhaps at his suggestion, Fall was named to the important post of ambassador to France and consequently

[11] Interview with government official, Feb. 6, 1966, Kaolack.

[12] The French administrators, tour of duty was normally two years. The Senegalese have no set time but have changed almost all their *prefets* and governors several times since independence. An extreme shakeup in the regional administration occurred after the Dia crisis, when the central government sought to remove all men loyal to Dia from important posts. Thereafter changes have continued but not on such a mass scale. See lists of national and regional administration issued by the government of Senegal, esp. for 1960, 1963, 1965.

removed from the governorship in 1964. He was replaced by another close friend of Falilou's, Lamine Lo, reportedly a Murid himself whose son is named for the khalif.[13]

Similarly, if the lower levels of the administration are considered one finds that the Murid khalif and his subordinates influence appointments for office. At the lowest levels, of course, one finds that in Diourbel, as in other regions, many of the *chefs d'arrondissement* are members of old and powerful families. Some are Murid and some merely have the approval of the Murid hierarchy. Others, like one relative of the khalif's general secretary, appear to be direct appointees of the rulers of the Murid *tariqa*.[14] At the next level, the *préfets* are liable to change as frequently as that of the governors, therefore this position is not usually held by the important local families. But the Murid leaders' influence at this level is clear. One finds in office men like Abubacar Sy, the present *préfet* of M'Backé, who is widely regarded as the former khalif's *serviteur*, or the *préfet* of Diourbel, Thierno Birahim N'Dao, who is a close friend of Falilou's powerful cousin Shaykh Awa Balla M'Backé.[15]

Not all of the administrators in the Diourbel region are appointees of the Murid leaders, although none of them are outright enemies of the brotherhood. Even the Murid khalif's demands are not always infallible: Fall was removed from his ambassadorship under pressure from the French governorment.[16] But the Murid leaders' tacit approval seems necessary if an administrator is to be effective in Diourbel. Indeed, when evaluating the significance of Murid influence on appointments at the regional level, acquiescence to the marabus' wishes should be seen not only as a game of patronage where the government allows the khalif to appoint his favorites as a reward, but also as a realistic maneuver to give the regional administration authority in Diourbel. Faced with an enormously powerful organization, the Muridiyya, the politicians in Dakar have carefully chosen men who can get along with the local leaders and therefore get things done. The problem, of course, is to choose men who will also implement government programs

---

[13] Interviews with a Murid disciple and with a government official, Feb. 6, 1966, Kaolack; Nov. 17, 1965, Dakar.
[14] Interview with Murid disciples and leaders, Oct. 8, 1965, Touba.
[15] Interview with Murid disciples and leaders, Nov. 17, 1965, Touba.
[16] Pointed out to me by William Foltz (private correspondence, 1967).

as they are supposed to be carried out even if this means infringing on Murid interests. Examples above indicate that the khalif's requests and those of his subordinates are sometimes turned down, which proves that some administrators, even if chosen by the Murids, attempt to fulfill their government roles even when these conflict with the interests of the marabus.

In the Tijani areas of the peanut zone the marabus' influence on appointments is much weaker than it is in Diourbel. For example, the governor of Thies and his predecessor are supposedly not appointees of the Tijanis. Nevertheless, the Thies administrators and those from other peanut regions are chosen under the assumption that they can get along with the Muslim leaders in their areas. In Sine Saloum, where Ibrahima Niass lives, the present governor—who is from the region—had never met Ibrahima before he took office. However, as he says himself, it is absolutely necessary for a governor on Sine Saloum to cooperate with Ibrahima; at present the two work closely together and extremely friendly relations have been established between them.[17] In non-Murid areas, then, the marabus' wishes are still taken into consideration when officials are named to office in the regional government.

Outside the peanut zone, marabus appear to have even less influence on administrative appointments, corresponding with their less important position in politics in general. Even in these regions, however, powerful marabus will exert pressure successfully on the government on certain occasions. A recent example occurred when the nephew of Saidou Nourou Tall visited administrators throughout the River Region in early 1966 to gain their support in order to obtain a position in the Regional Assembly. His efforts met with success: he was elected *questeur* of the Assembly although he reportedly cannot read or write French.[18]

Marabus in National Politics

The most powerful marabus, including both Murids and Tijanis, have a great deal of influence on appointments at the national level as well as in regional politics. When a politician

[17] Interview with governor of the Sine Saloum region, Feb. 6, 1966, Kaolack.

[18] A *questeur* has charge of the registration of debates, among his other responsibilities. Interviews with government officials, Mar. 14, 1966, St. Louis; Mar. 15, 1966, Dagana. Notice of the appointment is in *L'Unité africaine*, Mar. 24, 1966.

wishes to improve his own position he will not only try to gain support among his peers in the government and in the UPS, but also will trek to one of the major marabus for help. Once in office, he may continue to visit his marabu for help in carrying out the job. The most important marabu to see up to 1968, of course, was Falilou M'Backé; Murids and non-Murids alike traveled from Dakar to Touba to obtain his assistance. It is not yet clear how much power the khalif Abdu Lahat will wield, although as Falilou's heir he will naturally be the focus of many visits. To a lesser extent, other powerful Murid and Tijani marabus are objects of similarly motivated visits. Furthermore, a man may visit more than one marabu in order to have as widespread backing as possible, although this must be carefully maneuvered so that no marabu is offended by the appearance of one of his candidates at the court of a rival.

The importance of approval of a powerful marabu to any man holding a national position is openly recognized in Senegal. Most men, including even those who would like to see the affairs of the government carried on with less interference from the marabus, are forced to pay homage to them. An interesting example is a highly educated young Senegalese, married to a French girl, now an official in the Ministry of the Interior. On his return from studying in France he learned that to be promoted one needed the recommendation of a marabu. At first he doubted that the real source of power lay with the Muslim leaders, but gradually he realized that he would have to seek the marabus' help if he wished to advance himself. This skeptical Tijani (skeptical, that is, in many of his religious beliefs) joined the pilgrimage of officials to Touba. In 1966 he drove there almost every week (a three- or four-hour trip from Dakar) bringing gifts of fruit and soft drinks for the khalif Falilou and armed with money to pay off the khalif's many retainers, who regularly take their cut from the politicians who visit their master. These trips were expensive, but in the young man's mind necessary for promotion to an ambassadorship (or perhaps to a ministerial post, his desire). He made every attempt to be "one of the group" in the Murid capital and tried to make friends with the khalif's assistants because they could influence the khalif. His trips were not in vain, for the khalif came to know him; he would be admitted to Falilou's presence on arrival while some less fortunate politicians had to wait, and he also made firm friends among the khalif's sons and retainers.

114

The Government and the Brotherhoods

He became, in fact, the image of what a young man must be if he wishes to be promoted in Senegal.[19]

A trip to Touba may coincide with the visits of several national and regional officials who have also come, to obtain help from the Murid khalif. One of my visits to Touba in late fall 1965 coincided with that of three men (among many others) who called on the khalif: one was a deputy to the National Assembly from Sine Saloum who so pleased the khalif that he was rewarded with a round-trip ticket to Mecca for his wife and himself; the second was a presidential advisor who appears frequently in Touba and on one occasion was given an American car as a mark of Falilou's affection; third was a minister who often visits Touba, who was given help in carrying out a difficult program and assured of the further support he badly needs because he was once involved in the opposition and lacks support in the UPS.[20]

A similar trip to Tivouane or Kaolack will show that the volume of official travel to the court of the Tijani khalif and lesser Tijani marabus is not as great as to Touba;[21] nevertheless, the trip may coincide with the visit of a minister, a deputy, or another official. The same deputy who received the tickets to Mecca also visits Saidou Nourou Tall, who lives in Dakar. Former Minister of the Interior Valdiodio N'Diaye, who comes from the Sine Saloum, made weekly trips to see Ibrahima Niass, and many of today's ministers take any available opportunity to pay their respects to Niass. Others, especially those from Tivaouane, visit the court of Abdul Aziz or Cheikh Tidjane Sy frequently.[22]

The logical question at this point is: can one recognize certain special favorites of the marabus in the national government? In fact, yes, and it is relatively easy to do so. Without naming them it can be said that two ministers are widely regarded as appointees of the former Murid khalif, not including Minister of Foreign Affairs Doudou Thiam, who is a Murid and was liked by the khalif but was not his protégé. Other ministers, of course,

[19] I have disguised the identity of the official concerned, but this is a literal account of his actions and statements in 1965–1966.

[20] Interviews with the men described here and with Murid leaders, Jan. 10, 1966, Touba; Mar. 24, 1966, Dakar; Nov. 20, 1965, Touba.

[21] One reason that there was not as much traffic to the Tijani centers as to Touba at the end of Falilou's reign is that he himself no longer traveled, whereas the major Tijani marabus frequently visited Dakar and politicians contacted them in the capital. Nevertheless, there was a significantly larger number of visits by government leaders to the Murid khalif and his assistants than to his Tijani peers, including visits to the latter in Dakar.

[22] Interviews with the Tijani khalif and with Ibrahima Niass, Jan. 15, 1966, Dakar; Jan. 21, 1966, Kaolack.

Muslim Brotherhoods and Politics in Senegal

received Falilou's help but were not considered "his men."
In the National Assembly, all the deputies from the Diourbel
region are more or less "Murid men" in that they have the
approval of the Murid leaders and actively seek to keep that
approval. But two men came to be closely associated with the
former khalif Falilou, one a member of the M'Backé family
and deputy mayor of the town of M'Backé (of which Doudou
Thiam is mayor), the other a relative of Doudou Thiam and a
former secretary of Cheikh M'Backé. Individuals from other
regions of Senegal are identified with the Murid leaders, too;
for example, one deputy from Senegal Oriental is known to be the
representative of Falilou's eldest son.

The Tijani marabus also have their representatives and exert
pressure on their behalf in a variety of ways. Two men in the
National Assembly, one his relative from the River Region and the
other a long-time *taalibé* from Senegal Oriental, are considered
appointees of Saidou Nourou Tall. Abdul Aziz is known to have
three especially loyal *taalibés* in the National Assembly,
although it is doubtful that he actually appointed them since
he tries to stay out of politics. Many ministers are Tijani, but
none is as closely tied with the Tijani marabus as the
two mentioned above who are reportedly the Murid
"khalif's men." [23]

The president, too, participates in the system. He listens to the
requests of the most important marabus and personally attempts
to use their influence in implementing his policies. On a daily
level, he will probably not drive out to see the Murid khalif
or any other marabu, but he may consult with their delegates in
Dakar. In fact, a section in *Dakar Matin* lists those whom the
president officially receives each day, and the list frequently
includes a marabu or his delegate. The president officially confers
weekly with the general secretary of the Murids, and, less
frequently, he sees other Murid or Tijani marabus. During a
four-month period from December 1965 through March 1966,
for example, President Senghor officially received Al Hajj Dramé
thirteen times and in the same period he saw Modou Mustafa
Ibrahima Niass, Oumar Bousso, and Cheikh M'Backé once each;
he also saw Cheikh Tidjane once and received the latter's
personal representative twice.[24] Since the president receives

[23] Men in less important government posts are also considered Murid appointees, but they will not be listed here.
[24] See *Dakar matin*, December, 1965, and January, February, March, 1966.

116

The Government and the Brotherhoods

a maximum of ten to twelve people or delegations and usually less, this number of visits with marabus or their representatives is strikingly high. The only people whom Senghor officially sees with greater frequency are the actual members of the government; he also keeps in direct contact with the marabus by telephone and by letter so that even the number of official visits in Dakar is no real indication of the frequency of his dealings with the marabus. It is startling for a Western observer, but a fact of Senegalese politics, that at any time the Murid khalif can call the president about some matter as Falilou did in the course of an interview in 1965 when the question of appointment of one of his favorites was raised.[25]

Many national officials deplore the power of the marabus but try to view the situation with perspective. After all, the government does try to implement policies designed to reform the economy of Senegal and free the peasants from their subordinate position. In the meantime, while the marabus are gradually being undermined, they might as well be used as much as possible to help carry government programs in rural areas. Thus the officials assiduously pursue their contacts with the Muslim leaders and, like the French before them, attend Muslim ceremonies at which government goals are presented and given marabutic support. At Ibrahim Niass' Gamou in 1966 the Mayor of Kaolack, the Ambassador to Belgium (who comes from Kaolack), and the Governor of Sine Saloum were all present. Niass complimented the Governor and voiced his support for the government. The Governor in his turn underlined several administrative problems. He asked that all the disciples grow peanuts and that they also follow the example of Ibrahima Niass in trying to diversify their crops. He demanded that everyone pay back the loans they had received from the government—as Ibrahima had done—and requested the disciples' full cooperation with the government in whatever it asked.[26]

The kind of speech given at Niass' Gamou is repeated at Muslim ceremonies by regional and national officials whenever possible. At the Murid Magal in 1963 the President gave a speech that went beyond merely praising the cooperation of the brotherhood in seeming also to identify his government with the brotherhood. Senghor's speech was addressed to Falilou:

[25] Interview with Falilou M'Backé, Oct. 8, 1965, Touba.
[26] Speeches at Niass' Gamou, Jan. 21, 1966, Kaolack.

Muslim Brotherhoods and Politics in Senegal

Eighteen years ago . . . one day in November, I exposed the goal and the objectives of my policy to you. . . .

Immediately you understood me, you approved of me, you helped me. Since then, you have never abandoned me; you have adopted me as your son. In the worst moments of this long night . . . when all seemed compromised and the friends of yesterday abandoned me [reference to Mamadou Dia], I always found comfort, advice and support next to you. . . .

Although a certain infantile leftism tries to present the religious chiefs to us as "counterrevolutionaries" . . . it pleases me to give justice to these lies.

Again, what is Socialism if not essentially the economic-social system which gives primality and priority to work? Who has done this better than Ahmad Bamba and his successors. . . . People talk to me of rational, organized work. And you have always, in this sense, supported the effort of the Party and of the Government. . . .[27]

The Marabus' Privileged Position

The marabus, of course, use their power to demand all kinds of advantages for themselves, especially those that take the form of frequent and large gifts of money. Moreover, they often refuse to obey laws which they do not like. Government officials are likely to let the Muslim leaders act outside the law as long as they do not threaten the government itself. Consequently, one finds in Senegal a privileged group of individuals who act as they see fit and often cause problems for the government as a result. Cheikh Tidjane Sy is the best example of a marabu whose personal ambitions have caused difficulties for the government; but many other cases could be cited, for example, the sale by several marabus of American surplus grain in the summer of 1965, a very delicate situation for the government to handle.[28]

The marabus are not just important national figures, they are also international religious personalities, which is a problem for the government. The most important marabus maintain contacts with the leaders of their brotherhoods outside Senegal and some Senegalese marabus have numerous disciples in other countries.

[27] Republic of Senegal, *Compte rendu,* by Cheikh Ba Baidy.

[28] Seven marabus had taken the free grain and sold it to their *taalibés* rather than distributing it. They were not punished, though as a result of the scandal President Senghor decreed that only Ibrahima Niass, Abdul Aziz Sy, Lamine Diene, and Falilou M'Backé could distribute surplus grain. Interviews with Murid leaders, government officials, and Catholic Relief officials, Sept. 26, Oct. 29, 1965, Dakar; Jan. 18, 25, 1966, Dakar. See Falilou's speech in support of Senghor on this matter in *Afrique nouvelle,* Aug. 19–25, 1965.

The Government and the Brotherhoods

There are Murids in Gambia and in smaller numbers in other states throughout West Africa, although the Muridiyya remains mainly a Senegalese phenomenon. The Murids also maintain ties with the Qadriyya in Mauritania. The Tijani brotherhood as a whole has its motherhouse in Morocco and stretches from there throughout West Africa to Nigeria and beyond. The Senegalese Tijani leaders maintain their ties with Morocco and have many disciples in their own right in neighboring African states. Ibrahima Niass has the most disciples outside Senegal, reportedly thousands of *taalibés* in Mauritania, Mali, Ghana, and Gambia and from ten to thirteen million in Nigeria alone.

Difficulties for the Senegalese government stemming from the international position of the marabus arise because the marabus keep up their contacts outside of Senegal whether or not these contacts happen to run contrary to the interests of Senegalese foreign policy. Muslim leaders make trips to see their *taalibés* and visit other Muslim leaders on their way to Mecca even though the other leaders may come from a state which the government of Senegal is boycotting. Also, marabus conduct their own foreign relations with world leaders, Muslim or not. At times difficult situations result for government officials in Senegal.

Ibrahima Niass is an excellent example of the ways in which the international importance of a marabu can embarrass the government. In 1960, though the PSS had been dissolved, Niass was not in complete agreement with President Senghor and the UPS. This may have contributed to his interest in making widespread contacts with political leaders whom Senghor distrusted. Notably, Niass received the Egyptian Minister of African Affairs when he came to Dakar in 1960 and later accepted an invitation to Egypt, where he was received by President Nasser in 1961. Niass also met Premier Khrushchev at the dedication of the Aswan Dam. He refused a later invitation to the Soviet Union but did visit China, where he was received by the major Chinese political leaders.[29] Even after Niass had begun to collaborate more closely with the government of Senegal, after the defeat of Mamadou Dia, his international activities bothered the government. In early 1966, his opposition to Muslim reforms in countries like Tunisia

[29] Interviews with Niass' assistants, Jan. 15, Mar. 24, 1966, Dakar. I saw pictures of Niass with Krushchev and Nasser, and with Mao and others in China.

led him to publicly condemn the Tunisian regime although
the government of Senegal had recently received President
Bourguiba and Niass himself had accepted an award from
Bourguiba.[30] The government was displeased with Niass comments,
which were widely distributed in article form at the party congress
in Kaolack and later on the streets of Dakar. A representative
was sent to the marabu to ask him to modify his statement
but he did not publicly retract what he had said.

In 1966, the military coups in Ghana placed Ibrahima Niass in a
position that was quite distinct from the official policy of his
government. Nkrumah (who had earlier shown great respect
for the Guinean marabu Sharif Fanta Mahdi, who died in 1954)[31]
was a *taalibé* of Niass, to whom he sent money on various
occasions; it is even reported that Nkrumah sent a plane to take
Niass to Mecca annually.[32] When Nkrumah was removed from
office, the marabu came out publicly on his side. On the occasion
of a trip to Mali in March, 1966, Niass sent a telegram to the
President of Guinea thanking him for supporting Nkrumah.
At the time, the government of Senegal had already acknowledged
the military regime in Ghana and had definitely refused to
support the movement started by Sekou Touré to reinstate the
former Ghanaian president. Naturally the Guinean government
publicized Niass' telegram on Radio Guinea and Touré's official
message of thanks. In this instance the government of Senegal
felt obliged to ask the marabu to be more circumspect in his
actions, but these efforts were most unsatisfactory: Niass was
furious, for he felt the government had no right to interfere
between him and his *taalibé*. He wrote a letter to the
President in which he said that he had been humiliated by the
request and that he refused "categorically" to do as he had
been asked. Senghor, via the person of Cheikh Tahorou Doukouré,
apologized to the marabu and the incident was finished.
Niass did not retract his support of Nkrumah and flew off to
Djeddah for a meeting of the Commission of the World
Muslim Congress, of which he is an official.[33]

[30] Niass said Bourguiba should no longer be considered a Muslim. *Echos du Sénégal,*
January 1966.
[31] See reference to Nkrumah's respect for Fanta Mahdi in Morgenthau, *Political Parties in
French-Speaking West Africa,* p. 235.
[32] Interviews with Niass' disciples, Jan. 15, 1965, Dakar; Feb. 2, 1966, Taiba.
[33] Interviews with Niass, his disciples, and with government officials, Mar. 13, 1966,
Podor; Mar. 24, Mar. 25, 1966, Dakar; I also saw Niass' letter to Senghor.

The Government's Independence
from the Marabus

There are, of course, limits to the international activities of the marabus. The government, for example, could not permit a marabu to side openly with an avowed enemy of the regime or become involved in an effort to overthrow the government. In such a case, no matter who the marabu might be, Senegalese officials would be forced to act and the marabu would be imprisoned or exiled despite the national and international repercussions such a step would cause. The government, thus, tolerates the embarrassment caused by men like Niass and, whenever possible, uses the international position of the marabus to further its own goals. Niass, for example, prevented a motion demanding the release of Mamadou Dia from coming to the floor of the plenary session of the World Muslim Congress in 1965. He has also acted as the government's envoy on special missions to various Arab countries several times in recent years.[34] Senghor puts up with Niass' vagaries within certain limits. Notably, although the President was forced to retract his demand that Niass cease supporting Nkrumah, Niass himself did not challenge the government further by any substantial efforts on the Ghanaian leader's behalf. His support was limited mostly to messages of sympathy.

The marabus cannot be seen as free agents internationally. Moreover, they should not be seen as completely free or omnipotent nationally, either; despite their privileged position there are distinct boundaries to their influence on the government. It is significant that above the level of the *chefs d'arrondissement* most regional and national officials are men trained in Western schools or in Western professions, not scholars of Muslim law. This fact symbolizes the important degree of independence maintained by the Senegalese government. Throughout the colonial period, government in Senegal was the province of French Christian rulers educated according to Western standards who made policy decisions according to Western criteria. In independent Senegal the marabus have a greater role in choosing who is to fill an administrative post than they did

---

[34] Interviews with Niass' assistants, Jan. 14, Jan. 15, 1966, Dakar.

in the colonial era. Nevertheless, marabus in Senegal leave
the government to the modern elite, although they place their
favorites in office and sometimes oppose policies that directly
conflict with their interests. The Muslim leaders' one effort to
gain direct control over the government and its programs
was the abortive Superior Council of Religious Chiefs. Once
that had failed, the Muslim leaders seem to have accepted,
as they did under the French, that they must allow an alien
group—Western-oriented politicians—to run the country
according to their own set of rules.

Significantly, as a result, Senegal is not a Muslim republic
like Mauritania but a lay state. The neutrality of the government
in most religious matters is shown in a number of ways. Even the
President's former advisor on religious affairs, himself a Muslim
scholar, stresses that Senegal is not a Muslim state, pointing
out as evidence that the law in Senegal has remained secular.[35]
Although Léopold Senghor once espoused the creation of more
Muslim tribunals in the regional capitals of Senegal,[36] he has
never sought to implement this policy. The only concession
to Muslims in the law courts are the qadis—Muslim Courts
in the four old communes still exist, but their jurisdiction is
very limited. Indeed, the government of Senegal is in the process
of drawing up a new law code; but, although authors of the code
have consulted with scholars of Muslim law, the code is an
amalgamation of civil and religious laws of various types and
it is not congruent with the strict specifications of Malikite law
to which the Muslims of Senegal technically adhere.[37] Senegalese
politicians have taken symbolic steps to appease the Muslim
leaders: for example, establishment of the Muslim Institute
at Dakar University, the first head of which was the French
scholar Vincent Monteil. Arabic has been added as an
alternative language in secondary school; several Muslim
holidays have been made school holidays; the mosque in Dakar
was built. But the government has not made any substantial
concessions to Muslim law or customs because it has not been
forced to do so.

It is unlikely that the government would openly attack current
Muslim customs in Senegal as Habib Bourguiba did in Tunisia,

---

[35] Interview with Tahirou Doukouré, Jan. 7, 1966, Dakar.
[36] *Condition humaine*, July 25, 1950.
[37] Interview with Tahirou Doukouré, Jan. 7, 1966, Dakar. See also *Afrique nouvelle*,
July 14–20, 1966.

for the marabus could be expected to defend existing conditions as a unified group. President Bourguiba has been able to outlaw polygamy and nationalize the property of the brotherhoods. He has also attacked the institution of the Ramadan fast and asked that it not be observed to the extent that it proves itself incompatible with work.[38] Bourguiba's actions have been heavily criticized by many Muslims in Senegal including some highly placed in the government.[39] The Senegalese marabus, of course, were outraged at Bourguiba's policy and apparently determined that such a policy should not be introduced in their country. As Ibrahima Niass stated in an interview, the government would not dare to speak against Islam as Bourguiba did. In fact, Niass mentioned that Léopold Senghor had once asked him if he would condone a measure cutting down on fasting for Muslims, and the marabu had replied that he would not.[40]

But Senegalese government officials do try to undermine those Islam institutions which seem to conflict with their program of development. A good example is the government's efforts to limit pilgrimages to Mecca. These pilgrimages, a religious duty for any Muslim who can afford the journey, have only recently become very popular in Senegal. Between 1907 and 1911 only eleven pilgrims are known to have made the trip. But over the years, as the cost became more reasonable, wealthier elements of the population began to take advantage of the government's efforts to help the pilgrims. In 1961, when the cost of the trip was 200,000 CFA per pilgrim, one thousand people gathered in Dakar and left by boat for Mecca and five hundred others paid higher fees and went by plane.[41] In theory UPS leaders should have no reason to oppose the pilgrimages, except that they put Senegalese Muslims into contact with leaders of the pan-Arabic and pan-Islamic movements that Senegalese politicians, like their French predecessors, distrust. But in fact the pilgrimages are negative factors for the development of Senegal because they channel the savings of the Senegalese out of the country.

There is no question of the government making a public

---

[38] I. William Zartman, *Government and Politics in Northern Africa* (New York, 1963), pp. 79–80. and Charles F. Gallagher, "Tunisia," in Gwendolen M. Carter, ed., *African One-Party States* (Ithaca, 1962), pp. 72–73.

[39] Interview with government official, Jan. 7, 1966, Dakar.

[40] Interview with Niass, Jan. 29, 1966, Kaolack.

[41] Vincent Monteil, "Islam et développement au Sénégal," *Cahiers de l'ISEA*, ser. V (December, 1961), p. 49.

pronouncement recommending restraint in this matter. Such a speech would meet with instant and united opposition from all the Muslim leaders in Senegal. Instead, the government simply did not provide a boat in 1966 as it had, following the French example, in the years before. Nor did it permit the National Federation of Muslim Cultural Associations, a modern reform group, to provide its own boat. People were free to make the pilgrimage, but the only reasonable method was by plane and this was too expensive for any but the most wealthy travelers.[42]

The Marabus in Conflict with the Government

To really understand the limits of the marabus' influence on the national government one must examine carefully the outcome of a situation in which Falilou M'Backé, the most powerful marabu in recent Senegalese history, opposed a measure favored by Léopold Senghor and the UPS. Two examples of disagreement that occurred in 1965 and 1966 will be examined here even though all of their details are not yet clear. In the first case, President Senghor and Falilou M'Backé disagreed over the question of Al Hajj Dramé, the khalif's general secretary of approximately seventeen years.[43] A most intelligent and politically agile man whom Cheikh Tidjane Sy calls "one of the most important acquisitions of contemporary Muridism,"[44] Dramé had played a major role in the politics of the Murid brotherhood since Falilou had become khalif. However, Dramé became involved in a scandal the news of which rapidly spread throughout Senegal. As the khalif's secretary he had authority to order Murids to work, to borrow money, or to make purchases as he pleased, and he reportedly used his position to collect a fortune for himself, cloaking his activities behind orders given in the khalif's name. In the spring of 1965 he went to Mecca, and a group of men to whom he owed a large sum of money went to the khalif. Falilou, shocked and disgusted when he learned of the large sums of money his secretary had taken, made a speech on the radio in which he stated that Dramé was no longer his secretary. The rift between the two men was

---

[42] Interview with governor of the Sine Saloum region, Feb. 4, 1966, Kaolack; interview with members of Muslim reform group, Mar. 2, 1966, Dakar.

[43] Republic of Senegal, *Reportage d'un voyage à Touba*, by Emile Badiane for the Bureau de Presse et d'Information (June 13, 1959).

[44] Sy, "Traditionalisme mouride," p. 102.

then very much in the open and it seemed as if Dramé's career with the Murids was over.[45]

The khalif was determined to replace Dramé but, curiously enough, President Senghor was against his removal. Senghor has spoken on numerous occasions against corruption within the administration,[46] therefore his support of Dramé was surprising; but he apparently found Dramé too useful to let him be dismissed. During the years Dramé had been secretary to the khalif he had acted as intermediary between the Murid leader and Senghor. Gradually he had become a valuable assistant to Senghor, since he was an excellent source of information about what was going on in the Murid community. He could tell the president just who saw the khalif and what had been requested, as well as which matters were of particular concern to Falilou himself.

The conflict between Senghor and Falilou over Dramé did not become public, but it was notable in the spring and summer of 1965 that Dramé was not received officially by the President as the khalif's general secretary.[47] Furthermore, Dramé was not featured as the khalif's representative at the Magal in June, 1965, which President Senghor, Doudou Thiam, and other government officials attended; and Dramé traditionally has been the khalif's spokesman at these events.[48] Rumors were rampant over the disagreement, however, which was considered one cause of Senghor's appearance at the Tijani Gamou in Tivaouane in July, 1965. In the meantime, a number of conferences took place between Senghor and various Murid marabus over the matter. Eventually it was Falilou who conceded to Senghor, and Dramé again became the khalif's secretary. Once again his name figured prominently in articles on the Murids. In September, 1965, during an official visit by the President to Falilou's fields not far from Touba, the khalif's delegation was led by his two sons, Modou Mustafa and Bara M'Backé, and by his "secrétaire particulaire" Al Hajj Dramé.[49]

There are two ways to interpret Falilou's concession. In the first place, one can denigrate the whole affair because

[45] Interviews with government officials and Murid leaders, Oct. 7, Oct. 9, 1965, Touba; Nov. 3, Nov. 5, 1965, Dakar; Jan. 14, 1966, Dakar.

[46] See L'Unité africaine, Apr. 3, Apr. 24, Sept. 25, 1963. Also see Republic of Senegal Les Mésures de rigeur et d'austérité, by L. S. Senghor (Dakar, Sept. 13, 1963); and see Afrique nouvelle, Aug. 26–Sept. 1 and Sept. 2–7, 1965.

[47] See Dakar matin, April–June, 1965.

[48] Dakar matin, June 24, 1965. For comparison see Baidy, Compte rendu.

[49] "Le Président à Touba-Bogo," Dakar matin (Sept. 25, 1965).

it was not a direct challenge to the khalif's authority and thus not terribly important: the khalif could afford to keep Dramé because the president wanted him to, merely to keep good relations between him and Senghor. But this interpretation does not seem to do justice to the significance of the dispute. Falilou felt strongly that Dramé must be removed from office, but he was forced to obey the President's wish although the matter related to personnel inside the brotherhood. The general secretary's position as liaison between the president and the Murids is one of the most important posts in Senegal, significantly, in this case judgment was that the man for the job should be one whom the president trusts, not the khalif. Apparently the President exerted pressure on the khalif, who did not want to run the risk of a severe disagreement with Senghor. Falilou had no wish to lose the advantages that he and his brotherhood had from collaboration with the government, and he therefore gave in when it was obvious that the President was adamant. According to this second interpretation, which seems the more plausible, the dispute showed that the president can force the khalif to back down in certain matters because the latter is aware that he needs the government's help.[50]

The second period in which the khalif and the President found themselves at odds over a matter of importance was in late fall of 1965, lasting into the early months of 1966. This was an issue of even greater importance than Dramé's position, since it was closely tied with the economic interests of all the Murids and with the government's control of the Senegalese economy. The issue was the ten-percent tariff on the price of peanuts which the government felt compelled to levy on the harvest in 1965.

Because Senegal is economically dependent on peanuts, the government had been faced since independence with a potential crisis arising from the fact that France, which had provided a protected market for Senegalese peanuts and supported their price above the world market price, planned to end its support. Senegal was to be forced to adapt to the lower world market price and to face competitors for their peanut market in the European Economic Community.[51]

---

[50] Interviews with brotherhood and government officials and with anti-Murid Muslim scholars: Oct. 7, Oct. 9, 1965, Touba; Nov. 3, Nov. 5, 1965, and Jan. 14, 1966, Dakar.

[51] For information on peanuts in Senegal see Fouquet, *La Traite des arachides,* and Yves Péhaut, "L'Arachide au Sénégal," *Cahiers d'Outre-Mer,* 14 (January–March, 1961), 5–25.

The Government and the Brotherhoods

The Senegalese government had to find a way to lower the price of peanuts paid to the peasants and to improve the quality of the peanuts produced. The government also had to decrease the large amounts of peanuts lost between their original purchase by the state-approved stocking organizations and their final export by the Office de Commercialization Agricole (OCA). Losses occur because of stones and sticks weighed with the peanuts, shrinkage due to the sun, outright thefts, and a variety of other reasons.[52]

The marabus, some of the largest producers, were aware that the price had to be lowered because of the world market situation. The crisis in 1965, however, came because the government had announced publicly before the *traite* (the official period decreed by the government in which peanuts can be sold) that an agreement had been made with France to have the price of peanuts supported for another year. Shortly thereafter the government announced that ten percent would be taken off the peanut price, giving the peasants ninety percent of the price when they sold their crops and a paper credit for ten percent; the latter would be returned to the peasants after the costs of transportation (hitherto paid by the state) had been paid and after losses to the government between the original purchase and final exports had been made up. Dissatisfaction at this decision was widespread, for it was (correctly) assumed that transportation costs and government losses could effectively cancel out any returns to the peasants from the ten percent withheld originally.

Falilou M'Backé, as one of the largest producers of peanuts, was directly affected, as were his many subordinate marabus and his thousands of *taalibés*. He objected vigorously to the President, and consequently the opening of the *traite* was delayed. The Minister of Rural Economy spoke on the radio to assure the peasants that the ten percent was only a guarantee and would be returned. In the meantime, however, the khalif ordered his followers not to sell their peanuts, thus putting into effect one of his major holds over the government, his ability to cause the entire Murid community to cease cooperating with the government. The khalif apparently was the more intransigent because he had not completely recovered from his displeasure at the Dramé affair. In addition, he was reportedly

[52] See Republic of Senegal, Compagnie Générale d'Etudes et Recherches pour l'Afrique, *Commercialisation des arachides*, vol. I: *Situation actuelle* (Dakar, September–October, 1963).

angry that President Senghor had not brought President Habib Bourguiba to see him during the latter's visit to Senegal in early December. (Bourguiba had awarded the Croix de l'Ordre National de Tunisie to Saidou Nourou Tall, Abdul Aziz Sy, and Ibrahima Niass in Dakar.[53]) The situation was extremely serious, and Senghor met frequently with Dramé—on more occasions than were ever mentioned in *Dakar Matin*—and at one point with Modou Mustafa; he also sent delegates to talk with the khalif. People throughout the country were disturbed by the public disagreement between the President and the Murid khalif, and some Tijani marabus took sides in the dispute: Al Hajj Ibrahima Niass, for example, announced his support for the president at his annual Gamou in January, 1966.[54] In the end, President Senghor was forced to compromise and agree that no tariff would be taken off Falilou's peanuts. He reportedly also agreed to pay an eighty-million CFA debt of Dramé's, which eased the situation. Consequently, on January 24 the khalif called a council of Murid leaders and that evening made a radio speech in which he reaffirmed his support for Senghor. The Murid *taalibés* were ordered to sell their peanuts, and the major part of the crisis was over.[55]

The events of the winter of 1965-66 illustrate certain important factors in the relations of the President and Falilou. It is evident that the khalif was able to force the president to compromise by ordering his *taalibés* not to sell their peanuts. On the other hand, it is significant that the tariff was not withdrawn for anyone but the khalif himself. Quite possibly the government will decide, on the basis of the widespread opposition to the tariff, not to continue it; but in the crisis period, under extreme pressure, it was not abolished. In fact, the peanut crisis may be proof that a khalif, using his supporters in a most damaging manner, can gain concessions for himself but cannot dictate what policy is to be followed in the country as a whole. Indeed, this seems the best conclusion to draw about the limits of the marabus' influence in general. Other marabus in Senegal cannot exert any more pressure than Falilou did because none of them is as strong as he was. Moreover, *all* important marabus are

[53] See *Dakar matin*, Dec. 6, 1965.
[54] Speeches at Gamou, Jan. 21, 1966, Kaolack.
[55] Interviews with Murid leaders and with government officials, Dec. 31, 1965, Jan. 7, 1966, Dakar; Jan. 10, Jan. 14, 1966, Dakar; Jan. 22, 1966, Kaolack; Jan. 25, 1966, Dakar; Feb. 4, 1966, Kaolack; Feb. 7, Feb. 16, 1966, Dakar. Reference to solution of the crisis was made at the UPS Congress by Leopold Senghor in his evening speech, Jan. 28, 1966, Kaolack.

The Government and the Brotherhoods

aware of the boundaries to their political power; yet, barring open attack on Islam by the government, Muslim leaders in Senegal seem to be content with their status as privileged individuals who are courted with advantages of various kinds but who do not, and cannot, run the government.

6 The Impact of the Brotherhoods on the Government Reform Program

The politically radical Senegalese draw little comfort from the fact that the brotherhoods cannot control the government or draw up government policy. They ask whether in fact continued collaboration between the marabus and the politicians has not seriously vitiated attempts to implement social and economic reforms. The radicals admit that the marabus have supported some aspects of the development program and have been unable to prevent the government from planning reforms some of which the Muslim leaders disapprove. But the slow rate of change in rural areas indicates to left-wing Senegalese that the marabus are a serious brake to progress. Some day, they say, the government must inevitably come into conflict with the brotherhoods because two fundamentally opposite sets of values are involved: the government hopes to liberate the peasant, whereas the marabus' authority rests on the complete obedience of their disciples. By not directly attacking the negative aspects of the *tariqas*, these men insist, by allowing the marabus to be privileged citizens and using them to implement policies, the government is putting off the conflict and thus weakening its own position. Many members of the government, of course, disagree with this evaluation, which they see as unduly pessimistic. They insist that the marabus can be undermined despite the open cooperation between the government and the brotherhoods. Both sides in this dispute draw their evidence mainly from a study of the implementation of government reforms since 1960.

Government Regulation of Agriculture

The colonial government attempted to both encourage and regulate peanut production, the latter through such measures as the reduction of export duties and other taxes and rural campaigns urging peasants to grow the crop. The corollary regulations were quite complicated: the government, for example, set up granaries in the villages to which each producer contributed in order that enough seeds would be saved for the following planting season. In 1910 this system was replaced by the Sociétés de Prévoyance (SPs), presided over by the *commandants de cercle*, in which all producers were members. The SPs stocked peanuts and distributed seeds. Beginning in the early twenties, the seeds were in part selected seeds tested at the Agricultural Center in Bambey.[1]

[1] Fouquet, *La Traite des arachides*, pp. 41–46, 65–66, and Péhaut, "L'Arachide au Sénégal," p. 12.

131

Despite the interest of the government in regularizing the production and sale of peanuts, Senegalese peasants became dependent on a group of middlemen. These *traitants*, approximately three thousand in number and organized into a hierarchy headed by large French import-export houses like Peyrissac, dominated the peanut trade up to the end of the Second World War.[2]

In 1933, the SPs were permitted to organize the sale of part of the peanuts produced by their members. This was one of the first important efforts to eliminate middlemen: the SPs were more able than the individual peasant to bargain with the exporting firms.[3] The colonial administration also tried to eliminate middlemen by encouraging a cooperative movement. Cooperatives multiplied rapidly between 1947 and 1952, but they did not have the intended economic effect. In the first place they were not financially responsible and did not pay back the money they borrowed. Secondly, the cooperators often did not get back their investments, for marabus and other traditional leaders controlled the organizations and pocketed the surpluses after harvest. The administration enacted legislation regulating the cooperatives, and many, if not most, were abandoned. The administration then set up its own Entente Coopérative (ENCOOP), which was supposed to create pilot cooperatives of a more ideal type. But this system did not take root, in part because it was opposed by the *traitants*, who foresaw their own destruction should the cooperatives work.[4]

Based on the various policies of the colonial period together with the recommendations of Lebret's research team, the Senegalese government drew up its plans for rural reform in 1959 and 1960. One important step was the creation of stocking organizations which were managed either by cooperatives or approved individual traders. Only these organizations had the right to buy peanuts from the peasants, which severely reduced the role of the middlemen traders.[5]

[2] Péhaut, "L'Arachide au Senegal," pp. 14–15.

[3] Diarassouba, "L'Evolution des structures agricoles," p. 119. After the Second World War the SPs became the Sociétés Mutuelles de Production Rurale (SMPR) and in 1956 the Sociétés Mutuelles de Développement Rural (SMDR). These societies differed little from the old SPs in organization and purpose. *Ibid.*, pp. 119-121.

[4] *Ibid.*, pp. 119–120. See also Appendix D.

[5] Not all of the old *traitants* have been replaced and in some areas they still dominate, however: formerly powerful and wealthy traders in the M'Backé region, for example, complain bitterly about the government measures that "ruined" them. Interviews with Lebanese merchants, Oct. 8–9, Dec. 20–21, 1965, in M'Backé.

The Brotherhoods and Government Reform

The reforms also included the creation of the Banque Sénégalaise de Développement (BSD), which was to provide much needed credit to the cooperatives. Loans in materials—food, fertilizers and machinery—could be obtained from another new government organization, the OCA, which bought peanuts from the stocking organizations and exported them. The OCA headed a new cooperative system based on small groups formed in one village or a single village and its neighbors. Because of the availability of credit and the amelioration of conditions of sale (through the creation of the stocking organizations), post-independence cooperatives spread throughout Senegal, growing in number from 99 to 712 in 1960-1961 and to 1,423 in 1963. In 1963 they marketed 57.5 percent of the total peanut crop, as opposed to 47 percent in 1962.[6]

The cooperatives received technical assistance from the Centres Régionaux d'Assistance pour le Développement (CRAD) and the Centres d'Expansion Rurale (CER). The CRAD replaced the successor organization to the SPs in each region and distributed technical information, as well as acting as intermediary between the cooperatives and the OCA and BSD and supervising loans. The CER was a group of centers (two hundred were proposed in 1960) at which technicians specializing in agriculture, herding, water use, and forestry were located. A final part of the new reform was the Centres d'Animation Rurale (CAR), whose activity was integrated with the CER. The CAR educated selected peasants in new agricultural techniques in twenty-day training periods; the peasants were then sent back to the villages to spread the new methods they had learned.[7]

The agricultural reforms of 1960 were diverse and comprehensive. Through them the government hoped to control the price of peanuts received by the peasants and regularize the cooperatives. The latter were to be forced to

[6] Republic of Senegal, *Le Mouvement coopératif au Sénégal, Bilan et perspectives,* by Guy Belloncle for the Ministry of Rural Economy (Dakar, n.d. [1965]), pp. 5–12.
[7] The arrangement can be simplified into the following diagram:

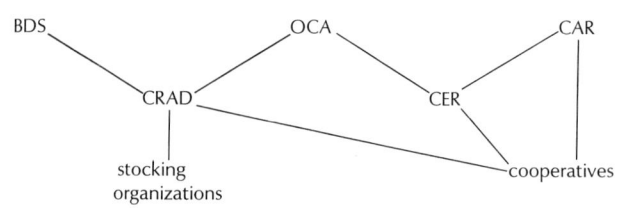

See *Le Militant UPS,* pp. 23–28, and Léopold Senghor, "Le Rapport politique général," *L'Unité africaine* (July 16, 1960).

pay their debts, since the stocking organizations would not
buy from them unless all debts were paid. The government
realized a marked improvement immediately in some aspects
of the rural problem: 93 percent of the total debt of the
cooperatives was paid in 1963-1964.[8] Moreover, the new plan,
through the CAR, gave the government a means of reaching
the peasants directly with suggestions for improved agricultural
techniques and collective action. The CAR, which began with
seven centers in 1960, had twenty-eight centers for men and
thirteen for women by 1966; each department in Senegal had
at least one center. In addition, seven to eight thousand
animateurs (peasants who had received training) had been
produced by that year.[9]

But the government still faced major problems in the
peasants' agricultural techniques. Use of fertilizers was not
widespread even where cattle were present and manure
therefore available. The scientific practice of crop rotation
was virtually unknown, and agricultural tools were few and
awkward. Moreover, the spread of peanut production
throughout the country was carried out with few precautions
to protect the soil, large areas of which had been overworked.
Nor had trees and bushes or grass been preserved to prevent
erosion which threatened a number of areas in Senegal,
especially in the Senegal Oriental region. And, of course,
the economy of Senegal still was dependent on peanuts and
thus on the fluctuations of the world market.

Table 1. Distribution of agricultural tools and fertilizer

Article distributed	1960	1961	1962	1963	1964
Seeders	1,510	4,589	12,000	24,906	23,437
Hoes	241	1,601	6,827	11,071	9,815
Ploughs	–	200	1,587	1,484	3,095
Fertilizer spreaders	–	–	1,750	3,140	105
Carts	–	–	257	–	2,654
Fertilizer	4,000 t.	11,669 t.	21,000 t.	29,000 t.	28,500 t.

Source: Republic of Senegal, *Le Mouvement coopératif du Sénégal, Bilan et perspectives,* p. 29.

[8] Chart on the debt and repayment by cooperatives used at the Ecole Nationale de
l'Economie Appliquée.
[9] Interview with Ben Mady Cissé, Mar. 7, 1966, Dakar.

Table 2. Principal products harvested by 1,000 t.

Products	1960	1961	1962	1963	1964 forecast
Mil	392	407	424	478	460
Niebes	11	15	13	14	15
Rice (paddy)	68	66	77	106	106
Corn	27	28	27	27	26
Manioc	168	139	157	153	156
Sweet potatoes	21	16	16	15	15
Beref	1	—	—	2	2
Fonio	3	4	4	4	4
Total traditional food crops	691	675	718	799	784
Truck garden crops	30	27	33	31	30
Peanuts	893	995	894	952	950

Source: Republic of Senegal, Situation économique du Sénégal, 1964, p. 27.

The government has taken a number of steps to solve these problems. For example, there has been an intensive effort to spread the use of fertilizers and equipment such as hoes, seeders, and ploughs through the cooperatives, and this effort has had some success (see Table 1). In addition, the growth of millet, the major food crop, and other crops has been encouraged to balance peanut production. A marked increase in millet production has occurred (see Table 2); but the significance of the increase is uncertain. The growth of millet is related to the terms of trade of peanuts versus rice: the peasants exchange peanuts for rice, which they prefer to millet, but when the terms of trade deteriorate the peasants tend to decrease their peanut production relative to their millet production.[10] Over the last few years it seems that the terms of trade from the point of view of the peasants have worsened, and this fact may explain the increased growth of millet.[11]

[10] For example, in the late thirties and early forties the terms of trade deteriorated markedly, with the result that peasants in the Sine Saloum Region decreased their peanut production in favor of their traditional food crop production. Fouquet, La Traite des arachides, pp. 114–115.

[11] If the terms of trade of peanuts versus rice had a value of 100 in 1961, then the value was 100 in 1962, 91 in 1963, and 93 in 1964. See Republic of Senegal, Situation économique du Sénégal, 1964 (Dakar, 1965), pp. 58–59. I am indebted to Marc Karp for pointing out the significance of the terms of trade in the expansion of millet.

Muslim Brotherhoods and Politics in Senegal

The government has also tried to control the spread of peanuts to fragile soil areas and to protect wooded areas. Controlling the use of land in Senegal has been a problem since the early colonial period. Individual land ownership did not exist traditionally, although peasants paid fees for the use of the land to their local rulers. These fees were outlawed repeatedly in the colonial period but they continued to exist. Moreover, laws passed in the colonial period to make all land not expressly granted to an individual—or at least all land which had been unused for more than ten years—the property of the state were ignored.[12] The Senegalese government made its most important efforts at land control when it enacted the *Loi sur le Domaine National* in 1964. The purpose of this series of acts was to ensure the rational utilization of land conforming to the priorities of the development plan. In effect, the law declared that the state owned all land except for those areas previously recognized as belonging to individuals, who were to register their land within six months after the decree. The government-controlled land was to be given to occupants organized in rural cooperative communities so that land division would be equitable. Traditional rights to use of the land would be recognized, but all forms of payment to local chiefs would be abolished once and for all. New areas of cultivation were not to be undertaken without specific permission of the state. The overall intention of the law was explicitly to liberate the peasants, end the activity of the "speculators" who had misused the land, and help the government to implement its development program.[13] The effect of this law is difficult to evaluate, since it has not been implemented at all in certain regions such as the Casamance and the River Region and has been unevenly applied in other areas of Senegal. Until more time has elapsed, its full influence cannot be properly interpreted.

The Economic Role of the Marabus

Throughout their efforts at agricultural reform, the governments of Senegal have used the marabus as their agents. A major reason for this has been the economic position of the latter. Muslim leaders individually are major agricultural producers.

[12] Diarassouba, "L'Evolution des structures agricoles," pp. 98–99.
[13] Republic of Senegal, *Lois, décrets, arrêtés et circulaires concernant le domaine national* (Dakar, 1966), p. 13 (documents are not consistently numbered).

The Brotherhoods and Government Reform

The important marabus possess some of the largest fields in the country. The average Wolof field has been estimated at 4.83 hectares,[14] whereas Ibrahima Niass, for example, has a private field of approximately 603 ha.[15] Falilou M'Backé, one of the largest producers of peanuts in Senegal, had enormous fields at his showplace at Touba-Bogo including over 7,000 ha. under cultivation.[16] The marabus are part of a tiny minority of large landholders whose position is demonstrated in Table 3.

Table 3. Land distribution

	Number of cultivations	Land area in ha.	Percent	Number of people	Percent
Poor peasants	—	—	—	489,560	21.6
a) without land	—	—	—	22,340	—
b) small peasant owners	70,700	36,235	3.0	466,720	—
Average peasant owners	260,300	1,015,377	84.1	1,753,480	76.4
Large landowners	7,400	156,730	12.9	47,400	2.0
Total	338,400	1,203,342	100	2,290,400	100

Source: Valy-Charles Diarassouba, "L'Evolution des structures agricoles du Sénégal," p. 227.

The major marabus are in an extremely high income bracket for Senegal. They are included in the 1 percent (12,623) of the population earning 100,000 francs or more per year. (56.5 percent of the population receives more than 20,000 francs but less than 100,000, and 42.5 percent earns less than 20,000 francs.)[17] Thus the marabus' crops alone can provide the government with significant tax revenues and consequently their payment or nonpayment of taxes has a substantial effect on state revenues. Their use of, or their refusal to use, new agricultural techniques affects a large proportion of the Senegalese peanut crop. Their payment or nonpayment of debts also has a notable effect on credit-providing agencies. Their investment

[14] Diarassouba, "L'Evolution des structures agricoles," p. 155.
[15] Interview with Ibrahima Niass, Feb. 1, 1966, Taiba.
[16] Amadou Moustapha Kane, "Touba-Bogo école de développement," L'Unité africaine (Nov. 4, 1965).
[17] Diarassouba, "L'Evolution des structures agricoles," p. 227. The statistics cited by Diarassouba are at best rough approximations; they are given here in the belief that poor statistics are better than none. His figures in any case reinforce a generally held assumption— that the marabus are exceptionally wealthy and extremely important producers of peanuts,

or noninvestment of their revenues in the economy of Senegal is an important factor in the country's development. In other words, they can exert considerable pressure on the government in ways analogous to the wealthy commercial and agricultural elites that influence numerous governments throughout the world. The marabutic pressure, of course, is made even more significant by the fact that they can direct the agricultural production of their disciples, aside from their individual holdings.

The reaction of the colonial authorities to the economic power of the marabus was an attempt to encourage their growth of peanuts as much as possible. This was true despite French recognition that the rapid spread of peanut cultivation was potentially dangerous for the soil reserves of Senegal.[18] The policy of unlimited encouragement to the marabus was only called into question after the Second World War. Not surprisingly, it was the Murids who were the focus of government criticism at this time. The Tijanis, too, raised peanuts, with methods little different from the Murids; but the Tijani taalibés were not as aggressive as the Murids, upon whom, as a result, the French concentrated their attacks. The French began to emphasize the danger to the soil from the poor agricultural methods used and the declining amounts of millet being produced by the brotherhood.

The most notable report on the subject was that by Roland Portères, which alarmed the government with its dire predictions and focused blame on the Muridiyya. Portères had a doctrinaire dislike of the brotherhood, which he viewed as a form of slavery,[19] and his dislike was reflected in page after page of his report. He found that pagan Serer farmers practiced crop rotation and used fertilizer, whereas Wolof farmers in general were less acquainted with these techniques and did not maintain any plant cover on their land. Worst of all was the "speculative" method of agriculture typical of the Murids in which no fertilizer or crop rotation was used, the soil was exhausted, and food crops were not grown. The Murids, said the report, paid no attention to the land but only to the money which they could get from it.[20]

[18] See DA, Commandant of Baol, "Rapport du Novembre 1913," Dossier, and "Rapport politique du Sénégal" (1916), no. 1178, 2G 16.5.

[19] Republic of France, L'Aménagement de l'économie agricole et rurale au Sénégal, Mission Roland Portères (Dakar, 1952), p. 105.

[20] Ibid., pp. 55–56. The navetanes, or migrant laborers, were also singled out for blame. See Péhaut, "L'Arachide au Sénégal," pp. 9–10.

The Brotherhoods and Government Reform

Portères' report was reinforced by the failure of the Boulel experiment, in which the French had attempted to combine modern techniques of agriculture with use of a labor force of Murid *taalibés*. The Boulel colony was established in 1947 near Kaffrine, and, by 1953, 3,000 ha. were under cultivation.[21] The Murids included in the experiment were *taalibés* of Bassiru M'Backé, whose representatives directed the disciples and distributed food and clothing to them. The administrators hoped that the inclusion of Murids in the experiment would give the brotherhood experience in using modern agricultural and land conservation techniques; they also assumed that the tight organization of the Muridiyya and the wealth and authority of the Murid marabus would facilitate the spread of new techniques both at Boulel and in general. In time, however, because the Boulel experiment was yielding relatively poor harvests at high costs, the administrators became convinced that their assumption had been unwarranted. The Murid disciples, they decided, were particularly unsuited to the experiment and to modern agriculture generally because they were working as slave laborers. The "feudal" Murid system left no place for individual initiative on the part of the disciples, who saw no direct monetary return from improvements they made or from the large harvests they accumulated.[22] It was decided that the Boulel experiment would not be workable as long as "slave" labor was used, as Portères wrote.[23] The experiment was converted into the Secteur Expérimental de Modernisation Agricole (SEMA), the working force of which was fifty-five volunteer families.[24]

The result of Portères' report, and the Boulel experiment, was a general condemnation by the colonial officials of past agricultural policy and, in particular, collaboration with the Murids and to a lesser extent with other brotherhoods. The Governor of Senegal called the Portères' report "a veritable evangel," and high-level administrative discussions took place on possible means of following up Portères' recommendations. But in fact little was done by the colonial government to change

[21] Péhaut, "L'Arachide au Sénégal," p. 10, and Paul Pélissier, "L'Arachide au Sénégal: Rationalisation et modernisation de sa culture," *Cahiers d'outre-mer*, 15 (July–September, 1951), 13–16.
[22] R. Bouchet, "Le Secteur expérimental de modernisation des terres neuves," resume from *Agronomie tropicale* (May–April 1955), in *La Region arachidière*, 1–5, A–2 (9–10) (Dakar, n.d.).
[23] Portères, *L'Aménagement de l'économie agricole*, p. 111.
[24] Péhaut, "L'Arachide au Sénégal," p. 11.

its policy of collaboration. The report itself was not even widely published for fear of possible repercussions due to its uncompromising denunciation of the Murids.[25] Furthermore, the Senegalese government, once self-rule had been granted, tended to reject the conclusions of the Portères' report and succeeding similarly oriented studies. Research done for the Senegalese government recognized the agricultural problems about which Portères wrote, such as a deficit in food crop production and lack of fertilizers, crop rotation, or land conservation. The Murids and the other brotherhoods, however, were absolved from blame. The marabus and their disciples admittedly practiced a crude form of agriculture, but this was not due to the brotherhoods but was typical of the Wolof in general.[26] A postindependence report admitted that pagan Serer traditional agricultural practices were better than others in Senegal although the Serer were less adaptable to new agricultural techniques.[27] In addition, the report recognized that cultivation techniques were particularly poor on the fields of chiefs, marabus, and absentee landowners (all of which had in common the fact that their workers did not own the land and tried to get the most out of it with the least effort).[28] Nevertheless, neither the Murid nor the other brotherhoods were to be blamed for the style of agriculture in Senegal; indeed, the Murids were commended for being excellent workers whose collaboration would, and should, be very useful to the government.[29] The report heralded a reversal of the post-World War II colonial emphasis and a return to the earlier stress on usefulness of the brotherhoods—a stress that was, of course, congruent with the continuing practice of the Senegalese government.

Even the 1960 report recognized negative features in the brotherhood agricultural system largely due to the subjection of the disciples. But the positive features of the marabus' collaboration were underlined. Thus, the balance sheet of the marabus' economic contribution was seen as positive from the government's point of view, particularly for the following

[25] See Republic of Senegal, *Procès verbal de la réunion de la Commission pour l'Etude du Rapport du Professeur Portères* . . . (Dakar, Aug. 23–Sept. 12, 1952).

[26] *La Région arachidière,* pt. 1, pp. 1–5 (20).

[27] *Ibid.,* pp. 1–4 (10).

[28] *Ibid.,* pp. 1–4 (3).

[29] *Ibid.,* pp. 1–5 (32). Portères and others who condemned the Murids' economic role tended to overlook additional factors that affected the experiment at Boulel and the economy in general: for example, the renowned Groundnut Scheme in East Africa, analogous to Boulel in many ways, failed without having any marabus present.

reasons. First, the marabus supported the government's campaign
to diversify crops and spread the use of modern agricultural
techniques; major Murid leaders were already experimenting
with modern equipment in their fields by the early 1950's.
Thus Falilou reportedly received a loan of 3,640,000 francs
with which he bought a Massey-Harris tractor, a plow,
a pulverizer, and twenty-one seeders, among other things.[30]
In the succeeding years Falilou continued his interest in
experimentation, and in 1965 the government labeled his fields
at Touba-Bogo a "school of development." In the fields were
3,000 ha. of peanuts and 2,500 of millet; he had planned to
grow fruit trees and truck-garden crops there as well.[31]
Falilou's example was followed by other Murid marabus like
Bassiru and Cheikh M'Backé, both of whom have made
extensive use of new equipment and techniques in their
holdings, and certain Tijani leaders. The size of the marabus'
property and their ability to invest large amounts in new
machinery, to say nothing of their growing investments in
commercial undertakings of other kinds in Dakar and
elsewhere, is an important consideration for the government.
Moreover, the marabus have forced their disciples to cooperate
with the government in such agricultural matters as the use of
selected seeds and some fertilizer. The collaboration of the
marabus is a significant factor in the increases shown by
government statistics in the distribution of agricultural
machinery, fertilizers, and seeds in recent years (see Table 1).

The marabus also have helped institute new government
organizations such as the cooperatives, although here their
record is more mixed. The postindependence cooperatives
have worked in a much more regular fashion than the early
cooperatives, as debts generally are paid and other contract
obligations met. However, many marabus still maintain control
of their disciples' cooperatives, though the cooperatives often
have officials selected from the ranks of the peasants themselves.
The members still give the money they receive to their marabu
together with the yield from the marabu's special field,
the *champs du mercredi*, in their village. Some changes have
occurred—for example, David Hapgood mentions that one
cooperative actually voted its marabu director out of office;[32]
but this example is not typical of the cooperatives, which

[30]Nekkach, "Unpublished Report."
[31]Kane, "Touba-Bogo école de développement."
[32]Hapgood, *Africa from Independence to Tomorrow* (New York, 1965), p. 123.

are generally subservient to the marabus. Nonetheless, the Muslim leaders' role in regard to cooperatives still may be seen as positive from the fact that the marabus support these organizations, which in the long run may challenge the brotherhood system.

There is, of course, a negative side to the ledger. The peanut crisis discussed in the last chapter is one example of marabu opposition to a government program that hindered the sale of peanuts and eventually resulted in an important exemption to the proposed tariff. Many other instances of marabu opposition to specific policies could be given as well. Falilou at first refused to help the CAR establish itself in Diourbel, with the result that the program was able to produce very few *animateurs* in this region. Eventually the khalif, under pressure from President Senghor, agreed to support the program, and in 1966 prognostications for Diourbel by the Director of Rural Animation, Ben Mady Cisse, were quite optimistic.[33]

The marabus' privileged status (which permits their disobedience of law has also been a serious hindrance to decrees on debt control. Many marabus are heavily in debt to the government although there are no figures to indicate the amount of money involved. When the BSD was established, the earlier Crédit du Sénégal, which had provided rural credit, was left in existence (up to 1964) specifically to make individual loans to "grand cultivateurs," artisans, and traders.[34] The marabus make up the bulk of the large producers, and the five hundred-million CFA deficit of the Crédit du Sénégal in the end of 1964 may be in large part owed by the marabus.[35] Many more marabus pay back the loans they receive than was the custom formerly— Ibrahima Niass, for example, was complimented at Gamou in 1966 on his repayment of money borrowed by the governor of Sine Saloum.[36] But many other marabus still remain heavily in debt, for example, the former khalif of the Murids.[37] He may not in fact have seen himself as in debt, since the money he received he felt was his due; and he gave away to needy disciples as much as he received. But his attitude and the similar "financial irresponsibility" of his colleagues are very

---

[33] Interview with Cissé, Mar. 7, 1966, Dakar.
[34] Senghor, "Le rapport politique général."
[35] Republic of Senegal, *Situation économique du Sénégal, 1964*, p. 70.
[36] Speeches at Gamou, Jan. 21, 1966, Kaolack.
[37] Interviews with Murid leaders and government officials, Feb. 6, 1966, Kaolack; Nov. 20, 1965, M'Backé.

difficult for the government to handle. No sanctions could be imposed on Falilou M'Backé for such a matter, and he continued to give an outstanding example of nonpayment of debts that influenced his disciples and, due to the large amounts he received, was a serious embarrassment to the credit associations.

The question of the uncontrolled expansion of cultivation by Muslim leaders has been an even profounder problem for the government. The *Loi sur le Domaine National* has been ignored by many major marabus. President Senghor advised the administrators implementing the decree to treat "eminent personages objectively," which was interpreted as meaning not to be too strict with the marabus—with the results that the administrators closed their eyes to the marabus' transgressions.[38] The examples of classified forests in Déali and Boulel, in Sine Saloum, indicate the consequences. Classified forests, according to the law, are to be left uncultivated to protect the plant cover of Senegal; but because six Murid marabus and the khalif of the Tijanis became interested in expanding into the area, the forests of Boulel and Déali were reclassified as "pioneer zones," which theoretically may be cultivated only by rural communities or cooperatives created or approved by the government and remaining under government control.[39] Pioneer zones are also to be cultivated according to government specifications that include use of hedges to prevent erosion and use of crop rotation and fertilizer, and provision for the inspection of agricultural techniques and workers' villages by government agents.[40] But even before laws defining the details of the administration of the pioneer zones had been published the marabus had begun to clear the forests without government supervision or control of any kind. The amount of land involved was quite large and included the following two allotments:

Forest of Déali:	*Parcel 1*
Falilou M'Backé	1,550 ha.
Bassiru M'Backé	1,000 ha.
Medina M'Backé	1,000 ha.

[38] Interview with government official, Mar. 26, 1966, Dakar.
[39] *Lois, décrets, arrêtés,* p. 4.
[40] *Ibid.,* pp. 51–58.

	Parcel 2
Falilou M'Backé	2,000 ha.
Mamoun M'Backé	2,000 ha.
Modu Awa	1,000 ha.
Awa Balla M'Backé	1,000 ha.

Forest of Boulel:

Abdul Aziz	1,000 ha.[41]

Nor were Boulel and Déali the only places where such events occurred.[42] In Dagana, in the River Region, 600 ha. were taken over by marabus who sent their *taalibés* from other regions to cultivate the new lands even though the law stated that only the occupants of a particular region would be permitted to cultivate it.[43] That the marabus have continued their unrestricted takeover of land is to some administrators, particularly those charged with implementation of the *Loi sur le Domaine National*, a significant indication of the futility of land reform efforts as long as the marabus remain outside the law.[44]

The Marabus' Attitude toward Education and Medicine

The brotherhoods have influenced the spread of Western education and the expansion of health programs, also prerequisites for the success of the government plan, as well as the Senegalese economy. In general, the more important marabus are concerned with their disciples' welfare and support any measure which they see as promoting the living conditions of Senegalese peasants. But the problem lies in the Muslim leaders' definition of what is a favorable measure. Not all of them are convinced, for example, that Western medicine is an improvement over traditional methods of dealing with illness, methods which include blessings by powerful marabus. Misunderstanding and mistrust have led certain marabus in the past to encourage their followers to oppose government-sponsored sanitation or vaccination campaigns or not to visit clinics. There have always been some, like Saidou Nourou Tall, who have promoted government health

[41] *Ibid.,* "Arrêté interministériel . . . dans le Département de Linguère."
[42] *Ibid.,* "Décret 66–45" (Jan. 19, 1966), and "Arrêté ministériel" (Feb. 19, 1966).
[43] *Ibid.,* "Décret no. 65–443" (June 25, 1965).
[44] Interviews with government officials, Mar. 1, Mar. 26, 1966, Dakar.

programs,[45] but there are others, equally important, who have
actively opposed the government in these matters. Most
significantly, the government has had great difficulty in winning
over the heads of the Murid brotherhoods.

The Murid khalif Falilou, shortly before his death, indicated
his support of the government's health program: during the
yellow fever scare in the fall of 1965 he consented to a mass
vaccination of the Diourbel region. At the Magal of 1965,
he made a point of thanking the administration for caring for
the "life and health" of the inhabitants of the region, specifically
for purifying the area around Touba, clearing away dangerous
insects (like the malaria-bearing mosquito) and sending a doctor
to live permanently in Touba.[46] But close associates of the
khalif state that he nevertheless did not approve of doctors
and preferred that his disciples seek healing through prayers.[47]
Evidence of the effects of the khalif's disapproval can be sought
in government statistics for the number of hospital personnel
distributed throughout the seven regions of the country.
The figures show that Diourbel has the highest and therefore
the worst ratio of people to nurses and the second highest
to doctors; only Sine Saloum, also a heavily Murid region,
has worse ratios. The figures are not at all conclusive and other
factors must be considered; for example, Thiès-ville has a
population of 69,100 out of a total regional population of
409,660, whereas Diourbel region has a population of 503,040,
only 28,660 of whom live in the only large city, Diourbel.[48]
The relatively higher degree of Thies' urbanization must affect
the ratio of medical personnel to inhabitants, since most doctors,
nurses, and other medical attendants find it easier to live in a
large town where medicine is available and patients are more
accustomed to Western medical care. Such facts also explain
to a certain degree the very high ratios of people to medical
personnel in the Casamance, a remote and unsettled region
with relatively primitive living conditions. (Ziguinchor has
29,800 people in a region of 529,860.)[49] Nevertheless, the
high ratios in Diourbel do indicate that the khalif's opposition

---

[45] See Chapter 2.

[46] Falilou M'Backé, "Discours prononcé . . . a l'occasion du Grand Magal de Touba, 1965"
(Dakar: D. L. No. 19–6–65).

[47] Interview with khalif's assistants, Nov. 21, 1965, Touba.

[48] Verrière, "La Population du Sénégal," p. 31, and Jacques Antonn, "L'Evolution
démographique au Sénégal," Sénégal d'aujourd'hui, no. 23, September 1965.

[49] Antonn, "L'Evolution démographique du Sénégal."

Table 4. Distribution of medical personnel

Regions	Population (thousands)	Doctors	Thousands of people per doctor	Midwives	Thousands of people per midwife	Nurses	Thousands of people per nurse
Cap Vert	517	81	6.4	90	5.7	223	2.3
Casamance	562	10	56.2	9	62.4	106	5.3
Diourbel	538	8	67.3	10	53.8	92	5.9
River	371	15	24.7	12	30.9	147	2.5
Senegal Oriental	162	4	40.5	1	—	45	3.6
Sine Saloum	766	11	69.6	14	54.7	146	5.2
Thies	442	15	29.5	12	54.7	95	4.7
Total	3,358	144	—	138	—	858	—

Source: Republic of Senegal, Situation économique, 1964, p. 22.

to modern medicine in the past has affected adversely the spread of medical improvements in his region.

Although Tijani leaders may not be very enthusiastic about modern medical care, none of the major Tijani marabus is identified with a public stand against the health program. Indeed, one of my interviews with the khalif of the Tijaniyya in the fall of 1965 coincided with a visit by his doctor, and in 1966 a trip to the village of Ibrahima Niass in Taiba revealed that Niass pays for a doctor and a small dispensary for the benefit of his disciples there.[50]

Falilou's disapproval of modern medicine, of course, is more significant than such an attitude on the part of any individual Tijani. Similarly, the fact that he objected to Western education probably has a more telling result than such opposition by Abdul Aziz or Ibrahima Niass. The entire question of education, in fact, has been more controversial, more disputed by all the marabus, than the health programs. The reason for Muslim leaders' displeasure in regard to Western education is obvious. The Western school system tends to break down the ties of the students to the brotherhoods. Most Muslim leaders, therefore, view the Western schools as injurious to the Muslim faith. Tijani marabus, however, come from a brotherhood whose emphasis on learning has been more pronounced than has that of the Murids and where the marabus interfere less in the daily lives of their followers than do Murid leaders. Thus it is not suprising to find that the Tijani marabus less actively oppose the Western system of education than their Murid counterparts.

I asked an identical series of questions of five of the leading Tijani and Murid marabus in 1965 and 1966 (the marabus included Abdul Aziz Sy, Ibrahima Niass, Saidou Nourou Tall, Serigne Modou Bousso, and Modou Mustafa) to see if any differences could be found in their attitudes toward education. If a question on education was posed in terms of support to the government's education program, all the leaders and their assistants (queried later) insisted that they obeyed the government in everything including Western education. But if I approached the subject by discussing the doctrine of Islam and the problems which other religions throughout the world have in holding the

---

[50] Interviews with Abdul Aziz Sy, Oct. 19, 1965, Dakar, and Ibrahima Niass, Feb. 2, 1966, Taiba. Some of Niass' wives have used the doctor's services, indicating his approval of modern medical care even for his family.

loyalty of their followers in the face of materialism,
industrialization, and modern education, all the marabus reacted
similarly and discussed the question at length. They agreed that
they would prefer a Muslim parochial to a secular school system.
Western education in general, particularly on the college level,
tends to dilute their *taalibés'* faith, according to these leaders.
Not one of them wanted his children to attend Western schools.
Their offspring are educated at home in Qu'ranic traditions
and Muslim law and, if further education is deemed wise,
their sons are sent abroad to Saudi Arabia or perhaps to Egypt,
where it is less likely that the fundamentals of their faith will
be shaken.[51]

Saidou Nourou Tall seemed the most reconciled to the school
system. He said that, following the foundation of the French
schools, people had had their choice about what kind of school
to attend. In his opinion Muslim schools were better for a
follower of Islam, but he refused to oppose the wishes of those
of his disciples who preferred a French school.[52] Abdul Aziz Sy
said that the members of his family did not go to French schools
although they learned French at home; he did not, however,
oppose the schooling of his *taalibés* in the French system,
and he was proud of the fact that there were a larger proportion
of Tijani than Murid functionaries in the government (in relation
to the size of their *tariqas*), which he thinks is due to the superior
education common to members of the Tijani order.[53]
Ibrahima Niass, who appears to be the most fundamentalist
of all Tijani leaders, agreed that Western schools hurt the faith
of young Muslims and stated that he did not send his children
to French schools but educated them at home and counseled
his *taalibés* to do likewise.[54]

Both the son of the former Murid khalif Falilou and the head
of the Bousso family, the latter of whom is renowned as the
intellectual leader of the Muridiyya, agreed completely with
each other concerning their own negative views of Western
education and concerning Falilou's similar opinion and the
traditional opposition of their order toward French schools.
The head of the Bousso family noted that Ahmad Bamba had not
"ordained" that his *taalibés* go to school and therefore they

[51] Interviews with the marabus named in Tivaouane, Touba, Kaolack, Guede, and Dakar,
1965 and 1966.
[52] Interview with Tall, Mar. 23, 1966, Dakar.
[53] Interview with Sy, Dec. 5, 1965, Tivaouane.
[54] Interview with Niass, Jan. 29, 1966, Kaolack.

never have done so. Falilou M'Backé maintained this attitude.[55]
Modou Mustafa elaborated that when people are confronted
with Western civilization they begin to question the faith and
traditions of their fathers. They lose their respect for the marabus
and their faith diminishes. Therefore the khalif Falilou preferred
to send his sons to Cairo or to Mecca, where they could study
without losing their beliefs, and did not approve of French
schools for his family or for his disciples in general.[56]

Falilou's opposition to Western education does not mean
that no Murids attend Western schools, or even that none of the
children of important Murid leaders do. Throughout Senegalese
history the French schools have never lacked for students,
even in strongly Muslim areas, since it was early recognized that
the road to wealth and advancement in the government is
through Western education. In 1965 the son of an important
Baye Fall marabu, for instance, was graduated from the Lycée
Delafosse, a technical secondary school in Dakar.[57] But Falilou's
stringent opposition has had a significant effect on the expansion
of school attendance in Murid areas. This effect can be observed
by comparing the number of Tijani to Murid functionaries,
as Abdul Aziz suggests; but statistics on school attendance
seem to be more significant indicators. Table 5 shows that
only six percent of Diourbel's male school-age children were
in French schools in 1961—the lowest figure for any region
except Senegal Oriental. The percent of girls of school age
who are in school is also very low in Diourbel. Moreover,
Diourbel has more children in Qu'ranic schools than any region
but the River Region. The published government figures give
considerably higher percentages of school attendance for
1963 and 1964 for Senegal as a whole and for each region but
still show that Diourbel has one of the lowest percentages
of school attendance (see Table 6).[58] Again the degree of
urbanization affects the figures presented because more
children attend French schools in the large towns than in the
countryside. Thus Senegal Oriental, which has a very low
population density (three persons per square kilometer,
whereas there are fifteen in Diourbel)[59] and no significant towns,

[55] Interview with Serigne Modou Bousso, and brothers, Nov. 21, 1965, Gueded.
[56] Interview with Modou Mustafa Dec. 9, 1965, Touba.
[57] Interview with Abdul Aziz Sy and assistants, Dec. 5, 1965, Tivaouane.
[58] See Republic of Senegal, *Situation économique du Sénégal, 1963* (Dakar, 1964), p. 23,
and Verrière, "La Population du Sénégal," p. 3.
[59] Verrière, "La Population du Sénégal," p. 31.

Table 5. African population: school attendance by thousands

Boys	Cap Vert	Casamance	Diourbel	River	Senegal Oriental	Sine Saloum	Thies	Senegal
Total ages 6–13[a]	38.6	56.0	46.2	35.1	14.3	70.0	42.3	302.4
Not in school	9.1	38.0	34.3	21.1	11.9	38.5	26.6	179.4
Qu'ranic school	5.1	6.0	8.9	9.0	1.6	13.4	7.2	51.3
Other school	24.3	11.5	3.0	4.9	0.8	18.0	8.4	71.0
Percent in school[b]	63.	21.	6.	14.	6.	26.	20.	23.
Girls								
Total ages 6–13[a]	38.7	51.9	38.9	30.0	9.6	65.9	38.0	273.0
Not in school	16.8	44.8	36.8	26.0	9.3	53.3	31.6	218.8
Qu'ranic school	4.8	1.5	1.0	1.9	0.2	3.5	1.4	14.4
Other school	16.8	5.1	1.0	1.9	0.1	8.9	5.0	38.8
Percent in school[b]	43.	10.	3.	6.	1.	14.	13.	14.

Source: Louis Verrière, "La Population du Sénégal," p. 84 (based on the 1960-1961 census).
[a]Including the nondeclared.
[b]Not including Qu'ranic schools.

Table 6. School attendance in Senegal by percentage

Region	Percent
Cap Vert	75.0
Casamance	33.9
River	41.5
Diourbel	16.2
Senegal Oriental	25.1
Sine Saloum	22.2
Thies	36.6

Source: Republic of Senegal, Situation économique, 1964, p. 15.

has a very low rate of school attendance of any kind. But the statistics still indicate that the Murid leaders' opposition to French schools has kept down the numbers of children obtaining a Western education in Diourbel. Indeed—symbolically—there is no French school permitted in the Murid capital, Touba.

It is equally significant, however, that both the numbers of children attending schools and the numbers of medical personnel have risen in all regions, including Diourbel. The absolute number of students in French schools went from 4,750 in 1906 to 109,800 in 1960.[60] Marabu opposition, though it slows the pace, has not prevented the gradual implementation of education and health reforms.

Evaluation of the Marabus' Effect on Reform

It is difficult to evaluate the marabus' total effect on governmental programs. They have supported or opposed specific aspects of social and economic reforms. Their choice of what to support and what to oppose often seems dictated by extraneous factors rather than the result of careful ratiocination about the effects of the proposed reform. Mistrust of and irritation at the president or other important politicians in a specific incident may be more likely to bring on opposition by the major marabus than the long-term conflict between goals of the plan and aims of the brotherhoods. Falilou's opposition to the peanut tariff in 1965 and 1966 can be

[60] Quellien, La Politique musulmane, p. 262, and Verrière, "La Population du Sénégal," p. 84.

seen as a personal reaction to President Senghor, a reaction that might not have occurred had not relations between the khalif and the president been somewhat strained at that point. Usually, the khalif's opposition was also due to his suspicion of a suggested reform's possible adverse effects on his disciples and himself. Fear of the tariff was an important factor in the peanut crisis along with Falilou's irritation at Senghor. Apprehension toward the reform's effect must also be the main reason for Falilou's opposition to health and education measures. A further factor to consider is that those parts of a reform program which the marabus do not directly oppose, and do not order their disciples to disobey, they often ignore. Thus the marabus have paid little attention to the *Loi sur le Domaine National* because its provisions, if obeyed, would hinder their economic activities. Such action constitutes opposition of a more subtle kind that is extremely important. Possibly all the people in nonmarabu-dominated regions, and all but the marabus in the peanut zone, may be brought to obey the new law; but the marabus' actions affect large areas of land and influence large numbers of people.

Extensive efforts by Senghor and his assistants to explain and justify certain measures, and to offer compensatory gifts, can mitigate a marabu's open or tacit opposition—thus Falilou was brought to support the CAR, which he had once opposed. Thus, too, he even more enthusiastically promoted technical-agricultural innovations which, he had been convinced, would promote the well-being of his disciples as well as the overall revenues of his brotherhood. Neither Falilou nor any of the major marabus was or is concerned about the long-term conflict between agricultural and economic reforms and the marabus' control of their disciples. In part, this is due to the marabus' own blindness or lack of foresightedness; but, more important, their lack of concern may be a realistic appraisal of the power structure in Senegal. The marabus' opposition to all reforms would deprive them of the many and varied advantages they receive from collaborating with the government. Moreover, they probably could not prevent a reform program from being adopted because economic and social reforms are accepted as necessary by all Western-educated Senegalese politicians who control the modern government structure.

What conclusions can be suggested about the impact of the Muslim leaders? On the one hand, the radical Senegalese

The Brotherhoods and Government Reform

accusation that the power of the marabus vitiates the government reform program must be accepted at least in part. But the marabus are not the only factor preventing successful implementation of the plan. Equally and perhaps more important are a combination of other factors which, given the focus of this book on the brotherhoods, have not been discussed here in detail. The difficulties of bringing about social and economic reforms in a traditional society—even in one with no marabus—are legion. For example, meaningful dialogue is almost impossible between a Western-educated politician, who thinks in terms of modernization and industrialization, and the subsistence farmer. Explanations to peasants resulting in widespread acceptance of changes and sacrifices necessary for development are hard for any government leader to achieve. The gap between the Western elite and the peasant is compounded by lack of money with which to build the infrastructure and provide widespread education. In Senegal there is little indigenous capital (aside from that held by the marabus), and the government is dependent on foreign loans that have not been forthcoming in large numbers or amounts. Investment, because of the poor sandy soil and few minerals, has been difficult to attract. Furthermore, myriad corollary problems plague African development programs, Senegal included. The great difficulty of reform and the lack of resources encourage an attitude of semi-irresponsibility on the part of many government officials. This attitude is combined with the necessity of satisfying traditional expectations in terms of jobs and money for the politicians' numerous retainers and relatives, plus the need to live up to traditional status requirements including lavish personal spending.[61] Despite appeals and attempts to discipline party members on the part of leaders such as Senghor, the resultant drain of money and inefficient use of time hampers the government in its activities. Senegalese politicians, like many other African leaders, are attempting to carry out major reforms rapidly with few or no resources in terms of money, natural resources, and trained and disciplined personnel. The notable lack of success of the renowned plan so far it quite understandable without even considering the marabus.

All of the foregoing affects an evaluation of the marabus' role. The Muslim leaders are in fact a resource of a kind, because they do act as intermediaries between the government and the

---

[61]See Ousmane Soce, *Karim* (Paris, 1966).

peasants. To an idealist the use of "feudal lords" who "exploit" their disciples is repugnant.[62] But the marabus definitely are useful instruments in enabling the government to reach people with new ideas. The disciples, because of the marabus, can be brought to accept ideas that the government by itself would have had great difficulty in spreading. Even if the marabus only promote selected features of some innovation or other, their support gives decided assistance to the government. Their opposition slows or hampers the government and must be considered a liability, but, on balance, their aid outweighs their hindrance. The point made by radical Senegalese that collaboration strengthened the marabus and thus defeated a major governmental goal of liberation may be irrelevant, or at least not as significant as other factors. If the only goal of the development program were to free the peasants, then collaboration with the marabus would not make sense; for the Muslim leaders are bolstered and made wealthier by the government. But the Senegalese Plan aims at many things including expanded agricultural production and diversification of crops. The marabus have helped and will help significantly in the attainment of some of these goals.

It is not obvious that an attack on the power of the marabus at this time would be in the best interest of the government. Eventually the government may be in a position to discard the Muslim leaders, but it might as well use them until it is strong enough to attack them and until it has alternative effective ways of disseminating and enforcing its program. Moreover, insofar as the spread of education through both formal schooling and training programs like the CAR's continues and ideas about individual and collective rights and responsibilities are spread, the government is undermining the temporal authority of the marabus. The process is a slow one, but there may be no alternative for the Senegalese to adopt. The government's use of the marabus, though it has definitely helped to build up the marabus, has not resulted in a defeat of the government's overall goals.

Indeed, there is no reason to assume that if the marabus did not exist or were less powerful the reform program of the government would be more rapidly implemented. The policies of more radical states like Guinea have not been so successful as to warrant a

---

[62] The Murids, of course, would resent such a condemnation. They consider their organization voluntary and not at all exploitative. See speech by Al Hajj Dramé for the Murid khalif, *Dakar matin*, Jan. 20, 1966.

conclusion that the Senegalese method of gradual reform using traditional leaders is not viable. The Senegalese government has decided that, given the economic crisis in which the country finds itself and given the persistent loyalty of the peasants for their marabus, the only possible approach is to use the marabus to implement its program; none of the evidence presented here indicates that this approach is necessarily self-defeating.

7 Muslim Opposition to the Brotherhoods

The interests of the brotherhoods of Senegal are focused on that nation and on the prospects which collaboration with its government offers. Individual marabus visit their foreign disciples or pay calls on Muslim and non-Muslim state leaders, but the Senegalese *tariqas* never have been involved after the nineteenth century in an interterritorial Islamic movement of any political importance. Nevertheless, the Islamic reform movements that have shaken various parts of the Muslim world have had echoes, albeit faint ones, in Senegal. The major brotherhoods and their leaders, however, are conservative in their doctrines and practice, which is congruent with their position as part of the "Establishment." Ibrahima Niass may have adopted the crossed-arms position for prayer which is symbolic of the Wahhabi reform group (to be discussed later), but he, like his Senegalese peers, has not accepted the need for major reforms or revisions in the *tariqas*, although their present organization and belief go back to the Middle Ages. The men who have been influenced by ideas of the various reform groups are the young intellectuals who have been sent to North Africa and/or the Middle East to study. Frequently these students are related to the marabus, who habitually send their relatives and disciples out of Senegal to Muslim universities so they will receive solid training in their religion as well as other subjects. Ironically, these students have returned to lead some of the most pointed and bitter campaigns against the brotherhoods.

Two major factors are involved in the Muslim intellectual opposition to the orders. The distortion of the doctrines of Islam allowed by the brotherhoods[1] revolts the young intellectuals, who wish to purify Senegalese Islam and make it conform to the basic tenets of the religion. They wish to force all disciples of the brotherhoods to practice the required Muslim prayers and rituals, relying less heavily on their marabus for spiritual salvation. Indeed, the role of the marabu as anything other than a religious adviser seems to the Muslim intellectuals a major perversion of the faith. Islam traditionally had no priests, and Muhammad never claimed to be more than a human prophet of Allah rather than a sacred being, much less a son of God. Thus the semiworship of the marabus is inconsistent with fundamental principles of Islam. Closely connected to the desire to purify Senegalese Islam is the other,

[1] See Chapter 1, pp. 13–17.

more clearly political factor that motivates the Muslim intellectuals: revulsion against the temporal subjugation of the disciples, which the intellectuals relate to conservatism and stagnation in the political and social system of their country.

The combination of puritan religious reform and political radicalism is not unique to Senegalese Muslim reform groups. It has often been seen, for example, in Middle Eastern movements whose ideas have influenced, both directly and indirectly, the Muslim groups in Senegal. Wahhabism, a puritan reform movement with strong political overtones, began in the eighteenth century in central Arabia. Muhammad ibn Abd al-Wahhab led a campaign against decadence in Islam directed at the worship of saints and other "heretical" innovations by the sufi orders. His movement took on the characteristics of a revitalization movement and was both militant and fanatic; Wahhabis fought to establish an Islamic state conforming to their ideas and even conquered Mecca for a short period in the early nineteenth century. The influence of their ideas outlived their political power and continues to be felt today, especially in Saudi Arabia.[2] Similarly, a reform movement in Egypt was conducted in the end of the nineteenth century by Jamal al-Din al-Afghani, who died in 1897, and his disciple Muhammad Abdu (died 1905). The latter in particular had an important effect on the younger generation of his time, whom he incited against the decadence of the brotherhoods.[3] Another puritanical reform movement followed—the Muslim Brotherhood, important in recent Egyptian politics.[4]

In general, Middle Eastern reform movements have not been directly represented in French-speaking West Africa, though some important exceptions can be named. Wahhabism, for example, was brought to Mali by wealthy Dioula traders returning from Mecca in the late forties. The Dioula used Wahhabi ideas as bases for asserting themselves against established social and ethnic groups which were tied to traditional sufism. The traders took over some of the most important mosques and installed Wahhabi imams; they also sponsored young Wahhabi teachers, who created

[2] Gibb, *Mohammedanism*, p. 128; Marcel Cardaire, *L'Islam et le Terroir Africain*, pp. 73–88.
[3] Gibb, *Mohammedanism*, pp. 134–135.
[4] Marcel Cardaire, *L'Islam et le terroir africain*, pp. 85–88.

schools to teach a reform version of Islam. Nevertheless, the effect of the Dioula Wahhabism on the theory and practice of Islam in Mali was not great. The Dioula were usually uneducated men who did not understand the principles of the Wahhabi movement. They copied the symbolic ritual gestures of certain Wahhabi masters, such as the crossed-arms position at prayer, but they were not interested in a profound widespread reform of the religion.[5]

In Senegal, where there are few Dioula, Wahhabism as a movement has not taken root. Instead, Muslim students have formed Muslim reform associations which are not identified with movements like Wahhabism although they are closer to the ideals of such Middle Eastern reform movements than Dioula Wahhabism was.[6] The Senegalese associations take the form of modern organizations with democratically elected officers. Members are assessed a required membership fee, usually paid annually, and extra contributions are sometimes collected to help individual members in crisis periods. Some groups meet regularly, others sporadically. Some sponsor lectures on Islam or plays (generally skits) with a moral about Muslim life. Many groups publish a newspaper which is distributed to members and nonmembers alike for a small fee that covers the cost of publication. The papers, which often appear irregularly, promote causes favored by the group in articles written by members or like-minded outsiders. Handbills are also issued to announce meetings or lectures or to explain the purposes of the association. Many groups sponsor schools in which the Qu'ran and Arabic, along with the basic tenets of Islam, are taught to both children and adults.

Not all the modern Muslim associations in Senegal are concerned with reforming Islam. Some, like the *dahira*, are directly connected with the brotherhoods, and others are completely absorbed in more limited tasks such as organizing mutual assistance societies or promoting Arabic teaching and state subsidies to teachers of Arabic. Even the groups concerned with reform have sought to cloak their opposition to the brotherhoods behind indirect attacks on the orders and careful indications that leading marabus approve of them.

[5] *Ibid.,* pp. 127–134.
[6] *Ibid.,* p. 135.

Muslim Brotherhoods and Politics in Senegal

The moderation or prudence of the reform groups is due to their desire to reach the average rural Senegalese, who are controlled by the marabus and will not understand a frontal attack on the brotherhood system of which they are members. The degree of moderation, however, varies from group to group and also has varied over the last thirty years. There is, in fact, a direct correlation between increasing open attacks on the brotherhoods and the growth of nationalism in Senegal.

The Muslim Fraternity

Not surprisingly, the oldest and best-known Muslim reform association, the Muslim Fraternity, was quite mild in the reforms it proposed in the pre-World War II period and quite restrained in its criticisms of the government and of the brotherhoods. The group was founded in 1935 and was led for many years by Abdel Kader Diagne.[7] The overall goals of the group announced after the war included substantial reforms, such as: 1) reform of Senegalese education to include Muslim ideas and Arabic, 2) reform of the brotherhoods, 3) opposition to the activity of Christian missions, and 4) rejection of the civilization and culture of the West.[8] But in the pre-1945 period the Fraternity was polite and circumspect in its dealings with both the tariqas and the colonial administration: one Fraternity official publicly characterized the French authorities as "you, the French government, the most benevolent and human of government, who takes the place of father and mother for us. . . ."[9] The major issues with which the group was identified at this time were relatively moderate and involved such matters as the exorbitantly high price of brides that prevailed then and still does in Senegalese urban areas.[10] Other examples can be taken from the 1937 Fraternity request that Muslim notables be used as advisors for the national mosque proposed by the French, and that the Service des Affaires Musulmanes, which had been dissolved years before,

[7] DA, Abdel Kader Diagne to Governor General (Nov. 18, 1936), 19G 38 (108) FM.
[8] J. C. Froelich, "Archaisme et modernisme; les Musulmans noirs et le progrès," Cahiers de l'ISEA, ser. 5 (December, 1961), p. 78.
[9] DA, Speech by Thierno Boubakar Ben Omar Hadj on the occasion of the arrival in St. Louis of the Minister of Colonies and the Governor General, 1936, 19G 38 (108) FM.
[10] DA, Diagne to Governor General (Dec. 4, 1936) and attached clippings and letters, 19G 38 (108) FM.

be recreated so that the French could have closer contact with the needs and desires of Muslims.[11]

None of the publicly supported Fraternity causes appeared to threaten the government; but the French distrusted the group because they feared ties with pan-Islamic, anticolonial North African associations. The Governor General refused to sponsor the Fraternity[12] and did not respond favorably to various requests for help in its several campaigns. Thus the proposed list of Muslim notables as advisors for the mosque was rejected; and the government, on grounds that it could not interfere in religious matters, refused to help reform marriage ceremonies, divorce proceedings, and other rituals that the Fraternity felt were not being conducted according to the laws of Islam.[13] The Fraternity did not openly ally itself with North African radicals, although it did have contacts with Senegalese politicians of whom the French government were unsure, such as Lamine Gueye.[14] Despite its relative moderation, the organization was kept under close surveillance.

The UCM

In the post-World War II period, the political climate in Senegal changed fundamentally. Throughout Africa a burst of national feeling became more and more evident and led to the liberation of French-speaking Africa within fifteen years. Simultaneously, the French relaxed their control of the areas they governed. Rights of free association were granted by the administrators, who tolerated increasingly radical demands by political groups forming in this era. In Senegal, as elsewhere, African politicians began to assert openly their demands that Africans be respected and given a significant role in their government in conformity with the democratic principles which the French, in theory, always had espoused. Muslim reform groups were affected by the spread of national feeling. They associated themselves with anticolonialism and also with attacks

[11] DA, Diagne to Governor General (Nov. 6, 1939), 19G 38 (108) FM.
[12] DA, Governor General to President of the Muslim Fraternity (Nov. 26, 1936), 19G 38 (108) FM.
[13] DA, Diagne to Governor General (May 24, 1937), and Governor General to Diagne (June 3, 1937), 19G 38 (108) FM. See also *Islam AOF,* journal of the Fraternity, esp. 1938–1940.
[14] DA, Diagne to Lamine Gueye (May 7, 1940); Director of Political and Administrative Affairs, "Report" (May 16, 1940), no. 1163 AP/2, 19G 38 (108) FM.

161

on the brotherhoods, which were so closely identified with
the colonial system. In the postwar period, however, the most
important reform group was not the Fraternity, although it,
too, became more openly radical; a new association called
the Union Culturelle Musulmane (UCM) was founded in 1953
and became the leading Senegalese Muslim reform group.

The UCM published a newspaper called Le Réveil islamique,
which stated its aims as the following: 1) to clarify Muslim
practices for the masses, 2) to answer questions about Islam,
3) to publish educational articles, and 4) to defend Islam against
attack.[15] In reality, the newspaper spearheaded a protest
movement against what the UCM considered to be the
anti-Muslim attitude of the French and the corruption and
distortion of Islam by the brotherhoods. The attack against
the French was conducted openly in Le Réveil. Cheikh Touré,
president of the association, condemned the colonial rulers
for trying to destroy the Qu'ranic schools, sponsoring Catholic
but not Muslim schools, exiling and imprisoning Muslim leaders,
and trying to divide the Muslim movement in Senegal against
itself.[16] Cheikh M'Backé added to the list of complaints against
the French by accusing them of opposing the evolution of
Islam and spreading rumors about the anti-French and
pro-Communist activities of students studying in Cairo and
North Africa.[17] The list of accusations was lengthened in a
Réveil article written by leaders of another reform organization, the
Association Musulmane des Etudiants d'Afrique Noire (AMEAN).
AMEAN deplored the existence of the Bureau des Affaires
Musulmanes—in striking, though logical, contrast to the
Fraternity demands of seventeen years before that the Service
be recreated—because the Bureau supposedly divided Senegalese
Muslims, spied on them, corrupted religious leaders, prevented
pilgrimages to Mecca, and tried to isolate Senegalese Muslims
from the rest of the world. Furthermore, AMEAN expressed
regret at French involvement in Muslim concerns such as the
appointment of qadis, called for the teaching of Arabic in
primary and secondary schools, demanded the recognition
of existing private Arabic schools, and condemned the

[15] Kandji Saliou, "Editorial," Réveil islamique, no. 1 (December, 1953).
[16] Cheick Touré, "L'Islam aoefien et le colonialisme," ibid., no. 7 (June, 1954).
[17] El Hadj Cheick Amadou M'Backé, "Avant qu'il ne soit trop tard," ibid.,
no. 17 (June, 1956).

appearance of non-Muslim administrators at Muslim festivals on the grounds that infidels profaned the religious character of such ceremonies.[18] The latter point could again be contrasted to the Fraternity's praise of Governor General de Coppet for appearing at Tabaski.[19]

The UCM was much more restrained in its attacks on the brotherhoods than in its diatribes against the French because its leaders still recognized the advantages to be gained from associating with some of the marabus. But the marabus' authority was called into question in thinly disguised critical articles in the *Réveil*. Oumar Dieng, the secretary general, tactfully wrote that the UCM did not oppose "real" marabus, who naturally must approve of the UCM since it was attempting to unify Islam, spread the knowledge of Arabic, and fight fanaticism and charlatanism.[20] More striking, however, were the series of moral tales about "Dial," a UCM member, and his friends, which Dial's actions point out features of the brotherhoods that the UCM condemned. One story shows how children in marabutic Qu'ranic schools learn the Qu'ran incorrectly; criticizes the traditional marks of respect for a marabu, such as kneeling in his presence; and questions the right of the marabus to contributions from their disciples. The story also condemns the political involvement of the Muslim leaders and includes the following uncompromising description of a marabu:

This great religious chief [is a] specialist in political and administrative interventions, whether to give a political mandate to a candidate without renown, or to make those faithful to him accede to different administrative cadres. . . . Very often, [he does these things] to the detriment of worthy men whose only flaw was to have marabus who prefer to teach the precepts of the religion rather than interfere in matters which demand a different competence.[21]

In another story, a marabu is condemned for taking advantage of his disciples' ignorance. He is described sarcastically as

---

[18] "Manifeste de l'Association Musulmane des Etudiants d'Afrique noire," *ibid.* (October, 1957).

[19] DA, Diagne to Governor General (Feb. 25, 1937) and Governor General to Diagne (Mar. 3, 1937), 19G 38 (108) FM.

[20] Oumar Dieng, "Union Culturelle Musulmane," *Réveil islamique*, no. 1 (December, 1953).

[21] Oumar Dieng, "Chez Serigne Dame," *ibid.*, no. 3 (February, 1954).

blessing his followers by spitting saliva "with all its microbes" on the hands of his followers.[22] (Traditionally, the saliva of Muslim holy men is believed to contain holy power from the marabus, who consequently do, at least symbolically, spit on their followers.)

Despite the critical attitude of the UCM toward the brotherhoods, some marabus allied themselves with the group. Abdul Aziz Sy, Ibrahima Niass, and Cheikh M'Backé at different periods supported it. Niass' support can be partly explained by his interest in reform,[23] though the main reason for his connection with the UCM, which also explains the association of Abdul Aziz and Cheikh M'Backé, was the opposition of the UCM to the UPS. In the fifties all three of these marabus were at odds with Senghor and his allies and were looking for political associations to balance the UPS. The UCM, with its anti-French orientation, was opposed to the relatively conservative UPS and therefore attractive to the rebellious marabus.[24] Most marabus, however, either ignored the UCM or condemned it for its dangerous influence, and the French also condemned it. Officials had feared possible ties between pan-Islamic groups and the Fraternity; now they could be sure that the UCM had such contacts and that the group opposed colonial rule. Consequently they closed the Arabic schools that the UCM opened, refused most of the group's requests, and kept UCM members under surveillance. But in line with the more liberal political climate, the administration did not jail the UCM leaders or ban the organization, which continued to conduct its campaigns quite freely up to independence.

Oddly enough, when the Senegalese took over the government the UCM suddenly dropped its leadership of the radical Muslim movement. No *Réveil* appeared between 1958 and 1962, and in 1962 an editorial explained that anticolonialism had been the basis for the old publication but that no need for such a campaign existed in independent Senegal. The UCM would still sponsor Arabic schools (including twenty-eight for all of Senegal in 1962) and would send, as it had already done, many

[22] Moustapha Sy, "Cheikh Abdou Djabar," *ibid.*, no. 13 (May, 1955).
[23] Cardaire, *L'Islam et le terroir africain*, pp. 148–149.
[24] Evidence of the three marabus' support for the UCM is their attendance at UCM meetings, their contributions of money and articles to the *Réveil*, and the favorable manner in which other *Réveil* articles refer to them. See hand bill, July 1, 1956, Imp. Diop D. L. 746, and "Grand Meeting d'information," *Réveil islamique* (June, 1956).

students to North Africa for higher studies, but reform campaigns were no longer as necessary.[25] The UCM leaders had decided that collaboration with the government was the best policy. They pointed out publicly that Senegalese officials were not opposed to Islam as were the French; thus the government of independent Senegal gave subsidies to teachers of Arabic, offered Arabic in secular schools, and opened a Muslim institute at the university. In addition, the Arabic schools started by Muslim intellectuals were no longer prohibited and extra vacation days were granted to school children for Muslim holidays. In reality, however, the policy of the Senegalese government toward the Muslim community is not much different from that of the French. The state is secular, and none of the concessions to Islam have been very profound. The explanation for the cessation of activity of the UCM has to be sought outside the public statements of its leaders. The obvious explanation that comes to mind, that the UCM leaders were older and more "reasonable" in 1959 and, therefore, willing to be "bought" by jobs in the administration, may be the correct one. J. C. Froelich wrote: "The UCM appears to be satisfied with official favors and the lucrative or honorific posts which the government has given to its leading members."[26]

UCM leaders themselves, of course, do not accept that interpretation. Privately they insist that the Senegalese government is, in fact, stricter than the French were with the UCM. The French could afford to let the Muslim radicals criticize them and their marabu allies; indeed, the French played off the reform groups against the brotherhoods. In contrast, the Senegalese government is under more pressure from the marabus to prevent attacks on the brotherhoods and less secure in its own position. Thus, it feels forced to limit severely radical groups like the UCM, whose leaders, consequently, have decided on collaboration that allows them to fulfill certain goals (such as teaching Arabic) rather than opposition, which would result in there being no activity permitted at all.[27]

Both explanations probably are true, which would explain why

---

[25] "Editorial" and Fall Assan, "Nos Activités," *Réveil islamique*, no. 9 (August, 1962).

[26] Froelich, "Le Reformisme et l'Islam en Afrique noire de l.ouest," *Revue de défense nationale*, 17 (January, 1961), 83–89. See also Marcel Cardaire, "Quelques Aspects de l'Islamisation sénégalais," *Academie des sciences d'outre-mer*, 17 (June 15, 1962), 259.

[27] Interviews with UCM leaders, Dec. 2, 1965, Mar. 2, 1966, Dakar.

the leaders of AMEAN, which remained strongly critical of the UPS and the marabus,[28] were much more moderate in their public attacks after independence than they had been before. *Vers l'Islam*, the AMEAN publication, had condemned the marabus for supporting the French, for making themselves into saints, and for using their position to extort money.[29] After independence, however, the organization restricted itself mainly to supporting conferences and lectures that taught a "pure" form of Islam but only indirectly attacked the brotherhoods. Publication of handbills or newspapers criticizing the government or the *tariqas* was almost completely discontinued.

The Federation

AMEAN is an organization for students and was not in a position to replace the UCM as leader of the Muslim reform movement in Senegal. Instead, the leading position was filled by the Fédération Nationale des Associations Culturelles Musulmanes du Sénégal, founded in 1962. The Federation is a union of modern Muslim associations ranging from Ansourdine, which is a *dahiratu*, to the UCM.[30] The diverse nature of the member groups, plus the more restrictive attitude of the government, seems to ensure that the Federation will stick to moderate demands such as increased educational facilities, scholarships for students in the Middle East, and other uncontroversial matters. Its stated aims are mild and include "the amelioration of the moral, social and material conditions of the Muslims."[31] The organization, through its president, Abdul Aziz Sy (a brother of Cheikh Tidjane Sy and a nephew of the khalif Abdul Aziz), has criticized the division of Islam in Senegal into sects and the general ignorance of Senegalese Muslims. Abdul Aziz also has demanded the religious education of all Muslims in Senegal to the point where their worship of

[28] From a talk by Ly Ciré, then an official of AMEAN, that I attended in Dakar in July, 1960, in which he was heavily critical of the marabus.
[29] "Lutte, anti-islamique en Afrique noire," *Vers l'Islam* (January, 1956) and Diallo Modibo, "Islam aoefien et évolution politique," *ibid.* (June, 1957).
[30] For a complete list see Moustapha Cissé, "Les Echos de la Fédération," *L'Afrique musulmane* (October, 1965).
[31] *Ibid.*

Muslim Opposition to the Brotherhoods

Allah would not require intermediaries such as the marabus.[32]
The latter phrase could be interpreted as an attack on the
marabus, but most of the Federation articles are more innocuous.
For example, Oumar Dieng, a UCM officer and Federation
leader, called for the formation of a Muslim Red Cross, to be
called the Secours Musulman, and asked for the involvement of
mosques in such civil matters as the registration of births, deaths,
and marriages.[33]

Federation leaders claimed in 1966 that, in its few years of
existence, their organization had a number of important
accomplishments to its credit. It had managed to unite widely
diverse groups and attract, at least initially, substantial monetary
support for its educational and cultural programs, specifically
for a large cultural center in Dakar. President Senghor himself
gave 2,000,000 CFA to leaders of the Federation for travel
in the Middle East and North Africa. On the trip they were
received by major Muslim leaders like King Faisal and President
Bourguiba, all of whom donated or promised donations of large
amounts of money. In all, the Federation collected 42,470,000 CFA
and was promised 5,000,000 more together with materials
and artisans for their center. Prior to the trip the governments
of Algeria and Libya had given 12,000,000 CFA and President
Senghor another 4,000,000. Marabutic support had been
forthcoming, too: 250,000 CFA from Cheikh Tidjane Sy and
100,000 from Cheikh M'Backé. The khalif Abdul Aziz announced
himself represented in the group through his nephew, the
president; Falilou named one of the assistant secretaries
general of the Federation as his delegate; and Ibrahima Niass' son,
a vice-president, was named his representative.[34] The Federation
also claimed that it had succeeded in persuading the
government to open a Franco-Arabic school, obtained
scholarships for students to go to Muslim countries, and
managed to have religious education introduced in public
schools. Moreover, Arabic schools run by associations in the
Federation numbered 1,500 by the end of 1965.[35]

---

[32] Abdoul Aziz Sy, "L'Islam et les Musulmans sénégalais," *L'Afrique musulmane* (October, 1965).

[33] Oumar Dieng, "L'Action sociale de la Fédération," *L'Afrique musulmane* (October, 1965).

[34] Cissé, "Les Echos de la Fédération."

[35] Oumar Dia, "L'Action culturelle et éducative de la Fédération," *L'Afrique musulmane* (November, 1965).

But the action of the Federation has been hampered by two problems which threaten to destroy or split the group.
One major difficulty arose from the government's distrust of the motives of Federation leaders. Senghor did grant subsidies to the group, although this may be interpreted as an attempt to control it; but by early 1966 government officials were openly expressing doubt about the group and proposing to form another Muslim organization called the Regroupement National des Enseignants et Etudiants d'Arabe—UPS. The Regroupement would help provide Arabic teaching, find work for the Arabists who have not found positions—many students returning from North Africa or the Middle East cannot find work—and provide official delegates to the world Muslim meetings.[36] Thus, despite the mildness of the Federation's proposals in general, it has been viewed by the authorities as radical in the same sense the UCM had been. The specter of a unified radical Muslim opposition frightened some Senegalese officials, who were aware of contacts between some Federation leaders and PAI and Pan-Arabic groups. Consequently, the Federation has been kept under close surveillance and its programs have not been given full cooperation from the government. Federation leaders cite as an example their plan to build a large cultural center on land purchased on Avenue Gambetta in Dakar,[37] which the governor of Cap Vert refused to expedite by never giving the necessary orders to remove the squatters whose huts fill the proposed site. The matter went to court but became bogged down in technicalities. The Federation had planned to have President Bourguiba inaugurate the Center in 1965 but could not do so because of the squatter issue. In desperation the group bought another piece of land across the street from their original purchase, but the same difficulties arose and the Federation was unable to get construction underway.[38]

The mistrust of the government for the Federation is reinforced by the second problem that has plagued the group, bitter disagreements dividing the leadership. Some leaders, indeed, have accused others of being spies of the government and of reporting all that the Federation heads have said to the authorities, even going so far as to make up stories that cast a bad name on the Federation. These spy-leaders, for example,

[36] Interviews with Tahirou Doukouré, Jan. 7, Jan. 11, 1966, Dakar.
[37] Cissé, "Les Echos de la Fédération."
[38] Interview with leaders of the Federation, Feb. 16, 1966, Dakar.

supposedly told the government that the Federation planned
to train anti-UPS commandos in its new center. As a result
the Council of Ministers voted to outlaw the Federation, but
other Federation leaders forestalled this motion by exposing the
falsity of the accusation. Nevertheless, the spy-leaders have
managed to give the government officials a very negative
impression of the Federation that has contributed to the
government's reluctance to assist the organization.[39]

The leaders suspected of spying maintained in 1966 that the
Federation was falling apart because of mismanagement by the
other directors. The "spy" leaders accused the latter of using
money received for the Federation for themselves and of not
allowing the member associations to have any part in running the
Federation. One leader in particular was singled out for having
taken Federation money, and the accusation was substantiated
by a letter and a list of recent lavish expenditures made by the
accused.[40] The leaders accused of taking money, of course,
indignantly denied that any of them had done so,[41] just as
those accused of spying denied that charge. Whatever the truth
of either story, the Federation leadership clearly was divided and
the future of the group was therefore uncertain. As a result of the
internal disagreements no issues of its journal, *Afrique Musulmane,*
appeared for several months after the first three issues (October,
November, December, 1965) and an all-Federation meeting
scheduled for February was hastily canceled at the last minute.[42]
Unless Federation leaders are able to overcome their suspicion of
each other—which they had not done by early 1968—the group,
under heavy pressure from the government, will be dissolved or,
perhaps, will remain in existence but only as an ineffectual body
of quarreling Muslim intellectuals.

Evaluation of the Reform Groups

The weakness of the Federation raised questions about the
significance of this or any of the reform groups. The Federation
did manage to unite a wide variety of Muslim associations, but
what effect did it have on the disciples or the leaders of the
tariqas or the political position of the brotherhoods? The answer

[39] *Ibid.*
[40] Interviews with other Federation leaders, Jan. 11, Feb. 17, Mar. 1, 1966, Dakar.
[41] Interviews with Federation leaders, Feb. 16, Mar. 2, 1966, Dakar.
[42] Interview with Federation leaders, Mar. 1, 1966, Dakar.

seems to be that these groups have had very little influence outside of the restricted circle of Muslim intellectuals in Senegal. From the preindependence period to the present the intellectuals have been ones who have given time and money to the organizations, read their newspapers, and supported their causes. Marabus have associated themselves with the groups because it was politically expedient to do so or because association with a group supporting the purification and extension of Islam seemed symbolically "right" despite the implied or open criticism of the brotherhoods. None of the major marabus has been seriously involved in the groups' reform campaigns; and in rural Senegal the peasants do not know of the reform groups and have not been noticeably affected by them. Nor have the groups been able to change the pattern of collaboration between the government and the brotherhoods, although the UCM, at least, strongly attacked the political involvement of the marabus.

The most that can be said for the reform groups in regard to their effect on Senegalese Muslims generally is that they have expanded the systematic teaching of Arabic in Senegal and they gradually are spreading knowledge of the Qu'ran to a wider group of people. Over time the building of a group of Muslims educated in their religion and in Arabic will affect the brotherhoods and especially the authority of the marabus. But, clearly, this process will take many years. Moreover, the extension of Western secular education and technical training is more rapid and widespread in Senegal because it is government supported. Western education is more significant in the changing pattern of Senegalese politics than the education offered by Muslim reform groups. All the same, reform groups can be expected to remain in existence and probably multiply, for they are the only means through which religious intellectuals can defend and promote their religion. These men have accepted the basic Western goals of material and social reform along democratic lines; but, like their counterparts in Muslim countries throughout the world, they insist that Islam is not incompatible with modern reforms.[43] Many scholars in the West deny that

---

[43] This view has not always been accepted by Western scholars, though currently most of the latter do not assert that Islam is inherently incompatible with modernization. See Jacques Austruy, *L'Islam face au développement économique*, vol. III: *Economie et civilisation* (Paris, 1961); Froelich, "Archaisme et modernisme;" Pierre Marthelot, "L'Islam et le développement," *Archives de sociologie des religions*, 14 (1962), 131–138; and Vincent Monteil, "Islam et développement au Sénégal," *Cahiers de l'ISEA*, ser. 5 (December, 1961), 44–68.

Muslim Opposition to the Brotherhoods

contention and predict the end of organized religion because of industrialization and modernization,[44] but to Muslim intellectuals this is a false view. For them Islam, purified and reformed, can give a badly needed focus to modern Senegal. Thus, Muslim reform groups will not only continue their efforts but may, in the long run, provide an alternative type of Islam for disciples who are in the process of rejecting the authority structure of the *tariqas*. As a motivating factor for political (and social and economic) changes these groups are not very important; however, in terms of their own religious aims they do have a role to play in the future.

[44] See Wallace, *Religion*, pp. 264–270.

Conclusion

Relations between the government and the marabus in Senegal change constantly, depending on various factors. The importance of issues in question, the relative stability or unity of the government in a particular period, and the strength of the specific marabus involved, within and without their brotherhood, are only a few of the points that must be considered when analyzing a particular situation in which the marabus conflict with or provide support for the politicians; and many other factors can arise to distort or shift the balance. A prolonged economic crisis or an unexpected coup that removed or seriously threatened the present political leaders could place the marabus in a stronger, or a weaker, position. Thus, too, the death of important marabus, many of whom are now quite old, could change the pattern of political pressure altogether. For example, early in 1966 Falilou M'Backé obviously was becoming feeble and his death was imminent. In summer 1966 his heir apparent, Bassiru, the third eldest son of of Ahmad Bamba, died, leaving an almost unknown successor—the next brother, Abdullahi (Abdu Lahat). Many observers expected that Cheikh M'Backé would renew his claims to the khalifat with a much greater chance of success than he had when his more powerful uncle Bassiru was alive. His claims could have split the Muridiyya, for although he is the most powerful Murid marabu aside from Falilou, many Murid leaders would not have wanted to see him become khalif.

Instead, however, when Falilou died on August 7, 1968, he was succeeded by Abdullahi, whose candidature had apparently been agreed upon by the other leading Murids.[1] Should Cheikh M'Backé have become khalif he might have been almost as powerful as Falilou, for he is a consummate politician and well acquainted with the power structure within Senegal. But he might not have equaled Falilou, and certainly any Murid khalif other than Cheikh M'Backé will be less powerful than Falilou was. Falilou's position was cemented by ties with Senghor when the UPS was trying to rise to power in Senegal. At present UPS politicians are relatively stronger than they were in the late forties. The new Murid khalif Abdullahi, who is in the position of trying to stabilize his own authority, may not be able to demand as much from the government as Falilou could and did. The Tijani marabus may gain in political power as a result of Falilou's death; equally possible, however, is the overall

[1] I am indebted to Donald Cruise O'Brien for information on events in the summer of 1968.

173

diminuation in political power for all marabus as the old
Muslim leaders die.

Another factor that may eventually affect the brotherhoods'
power is the adherence of the PRA-Senegal to the UPS.
On the surface PRA leaders appear to have given up their
radical demands for the reform of Senegal. They have accepted
positions in a government that has not changed its major goals
and policies. Still, some observers suggest that the PRA leaders
provide a core of men which stiffens the reforming tendencies
and counteracts the conservative leaders in the UPS. This core
may be a challenge to Senghor and also may threaten the
marabus, whose cooperation with the government may be
correspondingly devaluated.[2] In early 1968 the situation did not
appear to have changed in any major way because of the
PRA-UPS merger, but the possibilities of such a change have to be
considered.

The future position of the marabus, then, cannot be
accurately predicted. Present relations between them and the
politicians can be examined and explained, but prognostications
on any but a very general level must be avoided. It can be
safely said, though, that, barring any major coup or crisis, the
present pattern of relations will continue in the short run.
Moreover, it seems that an overall weakening of the marabus
politically can be expected in the long run, for, insofar as the
reform program of the government is spread, especially that
involving Western education, the marabus will lose temporal
authority. Exactly how this will occur or the effect it will have on
Senegalese politics is hard to foretell. The early naive assumptions
by African reformers and Western observers about political
developments in Africa have not been borne out by events of the
last few years. Early predictions about political development were
far too optimistic, and, unfortunately, the result of undue
optimism has been widespread disillusionment—and, in some
countries, the replacement of "democratic" governments
through military coups. African nationalism in the postwar
period was a combination of reaction against the colonialists
and their insistence on European superiority, and desire for social,
political, and economic development.[3] Once liberation had been

---

[2] This suggestion was put forward by numerous Senegalese students studying in the
United States, whom I interviewed in August, 1967.

[3] See John Kautsky, "An Essay in the Politics of Development," in Kautsky, ed.,
Political Change in Underdeveloped Countries: Nationalism and Communism
(New York, 1962), pp. 13–119.

achieved (or at least achieved inasmuch as economically
dependent countries can be liberated), Africans discovered
that the goals of economic and social reforms sometimes
conflict with each other and frequently challenge or threaten the
stability of the new governments.[4] Thus, on the one hand
peasants had been promised improved living conditions and
emancipation, while on the other sacrifices were demanded of
them in the name of economic progress: consequently the
peasants neither understood nor cooperated with many of the
government programs.

Various methods have been suggested for transforming the
African situation, varying from radical efforts to reform socially
and economically immediately no matter what the cost,
to the Senegalese method of gradual reform using traditional
leaders as intermediaries while attempting to build up support
for the Western government and its program. None of these
methods has had sufficient time for vindication. Idealistically,
like many other Western observers I am attracted to the more
dynamic ideas of such a leader as Julius Nyerere, who calls for the
immediate implementation of socialism.[5] But I recognize that the
Senegalese method should be given consideration as a feasible
means of reform, given the enormous difficulties which African
governments face; it is a method that may prove itself the only
workable one for Senegal and for many other African countries.
It is conceivable that the eventual weakening of the marabus
could be a negative factor for political development in Senegal
unless major changes take place in the social and economic
structure of the country and substitute leaders are found who can
communicate with and organize the peasants. Such a conclusion
is heresy to the radical Senegalese nationalist but seems to be
reasonable deduction from the facts presented in this book.

Possibly, also, the marabus could maintain their political power
in the long run; but this seems unlikely unless attempts to
implement the governmental reform program, or similar reform
plans, are abandoned altogether. On the off chance that the
marabus might maintain (or strengthen) their authority, the
status quo would not necessarily continue. The marabus,
particularly those enterprising and business-minded men like
Cheikh M'Backé, might expand their role as entrepreneurs in the

---

[4] See Samuel P. Huntington, "Political Development and Political Decay," *World Politics*,
17 no. 3 (1965), 386–430.

[5] See Julius K. Nyerere, *Freedom and Unity* (London, 1967).

growing industries of Senegal. Their dominant position in industry as well as agriculture could reinforce their authority over the disciples and permit a loosening of certain other aspects of the follower-leader bond: for example, the supernatural aspects of the marabus' position might be de-emphasized, although they would still be the spiritual and political guides for their disciples. Indeed, in the above circumstances, the religious reforms demanded by the Muslim reformist groups like the Federation could be permitted and even encouraged by the marabus without their losing political importance. Nevertheless, this chain of events seems unlikely, largely because elsewhere, under the impact of modernization, religious leaders have lost and are losing their authority; evidence of a countertrend in Senegal does not seem to exist.

The Senegalese experience with brotherhoods is unique. A specific combination of historical events and conditions in Senegal has made it possible for the brotherhoods to assume their present role. These events and conditions have not been reproduced identically in any other country, yet generally applicable relevant factors can be isolated from the Senegalese case and examined in other contexts. Briefly: the first factor drawn from the Senegalese experience is that brotherhoods (or other religious groups) are more likely to become politically powerful if they act at first as revitalization movements—among the Tukulor, in contrast to the Wolof, the brotherhoods did not act as revitalization movements and the marabus never replaced the clan leaders as political leaders. In addition, the greatest dynamism of a religious revitalization movement comes in the period in which it is trying to establish itself: it therefore becomes conservative later and may not exert as powerful a force of attraction to uncommitted citizens or as powerful control over its members. In Senegal, the brotherhoods in the later stages of revitalization maintained their political authority because the leaders were able to adapt to the forces of change around them. They became major economic leaders and intermediaries for reform programs and thus facilitated the adjustment of their disciples to modernization. This remarkable flexibility or adaptability may be seen as the second point to consider, the presence or absence of which profoundly affects the political position of the religious leaders involved. In contrast to Senegal, North African brotherhoods apparently have not been so flexible. In Algeria, for example, the tariqas were extremely powerful political forces, especially in rural areas, in the eighteenth and nineteenth centuries, but today they have

relatively little power and seem to be stagnant. Algerian brotherhoods seem not to have acted as vehicles facilitating the
adaptation of their members to changes brought by
Westernization.[6]

A third factor to consider is the relationship between colonial
rulers and leaders of the brotherhoods. The French were not the
only colonial power to use religious leaders as intermediaries—
a policy they pursued in many places other than Senegal.
The British decision to use a form of indirect rule in northern
Nigeria, for example, caused them to collaborate with Muslim
lords in the area and helped maintain those lords in power.
In contrast, Gambia may provide an example in which British
colonial authorities avoided using the marabus and building up
their power, despite large membership in the *tariqas;* as a
consequence, Gambian marabus appear to have less of a political
role today than do their counterparts in Senegal.[7] Collaboration
with colonial rulers can also be a reason for loss of political
authority by the brotherhoods if a strong and popular anticolonial
movement takes place—a fourth factor.[8] Such a movement has
not taken place in Senegal, but in other countries bitter and long
drawn-out anticolonial struggles have severely discredited
brotherhoods. The best example of this may be Algeria, where the
brotherhoods' rapid political decline appears related to the
association of the *tariqas* with the French.[9]

The fifth point, related to both the first and second, is the
deceptively obvious matter of the dynamism, or the lack thereof,
of individual religious leaders in a specific country. Leaders of
revitalization movements who have been flexible in tactics and
interests are more likely to be aggressive and forceful and
therefore politically important than retiring ascetics concerned
with meditation. This fact cannot be overemphasized. One has
only to compare such marabus as Ahmad Bamba or his son
Falilou, or Ibrahima Niass, to their less well-known relatives. Niass,
for example, built his branch of the Tijaniyya to its present
position because of his forcefulness of character, intelligence,

[6]Rinn, *Marabouts et Khouan*, and L. P. Fauque, "Où en est l'Islam traditionnel en Algérie?"
L'Afrique et l'Asie, no. 55 (1961), 17–22.
[7]Interviews with representatives of a major marabu and leader of the Gambian
parliament, Feb. 6, 1966, Bathurst.
[8]If a brotherhood had not established a cooperative relationship with the colonial
authorities, then a strong anticolonial movement could work to its advantage. This seems
to have been the case of the Hamalliyya in Mali, whose cause was espoused by the Union
Soudanaise.
[9]See Fauque, "Où en est l'Islam," pp. 17–22.

dynamism, and pragmatism. His envious brothers have never been able to emulate his achievements. Equally obvious and equally important is the sixth factor, involving the location and size of membership of a religious group for that group's political position in a particular country. When only a small ethnic group is affiliated with a brotherhood, or when powerful *tariqas* are located in only one region of a country, it is then possible for modern politicians to ignore the demands of the group leaders except in very local matters. In Senegal, the largest ethnic group and economically the most significant part of the population belong to the brotherhoods, whose leaders therefore cannot be ignored. The same is true, but on an even more extended scale, of Mauritania, where brotherhood leaders have a decidedly powerful role in politics.[10] In contrast, in Guinea the major marabus are concentrated in the central and northern sections of the country and have been displaced from national politics;[11] this was a difficult maneuver for politicians in Guinea, but even they could not have carried out such tactics in Mauritania.

A final point to consider is the presence or absence of strong modernizing Muslim associations or Muslim leaders and scholars not affiliated with the brotherhoods (or equivalent groups where other religious movements can be examined). In Senegal, despite the existence of *qadis* and others not affiliated to the brotherhoods, almost everyone belongs to a *tariqa.* There is no powerful independent group of Muslims to criticize the brotherhoods, and the reformist Muslim associations, made up of intellectuals who have broken away from the brotherhoods, have little influence. But in other countries such antibrotherhood Muslims play an important part in balancing or undermining the *tariqas,* as they seem to have done in Algeria.[12]

These seven factors can be taken as variables that determine whether or not the leaders of Muslim brotherhoods or other religious groups have a significant voice in the politics of their countries. They are not the only possible variables to isolate from the Senegalese case, but they seem to be the most important ones. Certain of them are not applicable in some countries, but in many

[10]Interviews with government officials, March, 1966, Nouakchott.

[11]For a description of the chiefs' removal from official government positions there (a good indication of Touré's methods with the marabus), see Sekou Touré, *Guinée: prélude à l'indépendence* (Paris, 1959), and Morgenthau, *Political Parties in French-Speaking West Africa,* pp. 219-254.

[12]Fauque, "Où en est l'Islam," pp. 17-22.

Conclusion

places the variables are inter-related and taken together may explain the political position of the Senegalese and other African brotherhoods and religious groups.

In addition, the role of the Senegalese marabus can be compared to that of other religious leaders on a very specific level. The same series of questions asked in this book about the relations between religious leaders and party and state officials will indicate reasons for differences and similarities between Senegal and other countries. Simple structural comparisons about the inclusion or absence of the religious group and its aims in the avowed goals and explicit organization of the government and of the political parties must be considered. Answers to such questions as how often the president or ministers consult with religious leaders, or how much of the volume of political requests is channeled through religious leaders in contrast to government officials, can also be seen as indicators of political authority. And, family and social ties between the governmental and religious leadership can be examined to see how closely the political and religious elite are interwoven. Moreover, cases of conflicting governmental and religious interests can be analyzed to identify the motivating factor in the final outcome. Specific comparisons like these are perhaps more difficult to accurately determine than the larger factors mentioned above, but they form the core of any adequate understanding of the political role of a particular religious or traditional group in a given country.

In conclusion, I would emphasize that the role of the Senegalese brotherhoods cannot be taken out of the Senegalese context as evidence of a political situation elsewhere. Indeed, taking the brotherhoods out of context even in Senegal is a danger to avoid. Too much emphasis on the *tariqas* and too little consideration of other factors is as misleading to an understanding of Senegal as is ignorance of the role of the marabus. Exterior and interior matters having nothing to do with the brotherhoods, for example, the significant role of the French even today, also shape the course of politics in Senegal. Aid from the French government in the form of loans in money, material, and personnel is still essential to the Senegalese government; French businesses, the heads of which control the powerful Senegalese Chamber of Commerce, cannot be ignored by politicians. Senegalese political leaders still attempt to satisfy demands by French authorities in order to maintain good French-Senegalese relations. French demands that oppose the interest of the brotherhoods are granted at times—the dismissal of Médoune Fall as ambassador to France may be a case in point.[13] Thus, too, the economic and administrative problems discussed in Chapter 6 influence politics. And of course such general factors as international events or currents of opinion have great significance in daily politics here as elsewhere. Obviously the spread of African nationalism, the "winds of change," brought about major developments in Senegal which the marabus neither understood nor controlled. But the brotherhoods still should be seen as a key factor in Senegalese politics; other factors are important, but none is as pivotal and as little understood generally as is the role of the *tariqas*.

[13] See Chapter 5, p. 112. Fall, whose appointment was promoted by Falilou, was dismissed under pressure from the French; pointed out to me by William Foltz (private correspondence, 1967).

Appendixes
Bibliography
Index

Appendix A
Dramatis Personae[1]

BROTHERHOODS

A. Qadriyya (adjective Qadiri)

Marabus
Si Muhammad Abd al-Qadar al-Djilani (d. 1116), founder

Muhammad Abd al-Karim al-Maghrib, fifteenth-century missionary to the Sahel

Al-Mukhtar ibn Ahmad (d. 1811), Kunta founder of the Qadiri center north of Timbuktu

Shaykh Sidia (d. 1869), major nineteenth-century Mauritanian marabu with numerous disciples in Senegal
Cheikh Sidia Al Hajj Abdoulaye, current successor of Shaykh Sidia

Shaykh Saad Bu (d. 1917), major nineteenth-century Mauritanian marabu with disciples in Senegal
Cheikh Talibuya, son of Saad Bu

Bu Kunta (d. 1914), founder of important Qadiri group in Senegal
Bekkai Kunta (d. 1929), son and heir of Bu
Sidi Lamine Kunta, brother and heir of Bekkai

B. Muridiyya (adjective Murid), offshoot of the Qadiri order

Marabus
Muhammad ibn Muhammad ibn Habib Allah (Ahmad Bamba), of the M'Backé family (d. 1927), founder

Shaykh Anta, brother of Ahmad
Shaykh Thioro, brother of Ahmad
Ibra M'Backé, brother of Ahmad
Balla M'Backé, brother of Ahmad

[1] This list includes only people and organizations mentioned in the text. Marabus on the list are separated by brotherhood and within brotherhoods by generation and/or subgroup of the brotherhood. The letters A, B, etc., are used to distinguish, first, among brotherhoods; in the section that follows, among political parties (each listed with its publications); then, among Muslim reform associations (each listed with its publications and leaders).

M'Backé Bousso, cousin of Ahmad, head of Murid branch, renowned
for scholarship
Shaykh Ibra Fall, disciple of Ahmad, founder of Baye Fall
Yassa Diene, disciple of Ahmad
Balla Fall, disciple of Ahmad
Mamadu Mustafa (d. 1945), son and heir of Ahmad
Falilou M'Backé (d. 1968), son of Ahmad and heir of Mamadu
Mustafa
Bassiru M'Backé (d. 1966), son of Ahmad and heir apparent to Falilou
Abdullahi M'Backé, son of Ahmad and successor to Falilou
Sokhna Muslimatou, youngest daughter of Ahmad

Serigne Modou Bousso, son of M'Backé Bousso
Cheikh Awa Balla M'Backé, cousin of Falilou
Modou Mustafa, son of Falilou
Bara M'Backé, son of Falilou
Cheikh M'Backé, son of Mamadu Mustafa and claimant to khalifat

C. Layenne, offshoot of the Qadiri order

Marabus
Cheikh Limamou Laye (d. 1909), founder
Cheikh Mandione Laye, son of Limamou, present head of order

D. Tijaniyya (adjective Tijani)

Marabus
Ahmad ibn Muhammad al-Tijani (d. 1815), founder
Muhammad al-Hafiz ibn al-Mukhtar ibn Habib al-Baddi, Ida ou Ali
missionary in the late eighteenth and early nineteenth centuries

Sharif Tidjane Muhammad al-Habib, current head of the order
in Morocco
Umar Tall (d. 1864), Tukulor warrior-marabu, founder of major
Tijani branch in the Futa Toro
Maba Diakhu (d. 1867), warrior-marabu, disciple of Umar, influential
in nineteenth-century conversion of the Wolof
Saermaty (d. 1887), Maba's son
Ahmad Shaykhu (d. 1875), warrior-marabu
Mamadu Lamine (d. 1887), Sarakolé warrior-marabu
Fode Sulayman Bayaga (d. 1908), Sarakolé warrior-marabu

Saidou Nourou Tall, descendant of Umar, current head of the most
important Tukulor Tijani branch but technically subordinate to
Abdul Aziz Sy
Mourtada Tall, Saidou Nourou's nephew

Al Hajj Malik Sy (d. 1922), founder of the most important Wolof
Tijani branch
Abubacar Sy (d. 1957), son and heir of Malik
Mansur Sy (d. 1957), son of Malik, heir apparent of Abubacar
Abdul Aziz Sy, son of Malik, heir to Abubacar, current head of
branch
Cheikh Tidjane Sy,[2] son of Abubacar, claimant to the *khalifat*

Ibrahima Diop, important Dakar marabu
Amadou Lamine Diene, imam of Dakar
Amadou Saidou, Tukulor head of Tijani branch in the Casamance
Cherif Maky Haidara, head of important Tijani branch in the
Casamance
Faty Seck Serigne Thienaba, head of important Tijani branch
in Thies

Abdoulaye Niass (d. 1922), founder of important Tijani branch in
Sine Saloum
Muhammad (d. 1957), son and heir of Abdoulaye
Umar, son of Abdoulaye and heir of Muhammad
Ibrahima Niass, son of Abdoulaye and founder of his own Tijani
branch

E. Hamalliyya, offshoot of the Tijani order

Marabus
Sharif Hamalla ould Muhammadu ould Saidina Umar (d. 1943), man
for whom this branch of the Tijaniyya is named
Cheikh Tahirou Doukouré, son of most important Senegalese
Hamali marabu

POLITICAL PARTIES

A. Bloc Démocratique Sénégalais (BDS), founded 1948, became Bloc
Populaire Sénégalais in 1956, which became Union Progressiste
Sénégalaise (UPS) in 1958; the UPS is the present dominant party
in Senegal

Newspapers: *Condition humaine, L'Unité, L'Unité africaine*

B. Section Française de l'Internationale Ouvrière—Fédération du
Sénégal (SFIO), founded in 1936, became Parti Sénégalais d'Action
Socialiste in 1957, merged with the UPS in 1958

Newspaper: *AOF*

[2] Cheikh Tidjane Sy is also the name of a Sengalese scholar who is a relative of the
Sy marabus but who should not be confused with the son of Abubacar.

C. Parti de Regroupement Africain—Sénégal (PRA-Senegal), merged with the UPS in 1966

Newspaper: *Indépendence africaine*

D. Parti Africain d'Indépendence (PAI), founded in 1957, banned in 1960

Newspapers: *La Lutte, Momsarev*

E. Parti de Solidarité Sénégalaise (PSS), founded in 1959, dissolved in 1960

F. Bloc des Masses Sénégalaises (BMS), founded in 1961, part merged with the UPS in 1963, part with the FNDS

G. Union Progressiste Musulmane (UPM), ephemeral party formed around Cheikh Tidjane Sy in 1963

SENEGALESE POLITICIANS

Blaise Diagne (d. 1934), elected deputy to French Chamber of Deputies, 1914

Galandou Diouf, opponent of Diagne, his successor in Chamber of Deputies, 1934

Lamine Gueye, founder of SFIO (opponent of Diouf and later Senghor), current president of Senegalese Assembly

Léopold Sédar Senghor, founder of the BDS, president of the UPS and of Senegal

Mamadou Dia, assistant to Senghor and prime minister of Senegal until 1962

Doudou Thiam, foreign minister of Senegal

Valdiodio N'Diaye, minister of interior during Dia's administration

Cheikh Anta Diop, a founder of the BMS

Ousmane N'Gom, member of Senegalese Assembly from Thies

Ibrahima Saidou N'Daw, powerful Muslim trader from Kaolack, founder of the PSS

Ibrahima Tall, former governor of Diourbel region

Médoune Fall, former governor of Diourbel region; former ambassador to France

Lamine Lo, governor of Diourbel region

Thierno Birahim N'Dao, *prefet* of Diourbel

Abubacar Sy, *préfet* of M'Backé

MUSLIM REFORM ASSOCIATION

A. La Fraternité Musulmane, founded 1935

Newspaper: *Islam AOF*
Leader: Abdel Kader Diagne

Appendix A

B. Union Culturelle Musulmane (UCM), founded 1953

   Newspaper: *Le Réveil islamique*
   Leaders: Cheikh Touré, Oumar Dieng

C. Association Musulmane des Etudiants d'Afrique Noire (AMEAN)

   Newspaper: *Vers l'Islam*

D. Fédération Nationale des Associations Culturelles Musulmanes du Sénégal, founded 1962

   Journal: *L'Afrique musulmane*
   Leaders: Abdul Aziz Sy, Oumar Dieng

E. Regroupement National des Etudiants d'Arabe—UPS, founded 1966; government-sponsored reform group

Appendix B
Statistical Exercise: Political Characteristics of the Early Twentieth-century Marabus

Because of their fear of the brotherhoods, various high-level administrators in the AOF tried to accumulate as much information as possible on the marabus. In 1906 a circular went out from the Governor General asking all the *commandants de cercle* to fill out a form on each of the leading marabus in their district. Governor General William Ponty reiterated this request in 1913.[1] Consequently, between 1906 and 1913 many hundreds of these forms pertaining to the best-known marabus of the pre-World War I period were filed in the government archives. The forms themselves were printed questionnaires including the following information about each marabu: name, brotherhood, tribe, present home area or place of origin, caste, relationship to other marabus or chiefs, status as a teacher, profession or occupation, degree of influence, amount of wealth, age, attitude to the colonial regime, knowledge of French and Arabic, occupation of students or their parents, home area of students, and propensity (the marabu's) to travel. Given the fact that the *commandants* had to fill out identical forms, and that *commandants* from all regions in Senegal at one point or another in this period submitted the required information, the filed information sheets provide an interesting source of information on the leading marabus in Senegal at this time—a source that seems, superficially, more reliable for precise characterizations of the marabus than the impressionistic personal accounts of individual administrators like Paul Marty. Not, of course, that one would necessarily expect the information sheets to contradict the assumptions of Marty, who was intimately acquainted with the Muslim leaders of Senegal and had carefully read all the information sheets himself. But at least the sheets provide a relatively impersonalized means of corroborating Marty's theories or of suggesting new ways of comparing the leaders of various brotherhoods and of various ethnic groups.

The information sheets might be expected to be centrally important to any historical evaluation of the political role of the brotherhoods;

[1] DA, William Ponty to governors (Dec. 26, 1911), No. 117c, 19G 1, and "Circulaire au sujet de l'enquête sur l'Islam" (Dakar, 1913), 19G 1.

this expectation is unwarranted because of the way in which the administrators handled the sheets. Although the questions were all identical (the sheets were printed) the individual *commandants* chose to interpret them in various ways and with varying degrees of precision. Thus only name, tribe, and brotherhood were filled in similarly by all respondents. The other information called forth a broad range of responses: for example, the question on attitude toward the French caused some administrators to comment on the present activities of a marabu, some on his past actions, and some on his general attitude. Age was given in approximate numerical terms or by exact dates in some cases, and with the words "old" or "young" in others. Family status and relationship to chiefs and marabus called forth a confusing series of answers. Some *commandants* were as precise as possible in terms of the status-group system of the ethnic group involved, other *commandants* used the terms "high" or "low" (caste) and many others ignored the question except to indicate the names of noble relatives where they existed. It is not clear that the commandants were aware of the amount of Arabic that the marabus knew, although their impressions of the amount of French spoken were probably more accurate. The respondents' knowledge of the kind and quality of the marabus' teaching or the characteristics of their students was quite sketchy, and their information on amount of wealth and degree of influence was anything but precise. Indeed, what the information sheets provide is a large number of impressions of marabus that are colored by the predilections and biases of the *commandants,* who did not understand Islam and Muslim brotherhoods as well as Marty did.

The inconsistency and lack of preciseness of the respondents in their answers are adequate reasons for omitting the questionnaires from anything but a cursory survey sufficient to indicate whether or not a major discrepancy exists between the questionnaire information and the general assumptions about marabus in this period. Such a discrepancy might raise questions about previously held generalizations, although no adequate substitute for Marty and other traditional sources could be provided by the questionnaires. But, in fact, a major discrepancy does not exist. Consequently, consideration of the questionnaires for the text of this book has been limited to their use as general background for the chapters on the brotherhoods' rise to power and the relations of the French and the marabus. In this appendix, however, I have attempted to carry out some statistical comparisons on the characteristics of the marabus from the information sheets as an indication of what suggestions might have been gathered from the sheets had they been treated more scientifically.

The attempt involved forcing disparate information into a series of categories—for example, pro- or anti-French, good family or low caste, relationships to marabus and chiefs, influential or not, agriculturalist or not, wealthy or poor, inclined or not to travel, origin and profession of

Appendix B

Marabu characteristics

	No information	Tijani	Murid	Qadiri
Total	12	124	131	35
		(Percentages in parentheses)		
Tribe				
No information	6 (50)	12 (10)	21 (16)	1 (3)
Wolof	3 (25)	55 (44)	100 (76)	18 (52)
Tukulor	1 (8)	24 (19)	1 (1)	1 (3)
Fula	0 –	7 (6)	3 (2)	2 (6)
Mandingo	0 –	0 –	0 –	5 (14)
Other	2 (17)	26 (21)	6 (5)	8 (23)
Family status				
No information	5 (42)	59 (48)	48 (37)	18 (52)
Good family	7 (58)	62 (50)	79 (60)	16 (46)
Low caste	0 –	3 (2)	4 (3)	1 (3)
Related to marabus				
No information	0 –	1 (1)	1 (1)	0 –
Related	7 (58)	76 (61)	81 (62)	21 (60)
Not related	5 (42)	47 (38)	49 (37)	14 (40)
Related to chiefs				
No information	1 (8)	11 (9)	11 (8)	1 (3)
Related	11 (92)	113 (91)	120 (92)	34 (97)
Pro- or anti-French				
No information	6 (50)	87 (70)	100 (77)	26 (74)
Pro-French	3 (25)	26 (21)	12 (9)	7 (20)
Anti-French	3 (25)	11 (9)	19 (15)	2 (6)
Teach or not				
No information	9 (75)	28 (23)	65 (50)	9 (26)
Teach	2 (17)	92 (74)	57 (44)	24 (69)
Do not teach	1 (8)	4 (3)	9 (7)	2 (6)
Influence				
No information	7 (58)	83 (67)	84 (64)	24 (69)
Very influential	4 (33)	15 (12)	20 (15)	7 (20)
Moderately influential	1 (8)	20 (16)	19 (15)	1 (3)
Not influential	0 –	6 (5)	8 (6)	3 (9)
Wealth				
No information	11 (92)	95 (77)	83 (63)	29 (83)
Wealthy	1 (8)	13 (11)	26 (20)	4 (11)
Moderately wealthy	0 –	11 (9)	19 (15)	1 (3)
Poor	0 –	5 (4)	3 (2)	1 (3)
Over 40 years of age in 1910				
No information	5 (42)	16 (13)	43 (33)	4 (11)
Over 40	6 (50)	79 (64)	58 (44)	29 (83)
Under 40	1 (8)	29 (23)	30 (23)	2 (6)
Occupation				
No information	7 (59)	71 (57)	42 (32)	17 (48)
Agriculture	2 (17)	43 (35)	80 (61)	15 (43)
Trader or other town occupation	2 (17)	1 (1)	4 (3)	1 (3)
Fisherman	1 (8)	0 –	0 –	1 (3)
Chief	0 –	6 (5)	3 (2)	1 (3)
Other	0 –	3 (2)	2 (2)	0 –

Appendix B

Marabu characteristics *(Continued)*

	No information	Tijani	Murid	Qadiri
Total	12	124	131	35
		(Percentages in parentheses)		
Educated in Arabic				
No information	11 (92)	59 (48)	43 (33)	21 (60)
Educated	1 (8)	57 (46)	72 (55)	12 (34)
Not educated	0 –	8 (6)	13 (10)	1 (3)
Poorly educated	0 –	0 –	3 (2)	1 (3)
Educated in French				
No information	11 (92)	73 (59)	78 (60)	24 (69)
Educated	1 (8)	2 (2)	1 (1)	1 (3)
Not educated	0 –	49 (39)	52 (40)	10 (29)
Student occupation				
No information	8 (67)	41 (33)	82 (63)	12 (34)
Agriculture	1 (8)	59 (48)	48 (37)	15 (43)
Town or trader	0 –	1 (1)	0 –	1 (3)
Fisherman	1 (8)	4 (3)	0 –	6 (17)
Mixture	0 –	4 (3)	1 (1)	0 –
Low caste	2 (17)	15 (12)	0 –	1 (3)
Student origin				
No information	12 (100)	73 (59)	99 (76)	20 (57)
Same or surrounding area	0 –	49 (40)	31 (24)	14 (40)
Different area	0 –	2 (2)	1 (1)	1 (3)
Propensity to travel				
No information	8 (67)	106 (85)	116 (89)	33 (94)
Travels	3 (25)	8 (7)	14 (11)	0 –
Does not travel	0 –	3 (2)	1 (1)	1 (3)
Traveled to Mecca	1 (8)	7 (6)	0 –	1 (3)

students, knowledge of Arabic and French, over or under forty years of age in 1910, and so on. Obviously this meant that the information sheets had to be interpreted to fit the categories even though in a large percentage of cases a certain distortion of information probably resulted. Where the answers provided could not be meaningfully interpreted, then "no information" was registered. Three hundred nine marabus were listed and a matrix of all known characteristics (according to these categories) was filled in. Many other marabus, approximately a hundred, could not be listed at all because their information sheets had not been completed in a way that could be categorized; fortunately, they were not concentrated in any one region or brotherhood. I then proceeded to carry out a series of tests to see if the brotherhoods could be distinguished from each other in terms of characteristics of the marabus.

The first step in the process was to hold constant the brotherhoods and list all the characteristics of the marabus in terms of the brotherhoods. The preceding table,[2] from which several points emerged, resulted. First,

[2]The percentages in some cases do not total 100 because of errors introduced by rounding numbers.

the "no information" total was extremely high, which meant that later tests done on the given information were, in fact, based on a small sample of the total population of outstanding marabus, especially in the important category of pro- or anti-French attitudes and in the less significant characteristic of propensity to travel.[3] Second, and more important in terms of meaningful results, it was clear that the number of low caste marabus was negligible; in fact, most marabus (over 90%) in all brotherhoods were related to chiefs, while a lesser but significantly high percent (60% or over) were also related to marabus.

I then proceeded to carry out chi square tests on characteristics that had been observed a sufficient number of times to allow such tests, and that were of most interest to me in terms of the distribution of political characteristics among the brotherhoods.[4] The results of the tests are summarized as follows:

Null hypothesis [5]	χ^2	Degrees of freedom	Null hypothesis rejected
a) Marabus' membership in a brotherhood (Tijani or Murid) is independent of ethnic group affiliation (Wolof, Tukulor, or other).	48.6	2	yes
b) The older marabus (over age 40 in 1910) are randomly distributed between the brotherhoods (Tijani, Murid).	1.6	1	no
c) The marabus related to other marabus are randomly distributed among the brotherhoods (Tijani, Murid, Qadiri).	.16	2	no
d) The attitude of the marabus toward the French (pro- or anti-French) is independent of brotherhood affiliation (Tijani, Murid).	6.1	1	yes
e) Whether or not a marabu is involved in agriculture is independent of his brotherhood affiliation (Tijani, Murid).	2.4	1	no
f) Whether or not a marabu is educated in Arabic is independent of his brotherhood affiliation (Tijani, Murid).	.82	1	no
g) Older marabus (over 40 in 1910) are randomly distributed among the tribes (Wolof, other).	1.04	1	no

[3] The later tests were done under the assumption that the distribution of characteristics among those for whom there was no information would be similar to the distribution among those for whom information was available.

[4] See Sanford M. Dornbusch and Calvin F. Schmid, *A Primer of Social Statistics* (New York, 1955), pp. 124–219, 236–243. I am indebted to Henry Teune and especially to Jere R. Behrman for explanations of how to use this material.

[5] Because of insufficient information, several data calls from the above tables were consolidated before the chi square tests were conducted. All tests were done at the 5% level of significance.

Appendix B

h) The marabus' age (over or under 40 in 1910) is independent of their occupation (agriculturalist or other).   2.57   1   no

i) The marabus' age is independent of their knowledge of Arabic.   .11   1   no

I found that the null hypothesis that marabus' adherence to a particular brotherhood is independent of their ethnic group membership could be rejected. A statistic based on binomial distribution further indicated that the null hypothesis that a Wolof marabu is just as likely to join the Tijaniyya as the Muridiyya order could also be rejected. I then found the null hypothesis that older marabus are randomly distributed among the brotherhoods could not be rejected, nor could these null hypotheses be rejected: that a marabu's occupation is independent of his brotherhood or that a marabu's knowledge level of Arabic is independent of his brotherhood affiliation. But I could reject the null hypothesis that whether or not a marabu is anti-French in attitude is independent of the affiliation to a brotherhood.

Following these tests, I held age constant to see how various characteristics were distributed in terms of marabus over or under forty. The following list resulted:

	Over 40 (total 171)[6]	Under 40 (total 41)
Tribe		
Wolof	105	39
Tukulor	17	8
Fula	7	2
Mandingo	4	0
Other	26	4
Family status		
Good family	96	35
Low caste	6	2
Related to marabus		
Related to marabus	69	23
Not related to marabus	1	1
Related to chiefs		
Related to chiefs	13	4
Not related to chiefs	0	0
Pro- or Anti-French		
Pro-French	29	5
Anti-French	17	4
Teach or not		
Teach	107	34
Do not teach	8	5
Influence		
Very influential	24	3
Moderate influence	25	10
No influence	10	5

[6] The totals in all categories are less than the overall total because of lack of information.

Appendix B

Wealth		
Wealthy	27	5
Moderately wealthy	20	7
Poor	6	3
Occupation		
Agriculturalist	79	26
Trader or other town occupation	3	2
Fisherman	2	0
Chief	5	4
Other	1	3
Arabic education		
Educated in Arabic	81	32
Not educated in Arabic	11	8
Poorly educated in Arabic	4	0
French education		
Educated in French	1	3
Not educated in French	63	26
Student occupation		
Agriculturalist	83	23
Trader or town	0	1
Fisherman	9	2
Mixture	2	2
Low caste	14	5
Student place of origin		
Same or surrounding area	63	19
Different area	2	1
Marabu's place of origin	1	0
Marabu's propensity to travel		
Travels	13	7
Does not travel	3	1
Has been to Mecca	3	2

Chi square tests indicated that the null hypothesis that the age of the marabu (over or under 40) is independent of ethnic group membership could not be rejected, nor could the null hypotheses be rejected that age is independent of occupation or of knowledge of Arabic.

Perusal of the results of the above tests indicates several points to consider. In the first place, one might have expected a greater degree of differentiation between Murid and Tijani marabus. The Murid order, after all, was founded in 1886, whereas the Tijani brotherhood had become the major order among the Tukulor by the death of Al Hajj Umar (1864). Umar's disciples, thereafter, attracted numerous Wolof disciples (for example, MaBa Diakhu, who died in 1867). The Tijani brotherhood might have been expected to exhibit the characteristics of an established order by the early twentieth century, in contrast to the Muridiyya—then a more dynamic order still in the reforming stage of revitalization (see Chapter 1). But, significantly, marabus of the Murid brotherhoods were not noticeably younger than those of the Tijani. Moreover, almost all marabus had definite ties with the ethnic aristocracy, indicating that the infusion of other status groups had already stopped for all brotherhoods including the Murids, and, perhaps, raising the question of how great the leavening effect of the Murid brotherhood had actually ever been (Chapter 1, pages 29–31).

The fact that few low-caste men became marabus in any order may not be significant at all. Neither Marty nor the other sources of his period reported many low-caste marabus. What they did report—which these results do not negate—is that the ruling group was broadened by the brotherhoods by consolidation between the aristocracy and the marabutic families who were not necessarily of the nobility but were not low-caste either. The lack of differentiation among the brotherhoods on this point may be interpreted in at least two ways. On the one hand, the Tijanis were recruiting among the Wolof concurrently with the Murids and were drawing disciples who were looking for a new organizing principle for their lives in the Tijani order as they were in the Murid order. No figures exist that distinguish between old and new Tijani branches among the Wolof, so that it is impossible to make relevant distinctions between the Murids and the Tijanis because the brotherhoods could be expected to exhibit similar characteristics at their earliest stages. On the other hand, it can also be assumed that since the statistics used were collected in the early twentieth century, they may be too late to indicate differences between the Murid and other orders as the former had had time to become established.

The only characteristics that, the results show, can be used to distinguish between the brotherhoods are ethnic group affiliation and attitude toward the colonial regime. Wolof marabus were more likely to be Murids and Tukulor marabus and those of other ethnic groups were less likely to become Murids. This observation reinforces the generally held assumption that the Murid order was a Wolof brotherhood, especially in its early years. The different attitude of the Murids and Tijanis toward the French is also understandable, given that the Murid order had recently been founded and that agitation with anti-French connotations was associated with Ahmad Bamba and his assistants throughout the period when the information was being gathered. Indeed, on this point, the revitalizing aspect of the Murid order as opposed to the Tijani is supported by the statistical evidence: the Murid marabus did appear to be more of a threat to the colonial rulers than did the Tijani or other marabus.[7] Nor does this observation necessarily conflict with the fact that, as far as leavening the ruling group was concerned, no differentiation among the brotherhoods can be made. Again, that there is no breakdown between old and new Tijani groups is significant; so, too, is the fact that Ahmad Bamba was more powerful than any anti-French Tijani marabus of this period, although the latter certainly did exist. The Murids stood out at this time as the major

---

[7] Here, of course, what is recorded is the administrators' perception of the marabu's attitude, which may have little relation to his actual point of view.

opponents of the French, and the most important Tijani groups did not have this reputation. Malik Sy, for example, was not interested in fighting the colonial rulers, nor were the other leading Umarian Tijani leaders. Thus, the anti-French attitude of the Murids as opposed to the Tijanis *and* the lack of distinction between the Murids and Tijani in terms of social affiliation of the marabus probably do not conflict with each other or challenge the generally held assumptions about marabus in this period.

The other results are less important, although they, too, corroborate the generally accepted notions about marabus at this time. Most marabus, for example, were involved in agriculture. Very few knew any French at all, while a notably larger number were acquainted with Arabic. Neither age nor brotherhood distinguishes between the marabus on these points. The other characteristics, not mentioned so far, such as wealth, degree of influence, and occupation of students, do not lend themselves to any very significant interpretations as far as expanding or reinforcing information on the political characteristics of marabus in the pre-World War I period.

In sum, the statistical evidence presented here, even if it could be considered reliable, does not introduce any new variables into a description of marabus in the colonial period. Probably only evidence from the marabus themselves, letters or family records, for example, could shed new light on the early Muslim leaders' political characteristics.

Appendix C
The
Modern
Associations
of the
Brotherhoods
The *Dahira*

To an outside observer the involvement of disciples of the Senegalese *tariqas* in modern formal associations such as *dahira* may seem somewhat incongruous. As mentioned in Chapter 3, these organizations of brothers are found in towns throughout Senegal and are usually headed by elected officers including a president and/or a director and a secretary and/or treasurer. The leaders of the groups are appointees of the major marabus, and thus the members have little to say about who is elected or how the organization is run.

The primary purpose of the *dahiratu* is to raise money for the brotherhood, and this objective is pursued in a variety of ways: a common method is through organized evenings of religious songs ("les chants religieux"). One or more *griots* will often lead the songs or chants; the almost hypnotic effect of an evening of song can produce large contributions, which will be sent to a marabu. "Les chants religieux" are a combination of two traditions: according to tribal custom in Senegal *griots* would sing stories at gatherings in return for gifts; religious song evenings were also found in brotherhoods centuries ago in the Middle East and North Africa. The latter sometimes included only fully initiated brothers, who would chant religious formulas, perhaps moving their heads or bodies slightly at the same time, until they fell into a trance or reached a state of ecstasy.[1] Senegalese evenings of song are different from these mystical exercises but they are rooted in the same concept of mass piety through the common recitation of religious formulas or songs.

In general, the present methods used by many *dahira* to promote their song evenings seem to an outsider a strange mixture of commercial selling techniques and old-world piety. Innumerable handbills, which are passed out to publicize the evenings, illustrate this combination. For example, the following notice advertised a song evening in May 1957:

[1] Depont and Coppolani, Les Confréries religieuses, pp. 156–157.

Appendix C

City of Dakar

Islam only Islam

For the first time the city of Dakar under the sponsorship of the Dahiratu Lakhimidiya tou Attidjania will organize Religious Songs in commemoration of the birth of the Prophet (Muhammad). . . .
The 11 and 12 May 1957
As usual these songs will be presided over by Al Hajj Abdul Aziz (son of our most venerated Al Hajj Malik Sy) may peace be upon him (Amen) and will take place in the habitual place of prayer (Avenue El Hadj Malick Sy). All Muslims without distinction of Sect are cordially invited

The Secretary General
Al Hajj Ibrahima Sene, General Direction of Finance

The Commissary General
Al Hajj Mamadou M'Bengue, Retired Chief of Workers

The President
Al Hajj Birane N'Diaye Gatta, Retired Chief of the Office of Railways [2]

The *dahira* find other ways of raising money from the town-dwelling faithful. Many of these methods also seem to blend modern techniques with traditional religious purposes. Al Hajj Bamba Gueye, one of the Dakar representatives of the Murid khalif Falilou, sponsored a film on the annual festival at Touba that was advertised on a handbill as follows:

The Grand Magal of Touba 1956

For the First Time . . . The Visit of the Great Mosque
The Tomb of the Venerated Serigne
The Prayer of the Grand Khalif
All the Great Ceremony

To come to this film is to find ourselves near the General *Khalif* of our brotherhood, it is to relive the unforgettable days of our Great Pilgrimage.

This is why we want you ALL to see and resee this film which will perpetuate in us the memory of this grandiose and memorable ceremony.

Al Hajj Bamba Gueye, Official Representative of the Khalif of the Murids [3]

Another method of raising money used by a *dahiratu* is sponsorship of a speech on a religious subject, for example, the "Conference on Islam" given by the Fraternité Khadria in 1954.[4]

[2] Printed handbill, Imp. Diop, D. L. 859, Dakar. See also examples in *Dakar matin*: on Feb. 10, 1966, e.g.' at Serigne Mayobe's annual Gamou, the paper noted that there were religious songs "animated by the best known composers" and attended by several important men who "contributed largely and generously" to the success of the evening.
[3] Printed handbill, G.I.A., D.L. 4286–10–56, Dakar.
[4] Printed handbill, Imp. Diop, D.C. 320, Dakar.

Appendix C

The *dahira* are numerous, and a *dahiratu* is an important adjunct to any brotherhood, which finds it an excellent source of funds. The Murid brotherhood has approximately thirty-three dahira, headed by Al Hajj Bamba Diaw, in the Cap Vert region. The Murids have the most organized and hierarchized *dahira* but there are hundreds of Tijani *dahira* and many Qadria as well. Ibrahima Niass has his many *dahira* organized in a powerful organization called the Association Ansourdine (Jamiyyat Ansa Al-Din—the Society of the Faithful), which he controls through his sons. It was interesting to note in the fall of 1965, as proof of the importance of the *dahiratu*, that Bamba Gueye, who was attempting to gain stature in the Murid brotherhood and assert his own importance, tried to bolster his position by organizing a *dahiratu* among low-caste artisans; he failed, however, because the khalif opposed him.[5]

[5] Interviews with Murid leaders, Nov. 5, Nov. 17, 1965, and Jan. 9, 1966, Dakar. Another interesting modern association of Muslims in Senegal is that formed by those who have completed pilgrimages to Mecca. See references to the Fraternal Union of Pilgrims of the ex-AOF, *Dakar matin*, Nov. 19, 1965.

Appendix D
Marabu
Cooperatives

Following the Second World War many Senegalese marabus formed cooperatives among their disciples. One of the earliest cooperatives was started by Ibrahima Niass and was known as COMAS. Niass was president, but the cooperative was managed by his secretary, Mor Abdiou N'Diaye, until its dissolution.[1] Cheikh Tidjane Sy is one of many important Tijani marabus of the Sy family who have headed large and quite successful cooperatives;[2] he drew a great deal of money from his, and it was a well-known cooperative throughout Senegal. Murid leaders, too, have headed large cooperatives with considerable numbers of members: in 1947, a few months after Niass had founded COMAS, for example, Cheikh M'Backé organized the Coopérative de Production du Baol, of which he was president and administrative director. Bassiru M'Backé soon followed with the Coopérative de Production et de Diourbel.

Bassiru's cooperative can be used to illustrate the marabus' role in their cooperatives. His cooperative had twelve hundred members. He was honorary president and the active president was Cheikh Yaba Diop, the *chef de canton* in the area. The vice-president was Bassiru's son, Mustafa; the treasurer was M'Backé Diakhaté, a notable of Diourbel; the secretary was Mor Khara Diop, a cultivator; and the secretary-accountant was Lamine Sarr, who was known as a protégé of Bassiru. All the officials were loyal disciples of Bassiru, who himself benefited from the cooperative through his right to dispose of all the profits as he saw fit. He became embroiled with the administration over his use of the cooperative's finances, borrowing large sums in the name of the cooperative which he used for personal matters and which were not repaid. He is also reported to have done such things as to buy a house, using his organization's funds, and then rent it back to the cooperative at a very high rate.[3] Not surprisingly, the administration was concerned with Bassiru's exploitation of the cooperators, especially since the cooperative went heavily into debt; but government officials could not afford to oppose him or his fellow marabus outright on the question.

Interestingly enough, Senegalese politicians in the early post-World War II period defended the cooperatives of the era. Mamadou Dia wrote that, despite the fact that some of the cooperatives were mismanaged

---

[1] Interview with Mor Abdiou N'Diaye, Jan. 21, 1966, Kaolack; Quesnot, "Les Cadres maraboutiques," pp. 143–145.

[2] Quesnot, "Les Cadres maraboutiques," p. 141.

[3] Nekkach, "Unpublished Report."

by their leaders, the French administration should not attempt to suppress them: such action would be reactionary, for the cooperatives offered considerable promise for development of the rural economy. Dia insisted French efforts to regulate the cooperatives were dangerous and short-sighted.[4] On the one hand, he and the other politicians who generally shared his opinion were using the cooperatives as an issue to drum up support among the marabus and their disciples, who were opposed to French intervention in this matter. On the other hand, the politicians were sincerely convinced that some kind of cooperative was better than none and that gradually the cooperators could be taught their rights and "mismanagement" of the organizations would cease. In any case, the politicians, as they began to receive a responsible voice in the government, pursued much the same policy as the French had done, putting pressure on the marabus and other rural leaders who controlled the cooperatives to force them to make the organizations financially accountable. Many of the marabus, because of this pressure, dissolved their cooperatives (Ibrahima Niass was one). Some marabus still remain in direct and open control of cooperatives; but the government has encouraged the development of "real" cooperatives throughout Senegal. In these cooperatives the members may still give large portions of their produce to their marabus but, nonetheless, they are more likely to receive a share of the cooperatives' receipts to use as they please.

[4]*Condition humaine*, Sept. 1, 1948.

Bibliography

Books

Abun-Nasr, Jamil M. *The Tijaniyya: A Sufi Order in the Modern World.*
London: Oxford University Press, 1965.

Adanson, M. A. *A Voyage to Senegal, the Isle of Goree, and the River
Gambia.* London: J. Nourse and W. Johnston, 1759.

Agger, Robert E., Daniel Goldrich, and Bert E. Swanson. *The Rulers and
The Ruled: Political Power and Impotence in American Communities.*
New York: John Wiley & Sons, 1964.

Allen, V. L. *Trade Unions and the Government.* London: Longmans, 1960.

Almond, Gabriel, and James Coleman, eds. *The Politics of Developing
Areas.* Princeton: Princeton University Press, 1960.

Almond, Gabriel, and Sidney Verba. *The Civic Culture: Political Attitudes
and Democracy in Five Nations.* Princeton: Princeton University
Press, 1963.

An Mustafa. *Hyyatu Ishaykhi Ahmadu Bamba,* 2 vols. Dakar: n.d.

André, P. J. *L'Islam et les races,* vol. II: *Les Rameaux (mouvements
regionaux et sectes).* Paris: Guethner, 1922.

Apter, David. *The Politics of Modernization.* Chicago: University of
Chicago Press, 1965.

Arberry, A. J. *Sufism: an Account of the Mystics of Islam.* London: George
Allen & Unwin, 1950.

Austruy, Jacques. *L'Islam face au développement économique,* vol. III:
Economie et civilisation. Paris: Editions Ouvrières, 1961.

Balandier, G., and P. Mercier. *Les Pêcheurs Lébou: particularisme et
évolution.* Etudes sénégalaises no. 3. St. Louis, Senegal: Institut
Français d'Afrique Noire (henceforth IFAN), 1952.

Bamba, Ahmadu. *Kitabu Misalika-Ijinaan lishaykhi Ahmadu Bamba.*
Dakar: Imprimerie A. Diop, 1962.

Bascom, William R., and Melville J. Herskovits, eds. *Continuity and Change
in African Cultures.* Chicago: University of Chicago Press, 1959.

Baumann, H., and D. Westermann. *Les Peuples et les civilisations de
l'Afrique: suivi des langues et de l'éducation,* trans. L. Homburger.
Paris: Payot, 1948.

Bérenger-Féraud, L. J. B. *Les Peuplades de la Sénégambie.* Paris: Ernest
Leroux, 1879.

Bibliography

Binder, Leonard. *Religion and Politics in Pakistan.* Berkeley: University of California Press, 1961.

Boilat, Abbé P.-D. *Equisses sénégalaises: physionomie du pays, peuplades, commerce, religions, passé et avenir, récits et légendes.* Paris: P. Bertrand, 1853.

Brevié, J. *Islamisme contre "Naturalisme" au Soudan Francais: essai de psychologie politique coloniale.* Paris: Ernest Leroux, 1923.

Brigaud, Félix. *Connaissance du Sénégal,* fasc. XI: *Histoire moderne et contemporaine du Sénégal.* Etudes sénégalaises no. 9. St. Louis: Centre de Recherches et de Documentation Sénégalaise (henceforth CRDS), 1966.

———— *Connaissance du Sénégal,* fasc. IX: *Histoire traditionnelle du Sénégal.* Etudes sénégalaises No. 9. St. Louis: CRDS, 1962.

Brosselard, M. Charles. *Les Khouans: de la constitution des ordres religieux musulmans et Algérie.* Algiers: A. Bourget, 1859.

Caillié, René. *Travels through Central Africa to Timbuctoo and across the Great Desert to Morocco, Performed in the Years 1824–1828,* vol. I. London: Henry Colburn and Richard Bentley, 1830.

Cardaire, Marcel. *Contribution à l'étude de l'Islam noir: mémorandum II du Centre IFAN, Cameroun.* Paris: IFAN, 1949.

———— *L'Islam et le terroir africain.* Koulouba: Imprimerie du Gouvernement, 1954.

Carter, Gwendolen M., ed. *African One-Party States.* Ithaca: Cornell University Press, 1962.

Chailley, M. *Le Soudan avant le réferendum: quelques aspects de l'Islamisation de l'Afrique Occidentale Française, L'Islam en A.O.F., l'Afrique précoloniale, les milieux Africains.* Dakar: n.d.

Chailley, M., A. Bourlon, B. Bichon, F. D'Aby, J. Amon, F. Quesnot. *Notes et études sur l'Islam en Afrique noire.* Paris: J. Péyronnet, 1963.

Charles R. *L'Evolution de l'Islam.* Paris: Calmann-Lévy, 1960.

Ciré, Ly. *Christianisme ou Islam?* Paris: Imprimeries Réunies, 1956.

Coleman, James S., and Carl G. Rosberg, Jr., eds. *Political Parties and National Integration in Tropical Africa.* Berkeley: University of California Press, 1964.

Crone, G. R., ed. *The Voyages of Cadamosto and other Documents on Western Africa in the Second Half of the Fifteenth Century.* London: Hakluyt Society, 1937.

Cultru, P. *Premier Voyage du Sieur de la Courbe fait à la Coste d'Afrique en 1685.* Paris: Emile Larose, Edouard Champion, 1913.

Dahl, Robert A. *Modern Political Analysis.* Englewood Cliffs, N.J.: Prentice Hall, 1963.

Delafosse, Maurice. *Haut-Sénégal-Niger (Soudan Francais),* vol. I: *Le Pays, les peuples, les langues;* vol. II: *L'Histoire.* Paris: Emile Larose, 1912.

Delavignette, Robert. *Freedom and Authority in French West Africa.* London: Oxford University Press, 1950.

Bibliography

Delcount, André. *La France et les etablissements français au Sénégal en 1713 et 1763: mémoires de l'IFAN*, no. 17. Dakar: IFAN, 1952.

Depont, Octave, and Xavier Coppolani. *Les Confréries religieuses musulmanes.* Algiers: Adolphe Jourdan, 1897.

Dia, Mamadou. *African Nations and World Solidarity*, trans. Mercer Cook. New York: Praeger, 1961.

———— *Réflexions sur l'économie de l'Afrique noire.* Paris: Presence Africaine, 1961.

Diop, Abdoulaye. *Société toucouleur et migration enquête sur la migration toucouleur à Dakar).* Dakar: IFAN, 1965.

Dornbusch, Sanford M., and Calvin F. Schmid. *A Primer of Social Statistics.* New York: McGraw Hill, 1955.

Durand, Jean-Baptiste-Leonard. *Voyage au Sénégal ou mémoires historiques, philosophiques et politiques sur les découvertes, les établissements et le commerce des Européens.* . . . Paris: Henri Agasse, 1802.

Faidherbe, Générale. *Le Sénégal: La France dans l'Afrique Occidentale.* Paris: Librarie Hachette, 1889.

Fernandes, Valentim. *Description de la Côte Occidentale d'Afrique (Sénégal au Cap de Monte, Archipels),* ed. T. Monod, A. Teixeira Da Mota, R. Mauny. Bissau: Centro de Estudos de Guiné Portuguesa, 1951.

Fisher, Humphrey J. *Ahmadiyyah: A Study in Contemporary Islam on the West African Coast.* London: Oxford University Press, 1963.

Foltz, William Jay. *From French West Africa to the Mali Federation.* New Haven: Yale University Press, 1965.

Fouquet, Joseph. *La Traite des arachides dans le pays de Kaolack et ses conséquences économiques, sociales et juridiques.* Etudes sénégalaises no. 8. St. Louis: IFAN, 1958.

Froelich, J. C. *Les Musulmans d'Afrique noire.* Paris: Editions de l'Orante, 1962.

Gamble, David P. *The Wolof of Senegambia.* Ethnographic Survey of Africa: Western Africa, pt. XIV, ed. Daryll Forde. London: International African Institute, 1957.

Geismar, L. *Récueil des coutumes civiles des races du Sénégal établi par L. Geismar, administrateur en chef des colonies.* St. Louis: Imprimerie du Gouvernement, 1933.

Gibb, H. A. R. *Mohammedanism: An Historical Survey.* New York: Mentor Books, 1955.

Golbery, Sylvain Meinrad Xavier de. *Fragmens d'un voyage en Afrique,* 2 vols. Paris: Treuttel et Wurtz, 1802.

Gorer, Geoffrey. *Africa Dances: A Book about West African Negroes.* London: John Lehmann, 1949.

Gouilly, Alphonse. *L'Islam dans l'Afrique Occidentale Française.* Paris: Editions Larose, 1952.

Greenberg, Joseph. *The Influence of Islam on a Sudanese Religion.*

Bibliography

Monographs of the American Ethnographic Society, no. 10. New York: J. J. Augustine, 1946.

Grenier, Philippe. *Rapport de la mission dans la région du Ferlo, Décembre 1956–Mai 1957: arrondissement de l'hydraulique du Sénégal.* Dakar: Etudes de Géographie Humaine, 1956–1957.

Hapgood, David. *Africa: From Independence to Tomorrow.* New York: Atheneum, 1965.

Hitti, Philip K. *History of the Arabs from the Earliest Times to the Present,* 6th ed. London: Macmillan, 1956.

Hodgkin, Thomas. *Nationalism in Colonial Africa.* New York: New York University Press, 1957.

Hoffer, Eric. *The True Believer: Thoughts on the Nature of Mass Movements.* New York: Harper & Row, Perennial Library, 1966.

Houtsma, M. T., A. J. Wensinck, T. W. Arnold, W. Heffening and E. Levi-Provencal, eds. *The Encyclopedia of Islam: A Dictionary of the Geography, Ethnography and Biography of the Muhammadan Peoples,* vol. XLII. London: Luzac, 1929.

Kane, Cheikh Hamidou. *L'Aventure ambigue.* Paris: R. Julliard, 1962.

Kautsky, John H., ed. *Political Change in Underdeveloped Countries: Nationalism and Communism.* New York: John Wiley & Sons, 1962.

Kestergat, Jean. *La Promenade africain.* Paris: Editions Berger-Levrault, 1965.

Key, V. O. *Politics, Parties and Pressure Groups.* New York: Thomas Y. Crowell Company, 1958.

Klein, Martin A. *Islam and Imperialism in Senegal: Sine-Saloum, 1847–1914.* Stanford: Stanford University Press, 1968.

Labat, Jean-Baptiste. *Nouvelle Relation de l'Afrique Occidentale,* 4 vols. Paris: Guillaume Cavelier, 1728.

Labouret, Henri. *Paysans d'Afrique Occidentale.* Paris: Gallimard, 1941.

La Palombara, Joseph. *Interest Groups in Italian Politics.* Princeton: Princeton University Press, 1964.

Leca, N. *Les Pecheurs de Guet N'Dar avec une note sur les Wolof, leur parler, les langages secrets par Henri Labouret.* Paris: Librarie Larose, 1935.

Le Chatelier, A. *L'Islam au XIXe siècle.* Paris: Ernest Leroux, 1888.

———— *L'Islam dans l'Afrique Occidentale.* Paris: G. Steinheil, 1899.

Lewis, I. M., ed. *Islam in Tropical Africa: Studies Presented and Discussed at the Fifth International African Seminar, Ahmadu Bello University, Zaria, January 1964.* London: Oxford University Press, 1966.

Lombard, J. *Connaissance du Sénégal,* fasc. V: *Géographie humaine.* Etudes sénégalaises no. 9. St. Louis: CRDS, 1963.

Mannheim, Karl. *Ideology and Utopia: An Introduction to the Sociology of Knowledge,* trans. Louis Wirth and Edward Shils. New York: Harcourt, Brace & World, 1966.

Marty, Paul. *Etudes sur l'Islam maure: Cheikh Sidya, les Fadelia, les Ida ou Ali.* Paris: Ernest Leroux, 1916.

Bibliography

———— *Etudes sur l'Islam au Sénégal,* vol. I: *Les Personnages;* vol. II: *Les Doctrines et les institutions.* Paris: Ernest Leroux, 1917.

Marty, Paul, and Jules Salenc. *Les Ecoles maraboutiques du Sénégal: La Medersa de Saint-Louis.* Paris: Ernest Leroux, 1914.

Massignon, Louis. *Essai sur les origines du lexique technique de la mystique musulmane.* Paris: Librarie Paul Guethner, 1914–1922.

Mauny, R. *Tableau Géographique de l'Ouest Africain au Moyen Age d'après les Sources Ecrites, la Tradition et l'Archéologie.* Dakar: IFAN, 1961.

M'Backé, El Hadj Falilou. *Discours prononcé par le Khalif Général El Hadj Falilou M'Backé à l'occasion du Grand Magal de Touba 1965.* Dakar: Impricap, 1965.

Mecham, John Lloyd. *Church and State in Latin America.* Chapel Hill: University of North Carolina Press, 1965.

Mollien, G. *Voyage dans l'intérieur de l'Afrique aux sources du Sénégal et de la Gambie fait en 1818 par ordre du gouvernement francais.* Paris: Imprimerie de Mme. Vᵉ Courcier, 1820.

Monteil, Vincent. *L'Islam.* Paris: Bloud & Gray, 1963.

———— *L'Islam noir.* Paris: Editions du Seuil, 1964.

Montet, Edouard. *Le Culte des saints musulmans dans l'Afrique du Nord et plus spécialement au Maroc.* Geneva: Librarie Georg, 1909.

Morgenthau, Ruth Schachter. *Political Parties in French-Speaking West Africa.* Oxford: The Clarendon Press, 1964.

Murdock, George Peter. *Africa: Its Peoples and Their Cultural History.* New York: McGraw Hill, 1959.

Ney, Napoleon. *Un Danger européen: les sociétés secrètes musulmanes.* Paris: George Cane, 1890.

Nicholson, Reynold Alleyne. *Studies in Islamic Mysticism.* Cambridge: Cambridge University Press, 1921.

Nyerere, Julius K. *Freedom and Unity.* London: Oxford University Press, 1967.

Oliver, Roland, and J. D. Fage. *A Short History of Africa.* Baltimore: Penguin Books, 1962.

Ousmane, Sembene. *God's Bits of Wood,* trans. Francis Price. Garden City, N.Y.: Doubleday, 1962.

Park, Mungo. *Travels in the Interior Districts of Africa: Performed under the Direction and Patronage of the African Association in the Years 1795, 1896, and 1797.* London: W. Bulman, 1799.

Parrinder, Geoffrey. *West African Religion: A Study of the Beliefs and Practices of the Akan, Ewe, Yoruba, Ibo, and Kindred Peoples.* London: Epworth Press, 1961.

Pautrat, René. *La Justice locale et la justice musulmane en AOF.* Rufisque: Imprimerie du Haut Commissariat de la République en Afrique Occidentale Française, 1957.

Bibliography

Potter, Allen. *Organized Groups in British National Politics*. London: Faber & Faber, 1961.

Quellien, Alain. *La Politique musulmane dans l'Afrique Occidentale Française*. Paris: Emile Larose, 1910.

Raffenel, Anne. *Nouveau Voyage dans le pays des Nègres suivi d'études sur la colonie du Sénégal et de documents historiques, géographiques et scientifiques,* 2 Vols. Paris: Imprimerie et Librarie Centrale des Chemins de Fer, 1856.

La Region arachidière: étude regionale, 2 vols. Dakar: Grande Imprimerie Africaine, n.d.

Rinn, Louis. *Marabouts et Khouan: etude sur l'Islam en Algérie*. Algiers: Adolphe Jourdan, 1884.

Roberts, Stephen H. *History of French Colonial Policy (1870–1925)*. London: P. S. King, 1929.

Robinson, Kenneth E., and W. J. M. MacKenzie, eds. *Five Elections in Africa*. Oxford: Clarendon Press, 1960.

Rondot, Pierre. *L'Islam et les Musulmans d'aujourd'hui,* vol. I: *La Communauté musulmane: les bases, son état présent, son évolution;* vol. II: *De Dakar à Djakarta: l'Islam en devenir*. Paris: Editions de l'Orante, 1958-1960.

Roux, Jean Paul. *L'Islam en occident Europe-Afrique*. Paris: Payot, 1959.

Samb, El Hadj Assane Marokhya. *Cadior Demb: essai sur l'histoire du Cayor*. Dakar: Imprimerie A. Diop, 1964.

Samb, Maghetar. *La Succession en droit musulman*. Saint-Louis: Imprimerie du Gouvernement, n.d.

Santarem, M. le Vicomte de. *Notice sur André Alvarez d'Almada et sa description de la Guinée*. Paris: Arthur Bertrand, 1842.

Senghor, Leopold. *Nation et voie africaine du socialisme*. Paris: Presence Africaine, 1961.

Shah, Idries. *The Sufis*. Garden City, N.Y.: Doubleday, 1964.

Sicard, Jules. *Le Monde musulman dans les possessions françaises: Algérie-Tunisie-Maroc-A.O.F.; races-moeurs et coutumes-savoir-vivre-Islam,* 2nd ed. Paris: Larose, 1931.

Sire, Abbas-Soh. *Chronique du Fouta sénégalais,* trans. Maurice Delafosse and Henri Gaden. Paris: Ernest Leroux, 1913.

Smith, Donald Eugene. *India as a Secular State*. Princeton: Princeton University Press, 1963.

Smith, Donald Eugene, ed. *South Asian Politics and Religion*. Princeton: Princeton University Press, 1966.

Smith, Wilfred Cantwell. *Islam in Modern History*. New York: New American Library, 1959.

Socé (Diop), Ousmane. *Karim*. Paris: Nouvelles Editions Latines, 1966.

Stewart, J. D. *British Pressure Groups: Their Role in Relation to the House of Commons*. Oxford: Clarendon Press, 1958.

Suret-Canale, Jean. *Afrique noire Occidentale et Centrale: géographie, civilisations, histoire*. Paris: Editions Sociales, 1964.

Bibliography

Tautain, L. *Etudes critiques sur l'éthnologie et l'éthnographie des peuples du bassin du Sénégal.* Paris: Ernest Leroux, 1885.

Thiam, Médoune. *Cheikh Ahmadou Bamba: fondateur du Mouridisme (1850–1927).* Conakry: Imprimerie Nationale "Patrice Lumumba," 1962.

Touré, Sekou. *Guinée: prélude à l'indépendence.* Paris: Presence Africaine, 1959.

Trimingham, J. Spencer. *A History of Islam in West Africa.* London: Oxford University Press, 1962.

———— *Islam in West Africa.* Oxford: Clarendon Press, 1959

Truman, David B. *The Governmental Process: Political Interests and Public Opinion.* New York: Alfred A. Knopf, 1964.

Villard, André. *Histoire du Sénégal.* Dakar: Maurice Viale, 1943.

Wallace, Anthony F. C. *Religion: An Anthropological View.* New York: Random House, 1966.

Watt, W. Montgomery. *Islamic Surveys: Islamic Philosophy and Theology.* Edinburgh: Edinburgh University Press, 1962.

Wehr, Hans. *A Dictionary of Modern Written Arabic,* ed. J. Milton Cowan. Ithaca: Cornell University Press, 1961.

Westermann, Dietrich, and M. A. Bryan. *The Languages of West Africa.* London: Oxford University Press, 1952.

Westermarck, Edward. *Survivances paiennes dans la civilisation mahométane,* trans. into French, Robert Godat. Paris: Payot, 1935.

Williams, John Alden, ed. *Islam.* New York: George Braziller, 1961.

Zartman, I. William. *Government and Politics in Northern Africa.* New York; Praeger, 1963.

Zolberg, Aristide R. *Creating Political Order: The Party-States of West Africa.* Chicago: Rand McNally, 1966.

Articles

"L'Acceuil de Sine-Saloum," *Condition humaine* (Apr. 7, 1948).

Alexandre, P. "Le Facteur islamique dans l'histoire d'un état du Moyen-Togo," *L'Afrique et l'Asie,* no. 65 (1964), 26–30.

———— "L'Islam en Afrique noire," *Marchés tropicaux du monde,* 13 (Oct. 12, 1957), 2385–2387.

Ames, David. "Belief in 'Witches' among the Rural Wolof of the Gambia," *Africa,* 29 (July, 1959), 263–273.

———— "The Selection of Mates, Courtship and Marriage among the Wolof," *Bulletin de l'IFAN,* 18, ser. B (January–April 1956), 156–168.

Antonn, Jacques. "L'Evolution démographique áu Sénégal," *Sénegal d'aujourd'hui,* no. 23 (September, 1965), 20–25.

Arnaud, Robert. "L'Islam et la politique musulmane française en Afrique Occidentale Française," *Renseignements coloniaux et documents publiés par le Comité de l'Afrique Française et le Comité du Maroc* (1912), 3–20, 115–127, 142–154.

Ashford, Douglas E. "The Political Usage of 'Islam' and 'Arab Culture,'" *Public Opinion Quarterly,* 25 (Spring, 1961), 106–114.

Bibliography

Aujus, L. "Les Sérères du Sénégal (moeurs et coutumes de droit privé)," *Bulletin du Comité d'Etudes Historiques et Scientifiques de l'Afrique Occidentale Francaise* (henceforth BCEHSAOF), 14 (July–September, 1931), 293–333.

Azam, P. "Les Limites de l'Islam africain," *L'Afrique et l'Asie,* no. 1 (January, 1948), 16–20.

Ba, Tamsir Ousman. "Essai historique sur le Rip (Sénégal)," *Bulletin de l'IFAN,* 19, ser. B (July–October, 1957), 564–591.

Beer, Samuel H. "Pressure Groups and Parties in Britain," *American Political Science Review,* 50 (March, 1956), 1–23.

Behrman, Lucy C. "Ahmad Bamba, 1850–1927," *Studies on the History of Islam in West Africa,* ed. John Ralph Willis. London: Cass, expected 1969.

———— "French Policy and the Senegalese Muslim Brotherhoods," *Boston University Papers on Africa,* vol. V, eds. Daniel McCall *et al.* New York: Praeger, expected 1969–1970.

———— "The Islamization of the Wolof by the End of the Nineteenth Century," *Boston University Papers on Africa,* vol. IV: *Western African History,* eds. Daniel McCall *et al.* New York: Praeger, 1968. Pages 102–131.

———— "The Political Significance of the Wolof Adherence to Muslim Brotherhoods in the Nineteenth Century," *African Historical Studies,* 1, no. 1 (1968), 60–77.

Bourgeau, J. "Notes sur la coutume des Sérères du Sine et du Saloum," *BCEHSAOF,* 16 (January–March, 1933), 1–65.

Bourlon, Abel. "Actualité des Mourides et du Mouridisme," *L'Afrique et l'Asie,* no. 46 (1959), 10–30.

Brown, Bernard. "Religious Schools and Politics in France," *Midwest Journal of Political Science,* 2 (May, 1958), 160–178.

Campistron, H. "Coutume ouolof du Cayor (cercle de Thiès)," *Coutumiers juridiques de l'Afrique Occidentale Francaise,* vol. I: *Sénégal.* Paris: Librarie Larose, 1939. Pages 117–146.

Cardaire, Marcel, "Quelques aspects de l'islamisation sénégalais," *Academie des Sciences d'Outre-Mer,* 17 (June 15, 1962), 249–262.

Cau, M. "L'Islam au Sénégal" (synopsis), *L'Afrique et l'Asie* (January, 1948), 43–44.

Chailley, Marcel. "Quelques Aspects de l'Islam sénégalais," *Academie des sciences d'outre-mer,* 22 (June 15, 1962), 249–262.

Cissé, Moustapha. "Les Echos de la Fédération," *L'Afrique Musulmane* (October, 1965).

David, Philippe. "Fraternité d'hivernage," *Présence africaine* (April–May 1960), 45–57.

Davis, Morris. "Some Neglected Aspects of British Pressure Groups," *Midwest Journal of Political Science,* 7 (February, 1963), 42–53.

Dia, Mamadou. "Le Président Dia trace un programme pour la politique d'indépendance," *L'Unité africaine* (June 11, 1960).

Bibliography

Dieng, Oumar. "Chez Serigne Dame," *Réveil islamique,* no. 3 (February, 1954).

Dulphy, M. "Coutume sérère de la Petite Côte (cercle de Thiès)," *Coutumiers juridiques de l'Afrique Occidentale Française,* vol. I: *Sénégal.* Paris: Librarie Larose, 1939. Pages 237–321.

———— "Coutumes de Sérères none (cercle de Thiès)," *Coutumiers juridiques de l'Afrique Occidentale Française,* vol. I: *Sénégal.* Paris: Librarie Larose, 1939. Pages 213–236.

"L'Ecole franco-mouride de Diourbel," *Bulletin de l'enseignement de l'Afrique Occidentale Française,* 21st year (July–December, 1932), 241–242.

Ehrmann, Henry W. "Les Groupes d'intérêt et la bureaucratie dans les démocraties occidentales," *Revue française de science politique,* 11 (September, 1961), 541–568.

Fauque, L. P. "Où en est l'Islam traditionnel en Algérie?" *L'Afrique et l'Asie,* no. 55 (1961), 17–22.

Fayet, M. C. "Coutume des Ouolof musulmans (cercle de Baol)," *Coutumiers juridiques de l'Afrique Occidentale Française,* vol. I: *Sénégal.* Paris: Librarie Larose, 1939. Pages 147–193.

———— "Coutume de Sérères N'Doute, (cercle de Thiès)," *Coutumiers juridiques de l'Afrique Occidentale Française,* vol. I: *Sénégal.* Paris: Librarie Larose, 1939. Pages 195–212.

Froelich, J. C. "Archaisme et modernisme: les Musulmans noirs et le progrès," *Cahiers de l'Institut Scientifique d'Economie Appliquée* (ISEA), ser. 5 (December, 1961), 69–97.

———— "Le Reformisme de l'Islam en Afrique noire de l'ouest," *Revue de défense nationale,* 17 (January, 1961), 77–91.

Gaden, Henri. "Legendes et coutumes sénégalaises: cahiers de Yoro Dyâo," *Revue d'éthnographie et de sociologie,* 3 (1912), 119–137, 191–202.

———— "Du Regime des terres de la Vallée du Sénégal au Fouta antérieurement à l'occupation francaise," *BCEHSAOF,* 18 (October–December, 1935), 403–414.

"La Grande Mosquée de Touba a été inaugurée le 7 Juin," *Industrie et traveaux d'outre-mer* (August 1963), 729–732.

Hewett, Lt. J. F. Napier. "On the Jolloffs of West Africa," *Proceedings, Royal Geographic Society,* 1 (June 22, 1857), 513–517.

Hodgkin, Thomas. "Islam, History and Politics," *Journal of Modern African Studies,* 1 (1963), 91–97.

———— "Islam and National Movements in West Africa, *Journal of African History,* 3 (1962), 323–327.

———— "Muslims South of the Sahara," *Current History,* 32 (June, 1957), 345–348.

Huntington, Samuel P. "Political Development and Political Decay," *World Politics,* 17, no. 3 (1965), 386–430.

Bibliography

Joire, J. "Découvertes archéologiques dans la région de Rao (Bas-Sénégal)," *Bulletin de l'IFAN,* 17, ser. B (July–October 1955), 249–333.

—— "La Place de Wolofs dans l'ethnologie sénégalaise." *Première Conférence internationale des Africainistes de l'ouest: comptes rendus.* Dakar: IFAN, 1951.

Kane, Abdou Salam. "Coutume civile et pénale toucouleur (cercle de Matam)," *Coutumiers juridiques de l'Afrique Occidentale Française,* vol. I: *Sénégal.* Paris: Librarie Larose, 1939. Pages 35–115.

Kersaint-Gilly, Felix de. "Les Guelowars: Leur Origin, d'après une legende très en faveur dans le Saloum Oriental," *BCEHSAOF,* (January–February, 1920), 99–101.

Kesby, John. "Muslims of Senegal," *West African Review,* 33 (September, 1962), 37–58.

Lebret, L. J. "L'Economie sénégalaise," *Africa,* no. 21 (November–December, 1961); no. 22 (January–February, 1962), 13–15, 35–37.

—— "L'Etude générale préliminaire au développement du Sénégal," *Europe-France-outre-mer,* no. 376 (March, 1961) 31-37.

Le Grip, A. "L'Avenir de l'Islam en Afrique noire," *L'Afrique et l'Asie,* 2, no. 10 (1950), 5–19.

Le Mère, P. "Petite Chronique du Djilor," *Bulletin de l'IFAN,* 8 (1946), 55–63.

McKay, Vernon. "The Impact of Islam on Relations among the New African States," *Islam and International Relations,* ed. J. Harris Proctor. New York: Praeger, 1965. Pages 158–191.

Marthelot, Pierre. "L'Islam et le développement" *Archives de sociologie de religions,* 14 (1962), 131–138.

Marty, E. "Les Mourides d'Ahmadou Bamba (rapport à M. Le Gouverneur Général de l'Afrique Occidentale)," *Revue du monde musulman,* 25 (December 1913), 3–164.

Mauny, R. "Baobabs-cimitières à griots," *Notes africaines,* 67 (July, 1955), 72–76.

Méynaud, Jean. "Essai d'analyse de l'influence des groupes d'intérêt," *Revue économique,* 2 (March, 1957), 177–220.

—— "Les Groupes d'intérêt et l'administration en France," *Revue française de science politique,* 7 (July–September, 1957), 573–93.

Méynaud, Jean, and Jean Méyriat. "Les 'Groupes de pression' en Europe occidentale, état des traveaux," *Revue française de science politique,* 9 (March, 1959), 229–246.

Monteil, Vincent. "Une Confrérie musulmane: les Mourides du Sénégal," *Archives de sociologie des religions,* 7, no. 14 (1962), 77–102.

—— "Islam et développement au Sénégal," *Cahiers de l'ISEA,* ser. V (December, 1961), 44–68.

—— "Lat-Dior, damel du Kayor, (1842–1886) et l'Islamisation des Wolofs," *Archives de sociologie des religions,* 8, no. 16 (1963), 77–104.

—— "Un Visionnaire musulman sénégalais (1946–1965)," *Archives de sociologie des religions,* 10, no. 19 (1965), 69–98.

Bibliography

Moreau, R. L. "Les Marabouts de Dori," *Archives de sociologie des religions,* 9, no. 17 (1964), 113-134.

Péhaut, Yves. "L'Arachide au Sénégal," *Les Cahiers d'outre-mer,* 14 (January–March, 1961), 5–25.

Pélissier, Paul. "L'Arachide au Sénégal: rationalisation et modernisation de sa culture," *Cahiers d'outre-mer,* 15 (July–September, 1951), 1–32.

N'Doye, Momar Cisse. "La Circoncision chez les sérère-sine," *Notes africaines* (April, 1948), 21–22.

N'Goma, Albert. "L'Islam noir," *Présence africaine,* no. 819 (March, 1950), 333–343.

Robin, J. "L'Evolution du marriage coutumier chez le Musulmans du Sénégal," *Africa,* 17 (July, 1947), 192–201.

Robin, J. "Le Marbat: marché au bétail de Louga," *Africa,* 15 (April, 1945), 47–60.

——— "D'un Royaume Amphibie et fort disparate," *African Studies,* 5 (December, 1946), 250–256.

Rousseau, R. "Le Sénégal d'autrefois: étude sur le Cayor, cahiers de Yoro Dyâo," *BCEHSAOF,* 16 (April–June, 1933), 237–298.

——— "Le Sénégal d'autrefois: études sur le Oualo, cahiers de Yoro Dyâo," *BCEHSAOF,* 14 (January–June, 1929), 133–211.

——— "Le Sénégal d'autrefois: étude sur le Toubé, papiers de Rawane Roy," *BCEHSAOF,* 14 (1931), 334–364.

——— "Le Sénégal d'autrefois: seconde étude sur le Cayor (compléments tiré des manuscrits de Yoro Dyâo)," *Bulletin de l'IFAN,* 3–4 (1941–1942), 79–144.

——— "Le Village ouoloff (Sénégal)," *Annales de géographie,* 42 (Jan. 15, 1933), 88–94.

Sarr, Alioune. "Histoire du Sine Saloum," *Présence africaine,* 5 (1948), 832–837.

"Simple erreur de regime," *L'Unité africaine* (Sept. 25, 1963).

"Sur les Chantiers de la révolution agricole," *L'Unité africaine* (Oct. 17, 1962).

Tapiero, Norbert. "Vue générale sur les aspects actuels de l'Islam en ouest-Afrique et plus particulièrement au Sénégal," *Images de Toumliline* (March, 1962), 7–22.

Thiam, Abdoulaye Gallo. "La Circoncision chez les Oulof," *Notes africaines* (April, 1952), 49–50.

Thiam, Bodiel. "Quelques Superstitions ouloves," *Notes africaines* (January, 1949), 13.

——— "Le Teuque ou bijoutier ouolof," *Notes africaines* (January, 1954), 22–25.

Unpublished Works

"Allocation prononcée par le Gouverneur Lami à l'occasion du Magal de Touba," unpub. ms. Dakar, Sept. 4, 1958.

Bibliography

"Allocution radiodiffusée en Arabe par M. Cheikh Tahirou Doucouré," unpub. ms., Dakar, 1964.

Bomba, Victoria. "The Course of Wolof History until 1820," unpub. diss. University of Wisconsin, 1961.

Brochier, J. "La Diffusion du progrès technique en milieu rural sénégalais," unpub. diss. University of Dakar, 1965.

Diarassouba, Valy-Charles. "L'Evolution des structures agricoles du Sénégal (déstructuration et réstructuration de l'economie rurale)," unpub. diss. University of Paris, 1965 (recently published [1968] as *Evolution des structures agricoles du Sénégal* [Paris: Editions Cujas]).

McCall, Daniel F. "Islamization of the Western and Central Sudan in the Eleventh Century," unpub. ms. Boston University, 1967.

"Resolutions de la Conseil Superieur des Chefs Religieux," unpub. typescript. Dakar, n.d.

Sy, Cheikh Tidjane. "Traditionalisme mouride et modernisation rurale au Sénégal: contribution à l'étude des rapports entre socialisme et Islam en pays sous-développés," unpub. diss. University of Paris, 1965.

Verrière, Louis. "La Population du Sénégal (aspects quantitatifs)," unpub. diss. University of Dakar, 1965.

Wilkes, Ivor. "The Transmission of Islamic Values in the Western Sudan," unpub. ms., Northwestern University, 1968.

Witherell, Julian Wood. "The Responses of the Peoples of Cayor to French Penetration, 1850–1900," unpub. diss. University of Wisconsin, 1964.

Government Publications

Republic of France

Aménagement de l'économie agricole et rurale du Sénégal. Mission Roland Portères, Gouvernement Général de l'Afrique Occidentale Française. Dakar: March–April, 1952.

Etude démographique dans la région du Sine-Saloum (Sénégal): résultats des années 1963–1964. Office de la Recherche Scientifique et Technique Outre-Mer, July, 1965.

La Moyenne Vallée du Sénégal étude socio-économique). By J.-L. Boutillier, P. Cantrelle, J. Causse, C. Laurent, and T. N'Doye. Ministère de la Cooperation, INSEG, 1962.

Procès verbal de la réunion de la commission pour l'étude du rapport du Professeur Portères . . ." Dakar: Aug. 23–Sept. 12, 1952.

Rapport d'ensemble 1913. Report of the Governor General of the AOF. Dakar: 1916.

Situation générale de l'année . . . 1908. Report of the AOF government. Dakar: 1909.

Situation générale . . . des années 1910–1912. Report of the AOF government. Dakar: 1913.

Situation générale . . . pour l'année 1907. Report of the AOF government. Dakar: 1908.

Bibliography

Republic of Senegal

Bulletin Statistique et Economique Mensuel. Statistical Service, Ministry of Planning and Development; 1964–1965.

Commercialisation des arachides, vol. I: *Situation actuelle.* Compagnie Générale d'Etudes et Recherches pour l'Afrique. Dakar: September–October, 1963.

Comptes économiques: années 1959–1960–1961–1962. December, 1963.

Comptes économiques du Sénégal: année 1959. Service de la Statistique et de la Mecanographie, Commissariat Général du Plan. Dakar: June, 1962.

Compte rendu de la cérémonie inaugurale de la Grande Mosquée de Touba et de la premiére prière de Vendredi le 7 Juin 1963. By Cheik Ba Baidy. Thies: June 10, 1963.

Conférence du Réverend Père Lebret d'économie et humanisme sur les problèmes du développement au Sénégal donnée à la Chambre de Commerce de Dakar le 31 Octobre 1958. . . . October, 1958.

Conférence de synthèse pour la définition de la problématique du développement du Sénégal sous la direction du R.P.L.-J. Lebret conseiller expert en développement . . . le 30 Decembre 1958. Committee of Studies of Economic Problems, 1958.

Constitution de la République du Sénégal. March, 1963.

Deuxième Plan quadriennal de développement économique et social 1965–1969, vol. I: *Introduction et analyse;* vol. II: *Plan;* vol. III: *Programmes régionaux.* July 1, 1965.

Doctrine et problème de l'évolution du mouvement coopératif au Sénégal. By Mamadou Dia, president of the Council. Mar. 21, 1962.

Exécution du 2ᵉ plan quadriennal de développement économique et social. By Léopold Sédar Senghor, 5th congress of the UPS. Jan. 28–30, 1966.

Jeune Sénégalais connais-tu ta patrie? Mémento de formation civique. Ministry of Popular Education, Youth, and Sports, 1962.

Journal officiel du Sénégal et dépendences (J.O.). 1902–1966.

Livre blanc sur les elections présidentielles et législatives du 1ᵉʳ Décembre 1963. Dakar: Ministry of Interior, 1964.

Lois, décrets, arrêtes et circulaires concernant le domaine national. Dakar: Ministry of Planning and Development, March, 1966.

Les Mésures de rigeur et d'austerité. By Président Senghor. Dakar: Sept. 13, 1963.

Le Mouvement cooperatif au Sénégal, Bilan et perspectives. By Guy Belloncle, ENEA. Dakar, n.d. [1965].

Pédagogie des chantiers-écoles et des collectives educatives para-colaires. Ministry of Popular Education, Youth, and Sports, 1962.

Plan quadriennal de développement 1961–1964. National Assembly.

Rapport général sur les perspectives de développement du Sénégal, 2 vols. Dakar: January, 1963.

Bibliography

Recensement démographique de Dakar (1955): résultats définitifs, 2 ème fascicule. Service de la Statistique et de la Mecanographie, Ministry of Planning and Development. Paris: Imps. Technigraphy, March, 1962.

Reportage d'un voyage à Touba. By Emile Badiane, Secretary of State for Information in Senegal. Bureau of the Press and of Information, June 13, 1959.

Le Rôle de l'arachide dans la croissance économique du Sénégal. Statistical Service, Ministry of Planning and Development, July, 1964.

Situation économique du Sénégal, 1962, 1963, 1964, 3 vols. Service de la Statistique et de la Mécanographie, Ministry of Finance and Economic Affairs and Ministry of Planning and Development. Dakar, 1963–1965.

Unpublished AOF and Senegalese Archival Material (Dakar)

The Dakar Archives contain an abundance of material on Islam in Senegal and in West Africa in general. The numbers listed here refer to the most important document categories I used. The phrase following the number is the title of the category *or* refers to its significant contents. No attempt can be made here to list the thousands of individual documents relevant to this book.

1G	56	Lucien Nekkach, "Rapport sur le Mouridisme" (cited in this book as "Unpublished Report").
2G		Rapports politiques.
11G	4	Robert Arnaud, "Rapports sur l'Islam," 1906.
13G	2	(2) Cheikh Anta M'Backé.
13G	67	La Politique musulmane, 1905–1917.
13G	68	Fiches de renseignements sur les Marabouts, 1912–1913.
13G	69	Fiches de renseignements sur les Marabouts, 1912–1913.
13G	72	La Politique indigène, 1910–1918
13G	74	L'Affaire de Marabout Bayaga, 1908–1910.
13G	75	La Politique indigène, 1913–1917
13G	76	Dossiers personnels, 1901–1910
13G	295	Correspondence des affaires politiques, 1885–1905.
13G	379	Casamance.
13G	382	Casamance, 1916–1917
17G	24	Fonds secrets, 1900–1919
17G	32	La Politique indigène, 1903–1917.
17G	39	La Politique indigène, 1908–1920.
19G	1	La Situation de l'Islam en AOF, 1906–1916.
19G	2	Les Questions musulmanes.
19G	3	(1) Les Questions musulmanes.
19G	4	Surveillance de l'Islam, 1906–1917.
19G	5	Surveillance de l'Islam, 1909–1916
19G	18	(108) FM Renseignements sur l'Islam, 1920–1926.
19G	19	(108) FM Pélérinages.
19G	20	(108) FM La Propagande musulmane, 1921–1924.
19G	22	(108) FM Le Panislamisme.
19G	25	(108) FM La Situation générale de l'Islam.
19G	29	(108) FM El Hadj Saidou Nourou Tall (untitled 2-vol. testimonial).

Bibliography

19G   30   (108) FM La Situation générale de l'Islam.
19G   38   (108) FM Renseignements sur les questions musulmanes, 1928–1939.
19G   63   (108) FM La Politique sociale indigène.
Dossier on Ahmad Bamba (referred to as Dossier), Office of Archives Director.

Periodicals

l'Afrique musulmane, 1965.
Afrique nouvelle, 1945–1966.
l'AOF, 1948–1958.
Condition humaine, 1948–1956.
Dakar matin, 1945–1966.
Echos du Sénégal, 1966.
Independence africaine, 1959–1960.
Islam AOF, 1938–1940.
La Lutte, 1957–1960.
Momsarev, 1959–1960.
La Nation sénégalaise
Le Réveil islamique, 1953–1958, 1962.
Sénégal d'aujourd'hui, 1965–1966.
Sénégal documents, 1960–1965.
L'Unité, 1956–1957.
L'Unité africaine, 1958–1966.
Vers l'Islam, 1954–1957.
Voix de l'Islam, 1955–1957.

Index

Index

Index

Index

Index

Index